The Big Book

of

Folktale Plays

Also edited by
SYLVIA E. KAMERMAN

(Hardcover)
THE BIG BOOK OF HOLIDAY PLAYS
THE BIG BOOK OF COMEDIES
THE BIG BOOK OF CHRISTMAS PLAYS

(Paperback)
CHILDREN'S PLAYS FROM FAVORITE STORIES
CHRISTMAS PLAY FAVORITES FOR YOUNG PEOPLE
HOLIDAY PLAYS ROUND THE YEAR
PATRIOTIC & HISTORICAL PLAYS FOR YOUNG PEOPLE
PLAYS OF BLACK AMERICANS

The Big Book

of

Folktale

Plays

*One-act adaptations of folktales
from around the world, for stage
and puppet performance*

Edited by

Sylvia E. Kamerman

Publishers　　　　PLAYS, INC.　　　　*Boston*

Library of Congress Cataloging-in-Publication Data

The Big book of folktale plays : one-act adaptations of folktales from
  around the world, for stage and puppet performance / edited by
Sylvia E. Kamerman.
    p. cm.
  Summary: A collection of thirty-two plays, including six suitable
for the puppet stage, adapted from folktales of various countries.
  ISBN 0-8238-0294-9
  1. Folklore—Juvenile drama. 2. Children's plays, American.
3. One-act plays, American. 4. Tales—Adaptations. [1. Folklore-
Drama. 2. Plays.] I. Kamerman, Sylvia E.
  PS627.F6B54 1991
  812'.041089282—dc20   90-16928
                                                      CIP
                                                       AC

plays, Inc.   35⁴⁰   12-21-92   b 2¹

Contents

Puppet Plays

■■■■■■■■■■■■■■■■■■■■■■■■■

The Big Book

of

Folktale Plays

■■■■■■■■■■■■■■■■■■■■■■■

The Bell of Atri

An Italian folktale

by Adele Thane

Characters

HERALD
PETER, *young boy*
CHILDREN, *3 or more*
TOWNSPEOPLE, *men and women, 7 or more*
KING
MAGISTRATE
ATTENDANTS
SIR ROLFO, *Knight of Atri*
TROJAN, *Sir Rolfo's horse*

SCENE 1

TIME: *The Middle Ages.*
SETTING: *Marketplace in the town of Atri, Italy. There is an archway up center, with open bell tower, from which a large golden bell hangs. Fastened to bell is long rope that reaches the ground. A platform is at left side of archway; bench and trellis overgrown with leafy vines are right. Behind archway is painted drop of distant hills. Market booths and carts are left and right. There is a stepladder in one booth.*

3

AT RISE: HERALD, *standing in archway, is pulling the rope. Bell rings loudly.* PETER *runs on left, beckoning off.* CHILDREN *follow him on.* TOWNSPEOPLE *enter right.*

PETER: That's the King's new bell. He had it put here in the marketplace.

1ST CHILD (*Looking up through arch*): See how it shines! It's almost as bright as the sun.

2ND CHILD: What's it for?

PETER: I don't know. There's never been a bell like that here before.

1ST WOMAN: Why does the town of Atri need a bell?

1ST MAN: Maybe it's to ring if there's a fire.

2ND MAN: Or to warn us of robbers coming down from the hills.

2ND WOMAN: I think it's to let us know the King is going to visit our village. Isn't that so, Herald?

HERALD (*Stopping ringing bell*): The King himself is coming here to Atri to tell you about the bell. (*Sound of fanfare from offstage.* KING *enters with* MAGISTRATE *and* ATTENDANTS. TOWNSPEOPLE *curtsy and bow, as* KING *and* MAGISTRATE *mount platform.*)

KING (*To* MAGISTRATE): Are all the townspeople present?

MAGISTRATE: All but Sir Rolfo the Knight, Your Majesty.

KING: And where is he?

MAGISTRATE: Away on a quest, with his noble steed, Trojan.

KING: A magnificent horse. Very well, Magistrate, I shall address the people. (*Fanfare*) People of Atri, you are wondering about this beautiful bell. You can see that its rope reaches to the ground. (*Pointing to* 1ST CHILD) Even a child can reach the rope and ring this bell. (*Crosses to* 1ST CHILD) Come, try it. (1ST

CHILD *tugs rope and bell rings.*) Well done, little one!
(1ST CHILD *returns to crowd.* KING *returns to platform.*) This bell is to be rung in case of need. If
anyone is ill-treated or wronged, he may ring this
bell. The Magistrate will come and see that justice is
done.

MAGISTRATE (*Nodding solemnly*): Aye, Your Majesty,
justice will be done.

KING: Rich and poor, old and young, all alike may use
it, for it is the bell of justice.

TOWNSPEOPLE (*Together*): Long live the King! (KING
and MAGISTRATE *exit, followed by* HERALD *and* AT-
TENDANTS. PETER *and* 3RD CHILD *cross to center.*)

3RD CHILD: Come and play, Peter.

PETER (*Shaking head*): I can't. I must wait for Rolfo to
return. He'll he coming here soon, on his way to the
castle.

2ND CHILD (*Joining them*): You're lucky to be Sir
Rolfo's stableboy, Peter. He has so many fine horses!

PETER: Yes, a hundred! And the finest of all is Trojan,
his favorite horse. Trojan has carried Sir Rolfo safely
through all his battles and daring exploits. (*Looks
off right, pointing*) That's Trojan now! (PETER *runs to
right.*) Sir Rolfo is back! (SIR ROLFO *enters, leading*
TROJAN. PETER *takes charge of the horse.* CHILDREN
surround SIR ROLFO.)

2ND CHILD: Did you kill any dragons, Sir Rolfo?

1ST CHILD: Did you rescue a damsel in distress?

3RD CHILD: How many battles did you win, sir?

SIR ROLFO (*Wearily; waving* CHILDREN *off*): All of that
life is behind me. Out of my way, children. I've no
time for you now. (CHILDREN *murmur disappoint-
edly. He sees rope, then bell.*) Why is this bell in the
marketplace?

1ST CHILD: It's the bell of justice, sir.

2ND CHILD: The King had it hung here.

SIR ROLFO (*Bitterly*): Justice, eh? I've seen enough of the world to know that only the rich get justice.

3RD CHILD: But you are a very rich man, Sir Rolfo.

SIR ROLFO: Not rich enough! I want to have more gold than anyone else in the world. And I mean to get it! (*To* PETER) Come along, you lazy boy. Take Trojan to the stable.

PETER (*Patting* TROJAN): Come, Trojan. You'll have some oats.

SIR ROLFO (*Sharply*): Don't feed him too much, Peter. Oats are costly! (*Exits, as* PETER *leads* TROJAN *off*)

1ST MAN: Sir Rolfo has changed.

2ND WOMAN: Once he sought adventure and good deeds and loved to tell us of his exploits. (*Curtain*)

* * * * *

SCENE 2

TIME: *One year later.*

SETTING: *The marketplace. Bell rope is shorter.*

AT RISE: TOWNSPEOPLE *are busily arranging vegetables and fruits in booths, flowers and pastries in carts.* PETER *and* CHILDREN *wander about.* THREE WOMEN *gather downstage.*

1ST WOMAN: It's just a year ago today that the bell of justice was hung in the marketplace.

2ND WOMAN: You know, I'd almost forgotten about the bell. Nobody has rung it for such a long time.

3RD WOMAN: True. Remember in the beginning, the bell was rung nearly every week?

1ST WOMAN: And each time the Magistrate came and tried the case.

2ND WOMAN: The Magistrate has done his job so well,

there's no need to ring the bell now. All the wrongs in Atri have been made right.

3RD WOMAN: The King will be pleased.

1ST WOMAN: He'll probably decorate the Magistrate.

2ND WOMAN: And we'll have a holiday! (*They cross upstage.*)

2ND CHILD (*Reaching for rope*): The bell rope has worn thin and broken off. (*Trying to reach rope by jumping*) I can't reach it.

2ND MAN (*Reaching for rope on tiptoe*): Even I can't reach it.

1ST MAN: This will never do! What if a child were in need of help? He couldn't ring the bell.

2ND MAN: The rope must be replaced. (*Turning to* 1ST MAN) Victor, you have strong rope in your shop. Will you get it?

1ST MAN (*Shaking head*): I sold the last of my rope yesterday to a ship's captain on his way to sea. I will have to send a messenger to the village of Terano for new rope, but that will take days.

3RD WOMAN: Isn't there any way to mend the old rope?

PETER: I have an idea. (*Runs to hanging vine on trellis*) We'll tie this grapevine onto the bell rope. It's long and strong, and it will serve until the new rope comes.

TOWNSPEOPLE (*Ad lib*): Good idea. Get a ladder! Help me with this vine! (*Etc.* CHILDREN *pull vine off trellis.* 2ND MAN *goes to booth and brings ladder to archway.*)

3RD MAN (*Setting it in position*): Let's put the ladder here.

4TH MAN: We'll hold it. (2ND MAN *climbs ladder and fastens vine to bell.*)

1ST WOMAN: That's better. Now even a child can reach

it. (3RD MAN *returns ladder to booth.* SIR ROLFO *enters, wearing shabby clothes. He crosses, pushing others out of his way.*)

1ST CHILD: Hello, Sir Rolfo!

SIR ROLFO (*Pushing* CHILD *aside*): Don't bother me with your chatter! (*Exits*)

2ND WOMAN (*Shaking her head, sadly*): Sir Rolfo has become so mean and miserly.

3RD MAN: He thinks of nothing but gold.

1ST WOMAN: They say that on one of his adventures he came upon a cave, filled with treasure—chest upon chest of gold coins. He dipped his hands into the piles of gold pieces, and the sound was sweeter to his ears than any music. He fought for that treasure—but he lost.

3RD WOMAN: I remember now. He vowed one day he would have a fortune of his own.

2ND WOMAN: I hear he has sold everything for gold—his castle, his flocks and herds, his orchards and vineyards.

4TH MAN: He lives in a small hut now, and spends his days counting his bags of money.

3RD CHILD: He sold all his horses, too, didn't he, Peter?

PETER (*Sadly*): All except Trojan, but he keeps that poor horse half-starved. One day I tried to take some extra oats to Trojan, but Sir Rolfo drove me away with a stick. He won't let anyone come near his place, for fear they will steal his gold.

2ND CHILD: What will become of Trojan?

1ST MAN: I don't know, but something should be done about Sir Rolfo! (*Curtain*)

* * * * *

SCENE 3

TIME: *Next day.*

SETTING: *The marketplace. Vegetables, fruit, flowers, etc., have been removed from booths and carts.*

AT RISE: *Marketplace is deserted. Sound of dogs barking offstage is heard.* TROJAN *limps on from left, slowly. Barking fades.* TROJAN *whinnies and limps wearily about stage looking for something to eat. He finally comes to grapevine hanging from bell, whinnies happily and starts to nibble the leaves. As he nibbles, he pulls on vine and bell begins to ring. Voices are heard offstage, and* TOWNSPEOPLE *and* CHILDREN *enter right and left.*

TOWNSPEOPLE *and* CHILDREN (*Ad lib*): The bell is ringing! What is wrong? Who rang the bell? (*Etc.*)

1ST MAN: Why, it's only a horse.

1ST WOMAN: He's so hungry that he is eating the leaves on the grapevine. That's why the bell rang.

2ND WOMAN: How thin the poor creature looks!

3RD MAN: What a pity to mistreat an animal this way!

3RD WOMAN: His master should be ashamed—whoever he is.

PETER (*Bursting onstage*): Trojan! It's Trojan! He's run away!

TOWNSPEOPLE (*Ad lib*): Sir Rolfo's horse! For shame! Such a noble steed! (*Etc.*)

2ND WOMAN: Sir Rolfo should be brought to justice!

HERALD (*Entering*): Make way for the King! His Majesty has heard the ringing of the bell and comes to see that justice is done.

TOWNSPEOPLE (*Ad lib*): The King! Make way! (*Etc. Crowd parts, leaving center stage and platform clear.* KING, ATTENDANTS *and* MAGISTRATE *enter.*)

MAGISTRATE: People of Atri, the King has heard the bell ringing.

KING: What injustice has been done, good people? Has someone been mistreated?

4TH MAN: Your Majesty, the bell has been rung by—a horse!

1ST CHILD: Here is the horse, Your Majesty. (*Indicates* TROJAN)

KING (*Incredulous*): A horse, you say!

MAGISTRATE: Only a horse! (*To* KING) Your Majesty, this is a mistake. You should not have come. The horse cannot know what the bell is for.

PETER: No, wait! Your Majesty, you said that all may come to ring the bell, if there has been an injustice. Surely even a horse may call for justice—and this horse has been cruelly treated.

KING: The boy is right. Let us investigate this, Magistrate.

MAGISTRATE: Whose horse is this?

1ST MAN: It belongs to Sir Rolfo, the Knight of Atri.

3RD WOMAN: Sir Rolfo has treated the animal most shamefully.

3RD MAN: He gives the poor creature scarcely enough food to keep him alive. That is why the horse rang the bell—it was starving, so it ate the leaves.

KING (*To* MAGISTRATE): I've heard enough. Send for Sir Rolfo.

MAGISTRATE (*To* ATTENDANTS): Bring Sir Rolfo before us. (ATTENDANTS *bow and exit.*)

KING: Good people of Atri, I have said that if a wrong has been done to any of you, it shall be righted. This pitiful horse deserves justice, and justice he shall receive. (ATTENDANTS *reenter with* SIR ROLFO.)

SIR ROLFO (*Angrily*): Take your hands off me!

ATTENDANTS (*To* KING): We found him just outside the square, Your Majesty.

KING: Is this the man who once was the brave Knight of Atri?

MAGISTRATE (*Sighing*): Alas, yes, Your Majesty. (*To* SIR ROLFO) Sir Rolfo, is this your horse, Trojan?

SIR ROLFO (*With a glance at horse; sullenly*): What if it is? (TROJAN *nibbles more leaves, and bell rings again.*)

MAGISTRATE: Listen to that bell, Sir Rolfo—it speaks for a once proud beast. Do you deny, sir, that you have mistreated this animal?

SIR ROLFO: I shall do as I please with what belongs to me.

MAGISTRATE: People of Atri, look upon this wretched beast. (*Walking around* TROJAN *as he speaks*) Does anyone recognize in this miserable creature the brave and noble steed that bore Sir Rolfo safely through many a danger?

TOWNSPEOPLE (*Shouting; ad lib*): No, no! Punish the miser! To the dungeon with him! (*Etc.*)

MAGISTRATE: Sir Rolfo, what have you to say?

SIR ROLFO: I can no longer afford to keep the horse. It costs more to feed him than he's worth, for he is of no use to me now.

MAGISTRATE: What of your hoard of gold?

CROWD (*Ad lib*): Yes, yes, you miser! (*Etc.*)

1ST MAN: Peter, you tell the Magistrate about Sir Rolfo's treasure.

PETER: If it please Your Honor, I was once Sir Rolfo's stableboy. He has a hoard of gold coins that he guards like a dragon, but he lets no one come near him.

MAGISTRATE: Sir Rolfo, your heart has grown as hard

as the gold you hoard. You have forgotten the days when Trojan saved your life and helped bring you victory and honor. Now hear my judgment: I command that one half of your gold be set aside to provide shelter and food for this horse. (*All cheer.*)

KING: I am well pleased with your judgment, Magistrate. (*To* SIR ROLFO) Sir Rolfo, you have shown lack of charity to this steed that served you so faithfully. Therefore, by royal decree, you shall be known henceforth as Rolfo, the Unknightly. Go and live alone, in disgrace, with your gold, but never attend my court again. (ROLFO *slinks off, as* KING *crosses to* TROJAN, *gently laying hand on horse's head.*) People of Atri, each year we will celebrate this day as a holiday to mark the occasion. The Bell of Atri has brought justice even to a poor creature that could not speak for itself. (*Crowd cheers.* KING *turns to* PETER) Ring the bell, lad, and I will lead Trojan to his new stall. He shall have a dinner such as he has not eaten in many a day, and you shall return to care for him.

PETER (*Joyfully*): Trojan has been saved! (PETER *rings bell joyously, as* KING *leads* TROJAN *toward exit.* TOWNSPEOPLE *continue to cheer as curtains close.*)

THE END

(*Production Notes on page 311*)

The Sleeping Mountains

A Mexican folktale

by Barbara Winther

Characters

KING PAPANTCO (*Pah-pahn'-ko*)
PRINCESS, *his daughter*
HIGH PRIEST
JAGUAR, *his son*
TWO GUARDS
KING IXTLI (*Eest'-lee*)
PRINCE, *his son*
SERVANT GIRL
TERANA, *attendant*
OLD WOMAN OF THE MOUNTAINS

SCENE 1

TIME: *A day when the world was young.*
SETTING: *The Courtyard of the Sun in the palace of King Papantco in the Valley of Mexico. There is a stone bench center, to the right of a well. To the left is a throne.*

AT RISE: SERVANT GIRL *is playing a lively tune on a flute.* 1ST GUARD *stands behind throne waving a large fan. There is a sword in his belt.* TERANA *enters right, ushering* PRINCESS *to bench.* SERVANT GIRL *bows and exits left.* 1ST GUARD *stands at attention.*

PRINCESS: Where is my father, the King, Terana?

TERANA (*Nervously*): The King and the High Priest have been holding a secret meeting all morning, my princess.

PRINCESS: I do not trust the High Priest.

TERANA: Softly, Princess. It is not wise to speak against him.

PRINCESS: He holds too much influence over my father. And as for the High Priest's son, Jaguar, every time I look at him, I am chilled. (*Sounds of drum roll and horn blast are heard offstage.*)

1ST GUARD (*Shouting*): To the Courtyard of the Sun comes King Papantco, the great Toltec ruler over all rich and green valley lands on the southern side of the mountains. (1ST GUARD *and* TERANA *prostrate themselves.* PRINCESS *rises and bows.*)

PAPANTCO (*Entering right, followed by* HIGH PRIEST): What a beautiful day! My daughter, you are as lovely as the feathers of the quetzal [*ket'-sahl*] bird. (*He sits on throne.* PRINCESS *sits on bench.* 1ST GUARD *waves fan over* PAPANTCO, *and* TERANA *stands behind bench.*) High Priest, bring your son, Jaguar, before me.

HIGH PRIEST: At once! (*Claps hands and makes magical gesture*) Itza! (JAGUAR *enters.*)

JAGUAR: Yes, Father! (*Bows to* PAPANTCO)

PAPANTCO: Jaguar, we have been discussing you.

JAGUAR (*In a fawning manner*): Oh, Magnificent King, I am honored that you would bring my name to your lips.

PAPANTCO (*To* HIGH PRIEST): He speaks well.

HIGH PRIEST: Of course.

PAPANTCO: His appearance is not the best I have seen.

HIGH PRIEST (*Quickly*): But, he is very loyal to you. I am teaching him many spells and potions. He will be a powerful friend for your empire.

PAPANTCO (*Rising and crossing to* PRINCESS): Little flower, the time has come for you to be married.

PRINCESS (*Gasping*): Not to Jaguar?

PAPANTCO: The son of the most expert magician in my land would make an excellent husband for you.

PRINCESS (*Shocked*): Surely you would not wish me to marry one to whom I am so unsuited!

PAPANTCO: It is said that the mother corn will survive even on the desert. So you, too, can adjust. (*Returns to throne*)

PRINCESS: But, Father—

PAPANTCO: Tomorrow your feathered wedding robe will be started. (*Sounds of drum roll and horn blast are heard.* 2ND GUARD *enters.*)

2ND GUARD (*Shouting*): To the Courtyard of the Sun comes King Ixtli, the poor Chichimec [*Chee-chee-mek'*] ruler over all lean brown mountain lands to the north.

PAPANTCO (*Leaping up angrily*): Cactus spines!

2ND GUARD (*Continuing*): King Ixtli's son accompanies him.

PAPANTCO: This is even more disgraceful. Two enemies in my palace.

HIGH PRIEST (*Sternly*): Why are they here?

IXTLI (*Entering left, followed by* PRINCE): I will be quick, for I find your land overrun with poisonous vines.

PAPANTCO (*Coldly*): Since you prefer your rocky wasteland, I can see no reason for you to enter my fertile valley.

IXTLI: Your subjects are using my streams for fishing.

PAPANTCO: That is not true!

IXTLI: It *is* true!

PAPANTCO (*Angrily*): You whine like a scrawny coyote.

IXTLI: My country is poor, but my people are proud. I will not take your insults.

PAPANTCO: Depart at once, or I will have you thrown into the deepest well. (GUARDS *draw swords.*)

IXTLI (*Sternly*): That would mean war.

PRINCE: Please, Father. Let me handle this.

IXTLI: Very well, my son, I must leave this foul-smelling land. (*Exits left*)

PAPANTCO (*Shouting after him*): Your land is full of prickly pears and rattlesnakes.

PRINCESS (*Crossing to him*): Please, Father. I would like to talk to the Prince about this matter.

PAPANTCO: Gladly! (*Rises, crosses right*) Guard, if the Chichimec Prince does the least thing to threaten the Princess, throw him into the well. (*Exits right, followed by* HIGH PRIEST *and* JAGUAR)

PRINCESS (*To* TERANA): Wait for me in the Room of Seven Paintings.

TERANA: But, it is not proper—

PRINCESS (*Gently waving her away*): Do not worry. I shall be careful. (TERANA *exits right.*) Guards, put your swords away and stand back. I do not need your protection. (GUARDS *stand at rear.*)

PRINCE (*To* PRINCESS): I am sorry. It is not a pleasant way to meet.

PRINCESS: Our fathers have always been at odds with each other.

PRINCE: Long ago they had a quarrel, and our two tribes fought. The reason for the quarrel is forgotten, but the bitterness remains.

PRINCESS: How unfortunate. Our tribes should unite and be friends.

PRINCE: I am certain that if my people could see the lovely Toltec Princess (*Bows to her*), they would forgive anything. I know I do.

PRINCESS (*Blushing, looking away*): The Chichimec Prince is most gracious, but he does not know me. (*Smiles shyly*) You must not only judge by my outward appearance.

PRINCE: A woman is only beautiful if she reflects goodness inside. In your face I see kindness, gentleness, and honesty.

PRINCESS: And I see goodness in yours. (*They stare at each other, then laugh in embarrassment.*)

PRINCE: Will you let me see you again? (JAGUAR *reenters stealthily, unseen by them, and hides behind well.*)

PRINCESS: I would like to see you very much, but my father has chosen Jaguar, a nobleman of my tribe, to be my husband.

PRINCE: Do you care for him?

PRINCESS: No! I dislike him!

PRINCE: Then, meet me in the forest tomorrow.

PRINCESS (*Crossing right, thinking, and crossing back to* PRINCE): If I should decide to meet you, where would it be?

PRINCE: Do you know the hut where the Old Woman of the Mountains lives?

PRINCESS: Yes. It is near the border which divides our kingdoms.

PRINCE: Meet me at the giant palm beside that hut.

PRINCESS: When the sun is rising. (*Loudly, to* GUARDS) Show the Chichimec Prince out.

PRINCE (*Bowing*): Princess, your courtesy is greatly

appreciated. (*Exits left, followed by* GUARDS)

TERANA (*Entering*): Ah, he has gone.

PRINCESS (*Excitedly*): I have much to tell you, Terana. First, you must promise by all of the gods we worship, to keep my secret. (PRINCESS *grabs her arm and pulls her along toward right.*) Do you promise?

TERANA: Of course, but I am disturbed by this excitement of yours. (*They exit.*)

JAGUAR (*Coming out of hiding*): This enemy comes into our land and tries to steal what is mine. So, the Princess does not wish to marry Jaguar! (*Almost hissing as he speaks*) She will be sorry. I shall make certain that evil befalls them both. (*Curtain closes as* JAGUAR *exits right.*)

* * * * *

SCENE 2

TIME: *That evening.*

SETTING: *The Courtyard, the same as Scene 1.*

AT RISE: PRINCESS *and* TERANA *are sitting on the bench.*

TERANA: This is a terrible thing you are going to do.

PRINCESS: Is it so terrible to meet someone?

TERANA: If your father knew, he would have the Prince killed.

PRINCESS: My father has little understanding of the heart of his daughter.

TERANA: My child, perhaps you will change your mind by morning.

PRINCESS (*Determinedly*): I will *not* change my mind. Come with me to the forest. It will give me more courage.

TERANA (*Tearfully*): Come with you? If I were caught, it would be the end of me.

PRINCESS: You are right. Forget what I have said. (*Rises*)

TERANA (*Rising*): Wait! I carried you on my back when you first visited the sacred well. I stayed beside you every moment you lay sick with the jungle fever. I will not let you go alone to the forest now.

PRINCESS: Thank you, dear Terana. I know I am asking much of you.

TERANA (*Patting her cheek*): Go to sleep now. I will awaken you before dawn. (PRINCESS *exits right.* TERANA *sighs and starts to exit left.* JAGUAR'S *voice is heard from off right. She pauses.*)

JAGUAR (*From offstage*): The Princess meets the Chichimec Prince tonight. (TERANA *quickly crosses to hide behind well, as* HIGH PRIEST *and* JAGUAR *enter.*)

HIGH PRIEST: We must change our plans.

JAGUAR: She does not wish to marry me, and I believe she will find a way to change the King's mind. How can I become head of the kingdom then?

HIGH PRIEST: A bit of underhanded magic is necessary. (*Pauses*) If something should happen to detain the Princess tonight, then King Papantco would do anything to bring her back. (*Smiles maliciously*) It might be amusing to change the Princess and Prince into two stones for awhile.

JAGUAR: You risk angering the gods.

HIGH PRIEST: The gods have never bothered me before. (*Pompously*) I think they are afraid of my powers.

JAGUAR: Your magic *is* powerful.

HIGH PRIEST: Come with me now. We shall mix a powder. You will take it to the meeting place and sprinkle it over the Princess and Prince. (*They exit left.*)

TERANA (*Running right, calling softly*): Princess! Princess! (*She exits. There is a moment's pause. She screams from offstage*) Princess, where are you?

1ST GUARD (*Running on, sword raised*): What is wrong? (TERANA *enters.*)

TERANA: Nothing! Nothing! I had a bad dream. Now return to your post!

PAPANTCO (*Entering right*): I heard a scream. What is wrong?

TERANA: It is nothing, Sire. I was dreaming—that's all.

PAPANTCO: But you are fully clothed. Guard, is the Princess safe? (1ST GUARD *starts to exit right.* TERANA *moves in front of him, blocking his way.*)

TERANA: She is fine. Do not disturb her sleep. Everything is well.

PAPANTCO (*Aside, to himself*): This woman is acting strangely. (*To* 1ST GUARD) See to the Princess. (1ST GUARD *exits. Nervously,* TERANA *begins to move in the opposite direction.*)

1ST GUARD (*Shouting, from offstage*): The Princess is gone! (TERANA *turns and runs out.*)

PAPANTCO: Guard! (1ST GUARD *reenters.*) Bring back the attendant, Terana. (*He points offstage.* GUARD *runs off. Offstage,* TERANA *screams, then* GUARD *reenters, dragging the struggling* TERANA.)

TERANA: Let me go! Let me go!

PAPANTCO (*Sternly*): Where is the Princess?

TERANA: I cannot tell. (*Sinks to knees, sobbing*) I am sworn to secrecy. I promised the Princess I would not tell.

PAPANTCO: You dare refuse the request of your King?

TERANA: Oh, please, please, forgive me. The Princess is in danger. I must warn her. Let me go.

PAPANTCO: You will go nowhere until you tell me everything. (HIGH PRIEST *enters left, followed by* JAGUAR.)

HIGH PRIEST: What is wrong?

PAPANTCO: Terana tells me the Princess is in danger, but she will not tell me where she is.

TERANA (*Pointing to* HIGH PRIEST *and shrieking*): He knows where the Princess is. Ask him!

HIGH PRIEST: The woman has lost her senses. I know nothing.

TERANA: You are evil. (*Whirls back to* PAPANTCO) Then I will tell you where she is. She has gone to— (HIGH PRIEST *raises hands in a magic gesture, and* TERANA *gasps and sinks to floor.*)

PAPANTCO: She has fainted.

HIGH PRIEST: I will take care of her.

PAPANTCO: Guard, send a detachment of warriors to search the surrounding area. (1ST GUARD *exits left.*)

HIGH PRIEST: I suggest, King Papantco, that you try to rest. I am certain that by tomorrow this woman will give me the information we need.

PAPANTCO (*Agitatedly*): What could have happened to my daughter? If you find out anything, call me at once. (*Exits*)

HIGH PRIEST (*To* JAGUAR): Take this powder and go quickly. (*Gives pouch to* JAGUAR, *who holds it at arm's length and smiles*) Quickly! (JAGUAR *stealthily exits left, and* HIGH PRIEST *bends over* TERANA *as curtains slowly close.*)

* * * * *

SCENE 3

BEFORE RISE: *Dawn.* PRINCE *enters left, before curtain, gazes right.* OLD WOMAN *enters right.*

PRINCE: Good morning, Old Woman of the Mountains.

OLD WOMAN: Ah, Prince, what brings you to this side of the border?

PRINCE: The Toltec Princess.

OLD WOMAN: I can see by the radiance of your face that you would go anywhere to meet her.

PRINCE: You are right, Old Woman.

OLD WOMAN: It is dangerous. (*Shakes her head*)

PRINCE: I know. Our fathers are always on the verge of war.

OLD WOMAN: What a pity! It appears very difficult to love outside of one's tribe. (PRINCESS *enters right, sees* OLD WOMAN, *and stops.*) It is all right, Princess. I wish you both well. (*Exits left*)

PRINCE (*Crossing to* PRINCESS): I was afraid you would not come.

PRINCESS: There were times when my courage left me.

PRINCE (*Looking around*): You came alone?

PRINCESS: I did not wish to endanger anyone else's life.

PRINCE: You are braver than you realize. All night I have been awake, wondering what I should do. I want to ask for your hand in marriage.

PRINCESS: My father would never consent.

PRINCE: But, I cannot let you marry Jaguar.

PRINCESS: I will go with you to *your* father.

PRINCE (*Shaking his head*): My father would never accept you.

PRINCESS: Is there nothing we can do?

PRINCE: We could run away and leave both kingdoms. It would be difficult.

PRINCESS: If you will stay beside me, I am willing to go.

PRINCE: I will always stay beside you. (JAGUAR *sneaks in, and* PRINCE *sees him.*) Halt! Who are you? (PRINCESS *whirls around, gasps, and hides behind* PRINCE.)

PRINCESS: It is Jaguar!

PRINCE (*Drawing his sword*): Stand back.

JAGUAR: Your sword will be of no use to you, Chichimec Prince. (*Opens pouch and scatters powder over them.*

PRINCE *and* PRINCESS *freeze, and* JAGUAR *laughs evilly.*) I shall return for you, Princess. Until our marriage takes place, the Prince will remain locked in his stone cage. (*Blackout*)

* * * * *

TIME: *Later that day.*

SETTING: *The palace courtyard.*

AT RISE: PAPANTCO *is seated on throne.* 1ST GUARD *stands behind him.* JAGUAR *sits on bench.* TERANA *kneels, bound and gagged.*

HIGH PRIEST: Terana has revealed everything, King Papantco. The Princess has run away to marry the Chichimec Prince.

PAPANTCO: What? (*Rises; furiously*) We shall march against the Chichimec kingdom. (*Sounds of drum roll and horn blast are heard.* 2ND GUARD *enters.*)

2ND GUARD (*Shouting*): To the Courtyard of the Sun comes King Ixtli.

PAPANTCO (*Interrupting*): He dares to return?

IXTLI (*Entering left; angrily*): Where is my son?

PAPANTCO: He kidnapped my daughter.

IXTLI: That is a lie. My son would not stoop to such a thing.

PAPANTCO: Stoop! Your son is a cucaracha.

IXTLI (*Sputtering*): I demand an apology!

HIGH PRIEST (*Crossing between them and raising arms*): O kings of the northern and southern lands, I have a solution to this problem. My son, Jaguar, has courageously offered to find the Princess and Prince.

JAGUAR (*Rising*): King Papantco, I will bring your daughter back by nightfall, if you will consent to our marriage this evening.

PAPANTCO: What makes you so certain that you can bring her back?

JAGUAR: My father has given me special magical powers. And, if I should not succeed, you may sacrifice me to the gods! I am most certain of my success.

PAPANTCO: Go, then! (*Sits on throne*) The wedding shall take place on your return.

IXTLI: What about my son?

JAGUAR: Later this evening he will be returned to your kingdom.

IXTLI: If he does not come back as you say, I promise to have every man in my kingdom armed with a club and on the march by morning.

SERVANT (*Entering right, excitedly*): There is a strange old woman here. The guards do not know how she managed to enter the palace.

PAPANTCO (*Rising*): Who is she? (OLD WOMAN *enters.*)

ALL (*In surprise; ad lib*): Who is it? How did she enter? (*Etc.*)

OLD WOMAN (*Looking at both* KINGS): Ah! Again the two enemy kings have met to snarl at each other.

IXTLI: Who are you?

OLD WOMAN: I am the Old Woman of the Mountains. Your son knows me well. I have lived long, longer than all of you together. (*Crosses to* HIGH PRIEST, *who backs away*)

HIGH PRIEST: Go away! You are not wanted here.

OLD WOMAN: Is that so, High Priest? Are you in charge of the world? (*Pointing at him*) Your magical powers have grown too large for your little mind.

HIGH PRIEST: How dare you speak to me in this manner! Away with you! (*Claps his hands and raises arms in magical gestures*) Itza! (OLD WOMAN *cackles, unaffected by magic.*)

OLD WOMAN (*In a loud, shrill voice*): The gods have grown angry with you, High Priest. You and your son have brought evil to this land. (*Moves toward them as they back away*) Henceforth, you are banished from the human race. You shall become animals, confined to the deserts and jungles, always hiding.

HIGH PRIEST: No! No! (*Turns and runs off left, followed by* JAGUAR. *Loud howling and roaring of wild animals are heard from off left. Others move away from* OLD WOMAN, *watching her as she unties* TERANA.)

PAPANTCO (*Cautiously stepping forward*): Old Woman of the Mountains, your powers are greater than ours. Can you bring my daughter back to me?

IXTLI (*Stepping forward*): And my son back to me?

OLD WOMAN: No! I do not choose to bring either of them back.

PAPANTCO: But, the Princess must not marry the son of my enemy.

IXTLI: I cannot allow the Prince to marry my enemy's daughter.

OLD WOMAN: How foolish you both are! (*Crosses to bench*) You are so embittered that you do not really care about the dreams of your children. I have taken them to a place where they will always be together.

IXTLI *and* PAPANTCO: Where?

OLD WOMAN (*Standing on bench and gesturing out over audience*): Look there. See those two beautiful mountains rising high above this valley? (*All stare in fear and wonder.*) Their names shall be Ixtaccihuatl and Popocatepetl. Side by side these mountains will live while kingdoms below rise and fall. Some day, when there is less hate, the Princess and Prince will awaken and return to be happily married. Until then, they will sleep. (KINGS *glower at each other and turn away.* TERANA *weeps quietly, and*

SERVANT *begins to play melancholy flute music, as* OLD WOMAN *shakes her head sadly, and slowly exits. Stage lights fade as curtain slowly closes and music fades away.*)

THE END

(*Production Notes on page 311*)

The Boy Who Went to the North Wind

A Swedish folktale

by Jean Feather

Characters

NORTH WIND
NED
MOTHER
INNKEEPER
WIFE
GOAT
STICK

SCENE 1

SETTING: *There are three acting areas. A table and two chairs, at right, represent Ned's kitchen. Up center is the entrance to inn, with sign reading* INN *on screen. Down left, another reads* NORTH WIND.

AT RISE: NORTH WIND *is swirling about down left.*

NORTH WIND (*Chanting*):
    I am the North Wind
    Loud and strong,

All in my path
I blow along.

I am the North Wind
Wild and free,
I have great power,
Beware of me.
(*He sinks to floor, as* NED *and* MOTHER *enter right.*)

MOTHER (*Picking up bowl from table*): Ned, please take this bowl and go to the storeroom for some flour.

NED: Yes, Mother. (*He takes bowl from her and exits.*)

MOTHER: We have very little flour left. I must see what else we have. (*She looks in cupboard.*) Only two potatoes and two apples. (*Sighs*) How can my son and I stay alive till harvest time? Two apples, two potatoes, and a little flour. (*She goes to table and sits quietly, head in hands.* NED *reenters, and starts toward house.* NORTH WIND *jumps up, swirls around* NED, *grabs handfuls of flour from bowl and scatters it.*)

NED (*Crying out*): Stop! The flour is blowing away. Please stop, Mr. North Wind. (NED *runs into house.* NORTH WIND *exits left.*) Mother, look. The bowl is empty. The North Wind blew it all away.

MOTHER: All gone? (NED *nods.*) What are we going to do now? We'll starve before the harvest time. (*She puts her head in her arms, and weeps quietly.*)

NED (*Putting his hands on her shoulders*): Don't cry, Mother. We'll think of something.

MOTHER: What?

NED: I don't know. (*Pacing*) I'll tell you what I'm going to do. I'll go to the North Wind and ask him to give our flour back.

MOTHER (*Bitterly*): What does the wind care about people?

NED (*Hopefully*): He might help us.

MOTHER: Go, then. You may as well do that as sit here and starve. (*She rises and exits.*)

NED (*Walking around*): Why, it's almost calm. Mr. North Wind must have gone home to rest. Well, I'll find out where he lives. I'll keep walking north until I come to his den. How dare he steal our last bit of flour! (*Comes to sign at* NORTH WIND's *den, and calls*) Mr. North Wind, come here, please.

NORTH WIND (*Entering from den*): Why do you call me?

NED: I want to talk to you.

NORTH WIND: Speak, then.

NED: When you just swirled across the land, you blew away all our flour, and left my mother and me to starve.

NORTH WIND (*Shrugging*): Why, that's too bad. But a wind can't choose, you know. We blow whatever is in our path.

NED: But couldn't you get our flour back?

NORTH WIND: Gracious me, no. The flour is scattered everywhere.

NED: Couldn't you give us some of your flour, then?

NORTH WIND: My dear young man, I have no flour. But if you are hungry, I'll go into my den and see what I can find for you. (*He exits into den.*)

NED (*Cheerfully*): I thought he'd try to make amends for what he did if I asked him.

NORTH WIND (*Entering, carrying tablecloth*): I have no food, but here is a magic tablecloth. Just spread it on a table and say, "Cloth, cover yourself," and you'll have a meal fit for a king.

NED (*Taking cloth*): Oh, thank you, Mr. North Wind.

NORTH WIND: Not at all. Glad I could help. (*He exits.*)

NED (*Walking toward inn*): Magic! I'm *so* excited. But

I'm tired, too. I'll stop at the first inn I see. Ah, here's a place. (*He knocks on inn door.*)

INNKEEPER (*Entering from behind screen center*): Good evening.

NED: Good evening. I wonder if I may spend the night here.

INNKEEPER: Certainly. But before I show you to your room, good sir, may I have a silver coin in payment?

NED: I'm sorry. I don't have one.

INNKEEPER: What! No silver? Have you any gold, then?

NED: Oh, no, indeed. I have never owned a piece of gold.

INNKEEPER: How can you expect to get a bed if you have no money?

NED: I have something better than money!

INNKEEPER: Better than money? What can that be?

NED: See this tablecloth? All I have to do is put this cloth on a table and say the magic words, "Cloth, cover yourself," and there will appear a meal fit for a king!

INNKEEPER: If the cloth is so wonderful, you're surely not going to part with it.

NED: Oh, no, indeed. But if I were to provide a good meal for everyone in the inn, wouldn't that pay for my bed?

INNKEEPER (*Uncertain*): I suppose so. But I'd better talk that over with my wife first. Will you wait outside, please? (NED *moves away a few feet.* INNKEEPER *calls.*) Wife! Come here, please.

WIFE (*Entering*): What do you want?

INNKEEPER (*Excitedly*): There's a young man outside who says he has a magic tablecloth. It will provide a meal fit for a king.

WIFE: A magic tablecloth? That would be a wonderful thing indeed. I could stay out of that hot kitchen, and never have to prepare another meal. Oh, we must have it! (*Pauses*) But how do we know it really is magic?

INNKEEPER: He says he'll provide a meal for us all tonight in exchange for his bed.

WIFE: Ah, that will give us our chance. Tell him to come into the inn right now and prepare that dinner. We'll see if it's true. Then we can make plans.

INNKEEPER (*Nodding, slyly*): That is very wise, my dear. (*He calls to* NED.) Well, my boy, let's just see the meal you will prepare for us. Go in, and we will watch. (NED *goes behind screen, as* INNKEEPER *and* WIFE *watch.*) He's done it! The food appeared by magic!

WIFE: I still don't believe it. (*They continue to watch.*) It *is* a magic tablecloth!

INNKEEPER: Truly, it's food fit for a king!

WIFE: Tonight, when he's asleep, you'll creep into his room, take the cloth, and put one of ours in its place. He won't notice the difference.

INNKEEPER (*Laughing*): Not till he tries to make the magic work.

WIFE: And we'll take things easy the rest of our lives. (*Curtain*)

* * * * *

SCENE 2

TIME: *The next morning.*

SETTING: *The same as Scene 1.*

AT RISE: MOTHER *sits at table in kitchen.* NED *comes out of inn, carrying tablecloth, and goes to her.*

NED: Mother, I'm home.

MOTHER: And did you get any food?

NED: No, Mother. But I have something much better. A tablecloth.

MOTHER: My poor, foolish boy. What good is a table-cloth without food?

NED: Ah, but this is a magic cloth. I just say, "Cloth, cover yourself," and in a flash it's covered with wonderful food.

MOTHER: I won't believe that till I see it.

NED: All right, then. Just help me spread this cloth on the table. (*They do so.*) Cloth, cover yourself. (*Pause*) Cloth, cover yourself. (*Pause*) What's the matter with it?

MOTHER: Oh, Ned, you didn't really expect food to appear, did you?

NED: Of course, I did. It happened at the inn. We had a marvelous feast.

MOTHER: You're sure it wasn't a dream?

NED: No, Mother. We all ate and ate.

MOTHER: But where did you get the cloth?

NED: The North Wind gave it to me.

MOTHER: Did he say it would work more than once?

NED: Of course. (*Pause*) Well, no, he didn't actually say it would work more than once. But I thought it would give food whenever I asked it.

MOTHER (*Scornfully*): You *thought*! Well, at least you had one good meal.

NED: Oh, Mother, I'm sorry. I should have come straight home. I'll go back to the North Wind to tell him what happened. (*He rushes over to* NORTH WIND's *den, as* MOTHER *exits.*) Mr. North Wind! Wake up, please, Mr. North Wind!

NORTH WIND (*Entering, yawning*): What do you want with me now?

NED: Oh, sir, I used the tablecloth you gave me before going home, and my mother didn't get any food. Could you give me something for her?

NORTH WIND: Why didn't you ask the cloth again?

NED: I did, but nothing happened.

NORTH WIND: Strange. (*Puzzled*) The magic was supposed to last forever. But let me see what else I have. (*He goes into den, then reenters, leading* GOAT.) Here you are, my boy. Just say, "Goat, make money," and she'll drop a gold piece from her front hoof. Now I'm going back to sleep. (*Exits, yawning*)

NED (*Calling after him*): Thank you, Mr. North Wind. (*Starting across stage*) Come on, Nanny, let's go. Oh, I'm so tired. (*As he reaches inn*) I'll have to stop at this inn again. (*Knocks*)

INNKEEPER (*Entering*): Good evening.

NED: Good evening. May I have a bed for the night?

INNKEEPER: Why, of course. Come in.

NED: I'll have to bring my goat.

INNKEEPER: Oh, very well. May I have a silver piece in payment?

NED: Silver? Oh, yes, the money. (*He turns to* GOAT, *then back again to* INNKEEPER.) Will you make sure that your wife will let me keep my goat in the bedroom tonight?

INNKEEPER: Of course she will, if you can pay.

NED: I can pay, but please go and ask your wife.

INNKEEPER: If you insist. (*He goes out, but sneaks behind screen and watches.*)

NED: I'm not taking any chances this time. It's better not to let anyone know what this goat can do. Goat, make money. (GOAT *drops out gold coin.*) A piece of gold. Thank you, my friend, thank you.

INNKEEPER (*Coming from behind screen*): Yes, young man. You and your goat may have a room. (WIFE *enters and stands near screen.*)

NED: Thank you. Perhaps you can give me change for this gold piece. (*Hands him coin*)

INNKEEPER: Certainly. (*Hands him coins*) Here's your

change—nine pieces of silver. And now let me show you to your room. (*They exit.*)

WIFE: A gold piece, eh? That's the young man who had nothing but a magic tablecloth when he stayed here before. (INNKEEPER *reenters.*) Where did he get the gold piece?

INNKEEPER: You'll find it hard to believe. The piece of gold came out of the goat's front hoof.

WIFE: Really? Do you think the goat has any more?

INNKEEPER: As far as I can tell, it's more magic. He just said, "Goat, make money," and she gave him the gold piece.

WIFE (*Excited*): We must have that wonderful animal. The tablecloth is miraculous! I haven't cooked a meal since we got it. But a money-maker like this? We must get it somehow.

INNKEEPER: It will be as easy as before. When he's asleep I'll take his goat and put our old nanny in its place. He'll never notice the difference.

WIFE: Not till he says, "Goat, make money." (*They laugh, as curtain falls*)

* * * * *

SCENE 3

TIME: *The next morning.*

SETTING: *The same as Scene 1.*

AT RISE: NED *comes from inn with hobby-horse goat and enters kitchen.*

NED (*Calling*): Mother, I'm home.

MOTHER (*Entering*): What have you got this time? (*Stops*) A goat? Well, at least we'll have some milk and cheese.

NED: Something much better than milk and cheese. Gold!

MOTHER: Gold?

NED: Yes, Mother. I just have to ask and Nanny will give me a gold piece. Just watch. (*Turns*) Goat, make money. (*Pause*) Goat, make money. (*Pause*) What's the matter with you, Nanny? You gave me a gold piece yesterday.

MOTHER (*Sighing*): Dreaming again, my son?

NED: No, Mother. I gave the gold piece to the innkeeper and he gave me these silver pieces in change. Look. (*He puts money on table.*)

MOTHER: I don't understand.

NED: The goat did give me a gold piece, and I'm sure she should do it again. I'm going back to ask the North Wind. I'll just take one silver piece in case I stop at the inn. (MOTHER *picks up coins and exits with goat.* NED *crosses to* NORTH WIND's *den, calls.*) Mr. North Wind! Come out, please, Mr. North Wind!

NORTH WIND (*Entering*): It's you again.

NED: Yes. Mr. North Wind, do you know if that goat had any more than one gold piece?

NORTH WIND: Yes, indeed. That goat will give you a gold piece whenever you ask her.

NED: Oh, no, she won't.

NORTH WIND: That's strange. I suspect, my boy, that someone has played a nasty trick on you.

NED: I thought of that, but who?

NORTH WIND: Who knew about your magic?

NED: Everyone at the inn knew about the tablecloth. But I didn't let anyone see the goat make money. Not anyone.

NORTH WIND: Well, someone must have found out. Let me see now. Ah, yes, I have something that should help. (*He exits, returning immediately with* STICK.) This is a magic stick.

NED: What can it do?

NORTH WIND: When you say, "Stick, lay on," it will beat everyone in sight except you, until you say, "Stick, lay off."

NED (*Disappointed*): Oh.

NORTH WIND: It's not food or money.

NED: No.

NORTH WIND: But perhaps it could help you get your goat and tablecloth back, eh?

NED: Oh, that would be great! Thank you.

NORTH WIND: Not so fast, young man. This stick will obey only one person—me. I'd better transfer its magic to you. (*Chanting*)

Magic mustard, tumble faster,

Stick, be transferred;

Ned's your master.

Now you may go. And good luck. I have nothing else to give you.

NED: Thank you, Mr. North Wind. You've been very kind. (NORTH WIND *nods and exits.*) Now, my friend, we'll put you to the test. We'll soon find the thief. (*Crosses to inn with* STICK) I'll stay at the inn again. (*He knocks.*)

INNKEEPER (*Entering*): Good evening.

NED: Good evening, sir. May I have a room for the night?

INNKEEPER: Of course. Why, it's my young friend of the magic tablecloth. How has it treated you?

NED: Not at all well. I thought it would cover itself with food whenever I asked it. But it worked only once—that night I stayed at your inn.

INNKEEPER: That's too bad. And have you any magic with you this time?

NED: I have only this old stick to help me in my travels. But I do have a silver piece to pay for my room. (*Hands him money*)

INNKEEPER: Thank you. I'll put you in the same room as before. Follow me. (*They exit.* WIFE *enters.*)

WIFE (*Putting down her basket as she calls*): Husband! I wonder where he is.

INNKEEPER (*As he reenters*): Wife, you'll never guess who has just arrived.

WIFE: Not the young man with the magic cloth and goat!

INNKEEPER: The very same.

WIFE: Is he suspicious?

INNKEEPER: No, he's too stupid. I asked about his magic tablecloth and he told me it worked only once.

WIFE: And the goat?

INNKEEPER: I didn't mention it at all.

WIFE: What does he have this time?

INNKEEPER: He says he has nothing. And he paid me this silver piece. But I'm sure it's one I gave him in change last time.

WIFE: Surely he has something special with him?

INNKEEPER: No. Just an old walking stick.

WIFE: An old stick. I wonder what that could be good for.

INNKEEPER: Nothing, I'd say.

WIFE: Nonsense. He had a magic thing with him before. He must have something this time.

INNKEEPER: That's what I thought. But I watched him through a crack in the bedroom door. He just put the stick in a corner and went to bed.

WIFE: I wonder if he's asleep.

INNKEEPER: Why?

WIFE: You could get the stick, and we'd try to find out how it works.

INNKEEPER: I don't think that stick is magic, but we may as well find out.

WIFE: Go and see if he's asleep. Then get the stick.

(INNKEEPER *exits.*) I'm going to ask it to give me jewels. I'd like that.

INNKEEPER (*Reentering with* STICK): Here it is.

WIFE: Let me try it. Stick, make diamonds. (STICK *does not move.* NED *appears quietly next to screen.*) Make rubies. (*Pause*) Well, make any kind of jewels.

INNKEEPER: Give it to me. Stick, transform this old inn into a castle. (STICK *does not move.*)

NED: Stick, lay on. (STICK *starts to beat* INNKEEPER *and* WIFE. *They run and yell, then crouch down, covering their heads with their hands.*)

INNKEEPER *and* WIFE: Make it stop. Please, make it stop.

NED: Stick, lay off. (STICK *stops.*) Good. (*They stand up and look at* NED.) Now, I wish to collect my tablecloth and my goat.

WIFE: What are you talking about?

NED: I'm talking about the tablecloth and the goat you stole from me when I was here before. Return them to me at once!

WIFE: My dear sir, if you've lost a goat, I'm sure it's no business of ours. As for your tablecloth, you took it with you.

NED: Stick, lay on. (STICK *starts to beat them; they cry out as before.*) Stick, lay off. (STICK *stops.*) Well?

WIFE: I'll get the tablecloth. (*She exits.*)

INNKEEPER: I'll get the goat. It's just outside in our barn. (*He exits center.* WIFE *reenters with cloth.*)

NED (*As he receives tablecloth*): It gives good food, eh?

WIFE: The best I ever tasted. I haven't cooked a meal since we had it. (*She weeps.*)

NED: I hope you enjoyed your holiday while it lasted. (INNKEEPER *reenters, leading* GOAT *on rope, gives rope to* NED.) Thank you. And now goodbye. Come, my goat and stick. We must go and surprise my mother. Our troubles are over. We will never be hungry again. (*Crosses to kitchen with* STICK *and* GOAT) Mother, I'm home. (*Curtain*)

THE END

(*Production Notes on page 312*)

A Triumph of Wits

A Chinese folktale

by Margaret Hall

Characters

ROSE, *an elderly Chinese woman*
LOTUS FLOWER ⎤
MOON BLOSSOM ⎦ *her daughters-in-law*
LONG FOO, *her son*
INDIGO, *a poor orphan*

SCENE 1

TIME: *Several centuries ago.*
SETTING: *A Chinese garden, in front of a doorway.*
AT RISE: ROSE *is seated majestically on large chair. A tea table is beside her.* LONG FOO *stands left.*
ROSE (*Impatiently*): Why has my tea not been brought to me, Long Foo? I fear that those girls your brothers married are silly and thoughtless. They do not show me the respect a mother-in-law deserves.
LONG FOO: Lotus Flower and Moon Blossom are still very young, Mother, and they do treat you with great respect. Even now they are preparing your tea and rice.

40

ROSE (*Relenting*): They are good and obedient, but the village they grew up in is far away, and I know they are homesick. (*Firmly*) When you marry, my son, be sure to choose a wife from our own village. (LOTUS FLOWER *and* MOON BLOSSOM *enter left, each carrying a tray of covered dishes, which they set on table.*)

LOTUS FLOWER (*Bowing*): Honored Mother-in-law, here is your salted fish and rice.

MOON BLOSSOM (*Bowing*): And I have brought your stewed meat and vegetables, Honored Lady. The tea is almost ready.

ROSE: Thank you. Everything smells delicious. (*Girls remove covers from bowls.* ROSE *picks up chopsticks and dips into nearest bowl. She tastes food and nods.*) The food is tasty indeed, my dears. Now you may go eat your own dinner.

LOTUS FLOWER (*Bowing*): But, first, Honorable One, we have a request. We hope you will grant it.

ROSE (*Suspiciously*): What is it that you want?

MOON BLOSSOM: We wish only that you let us visit our native village for a few days.

ROSE: Again? You went there not more than two moons ago.

MOON BLOSSOM: I know, Honorable One, but it is the place where we were born, and we love it very much. Our husbands are willing to let us go, but they always ask your opinion in everything. If you give us your permission, they are ready to grant theirs.

LOTUS FLOWER: Our kind husbands like to see us happy. We have never asked another favor of you.

LONG FOO: Why not let them go, Mother? You have plenty of servants to wait on you, and you will not suffer if your daughters-in-law are absent for a few days.

MOON BLOSSOM: You are kind, Brother-in-law.

ROSE (*Sternly*): Since I have no daughters, I was hoping
for companionship from my sons' wives. But you
young, thoughtless girls wish to leave me again to
visit your old home. I mean to discourage this be-
havior. (*Pauses*) Yes, my little pheasants, you may go
to visit your families.

MOON BLOSSOM (*Excitedly*): May we truly? May we
leave today?

ROSE: Yes, you may leave as soon as you like. But this
time I am making a condition. There are two things
I desire, and you may not come back to your husbands without them.

LOTUS FLOWER (*Eagerly*): Of course, we shall bring you
anything you wish, Honored One.

MOON BLOSSOM: It will be our chief delight to fetch you
whatever you desire. Tell us what it is.

ROSE: It may not be as easy as you think. (*Pauses*) You
know how thin and fragile a piece of paper is. (*Turning to* LOTUS FLOWER) You, Lotus Flower, are to bring
me fire wrapped in a paper.

LOTUS FLOWER (*Astounded*): But how shall I wrap fire
in a paper? Why, paper will burst into flames if it is
placed near fire.

ROSE (*To* MOON BLOSSOM): As for you, Moon Blossom,
you shall bring me wind in a paper.

MOON BLOSSOM (*Bewildered and upset*): Wind in a
paper? That's impossible! The wind is not an object
we can see or touch. How could it be contained inside
a paper?

LOTUS FLOWER (*Tearfully*): I never heard of such a
thing. (*Turning to* LONG FOO) Do you know how we
may do either of these things, Long Foo?

LONG FOO (*Shaking his head*): I confess, I am unable to
help you. But, my honorable mother is wise and just,
so there must be a way.

LOTUS FLOWER (*Firmly*): If there really is a way, we shall find it. Surely by putting both our minds to work, we will think of something. (*To* ROSE) We shall bring back what you ask, Honorable One.

MOON BLOSSOM (*Bowing*): We shall do as you wish. May we go?

ROSE (*Bowing her head*): Certainly. Pack what you need and be off. (MOON BLOSSOM *and* LOTUS FLOWER, *smiling, bow to* ROSE *and* LONG FOO, *and run off.* ROSE *sighs.*) At least we shall have relief from their chatter for a few days.

LONG FOO: The time may be much longer than that, Mother. I confess that I don't see how they are to fulfill your request. They may never return here. (*Shaking head*) That will be a sad thing for my brothers.

ROSE: Your brothers may then see their wives for the silly creatures they are. Meanwhile, you may join me in eating this tasty meal, Long Foo. (LONG FOO *sits beside her, picks up chopsticks, and they begin to eat as curtain falls.*)

* * * * *

SCENE 2

TIME: *A few days later.*

SETTING: *A country road. This scene may be played before curtain.*

AT RISE: LOTUS FLOWER *and* MOON BLOSSOM *enter left, each carrying a bundle of clothing. They stop at center.*

LOTUS FLOWER: Now that we have had a delightful visit with our parents, Moon Blossom, we must make the long journey back to our dear husbands.

(*Sighs deeply*) But what about that rash promise we made to our mother-in-law?

MOON BLOSSOM (*Sadly*): I am afraid that the tasks seem impossible. (INDIGO *enters right, unseen by* MOON BLOSSOM *and* LOTUS FLOWER. *She stops to listen.*)

LOTUS FLOWER: How can I ever find fire in a paper to take to her? The paper will burn, and I will never see my dear husband again.

MOON BLOSSOM: It is no easier for me to put wind in a paper. The wind will blow the paper away and I, too, will be without a husband. (*Sadly*) Oh, what shall we do?

LOTUS FLOWER: We were so eager to go, we never thought it meant we had to choose between our husbands and our families. (INDIGO *goes to them.*)

INDIGO: Forgive me, but I could not help overhearing. I would like to help you solve your problem, since it is so important to you.

MOON BLOSSOM: It is no use! Who could wrap wind or contain fire in a paper? (*They sit and bury their faces in their hands, crying.*)

INDIGO: Now, now. Crying never mended a broken fishnet.

MOON BLOSSOM (*Looking up*): Who are you, kind stranger?

INDIGO (*Cheerfully*): I am an orphan, and the people who raised me never bothered to give me a name. As long as I do my share of work, they are pleased. But, sometimes they call me Indigo, for the long hours I spend working in the indigo fields. (*She sits.*)

LOTUS FLOWER (*Intrigued*): An orphan! I am sure your parents were noble people, Indigo, for it is kind and generous of you to help two strangers.

INDIGO (*Shrugging*): Perhaps . . . I know nothing about

them. (*Intently*) But let's concentrate on your tasks. If we all use our wits, we can surely find some way to keep your promise. (*They are silent for a moment. Then* INDIGO *springs to her feet, excited.*) I think I have the answer! All you really need are two pieces of paper and a small candle. If you will come home with me, I'll find them for you.

MOON BLOSSOM (*Doubtfully*): I don't quite see what good those will do, (*Firmly*) but I trust you, Indigo.

LOTUS FLOWER: How could the answer come into your mind, when it would not come to us?

INDIGO (*Laughing*): Because it is easier to think when your mind is not filled with worries! Come! (*They follow her out.*)

* * * * *

SCENE 3

TIME: *A few hours later.*

SETTING: *The same as Scene 1.*

AT RISE: ROSE *and* LONG FOO *are seated side by side.* LOTUS FLOWER *and* MOON BLOSSOM *enter, followed by* INDIGO. MOON BLOSSOM *and* LOTUS FLOWER *hold paper,* INDIGO *holds flashlight "candle" and candlestick. They bow respectfully to* ROSE, *as* INDIGO *stands behind them, looking around.*

MOON BLOSSOM: Honorable One, we have enjoyed a visit with our relatives, and we now return to your respected presence. (*Turning to* LONG FOO) Greetings to you also, Long Foo. We hope you and our husbands have enjoyed good health in our absence.

LONG FOO: Welcome home! (*Points to* INDIGO) Who is this lovely girl you have brought along?

LOTUS FLOWER: This is Indigo, (INDIGO *bows to him.*)

who helped us with our tasks. She is poor in worldly goods, but rich in imagination and good sense.

ROSE: Qualities like those are a form of wealth in themselves. But you astonish me. (*Sternly*) You two flighty daughters-in-law are not obeying my requests. You know I said you could come home only if you bring wind in a paper and fire in a paper.

LONG FOO: Wait! They have something in their hands. (*Turns*) What are you carrying?

LOTUS FLOWER (*Triumphantly*): You will see. (INDIGO *gives her a small flashlight disguised as a candle, then "lights" candle as* LOTUS FLOWER *turns on flashlight and places it in candlestick on table.*) You see the flame burning before you. Now I will make a lantern from this paper (*Holding up paper*) to surround the flame. Observe. (NOTE: *A finished paper lantern is set behind table, out of view of audience.* LOTUS FLOWER *lowers the lantern over the candle.*) The paper is wrapped around the candle. See? And the flame glows through it. (*All gasp in amazement.*)

ROSE (*Excitedly*): How pretty that looks!

LONG FOO: I see! By leaving a hole in the top of the paper, the paper does not burn.

ROSE: Wonderful! (*Suddenly, to* MOON BLOSSOM) What about the wind in the paper? How can you manage that?

MOON BLOSSOM: Please watch closely. (*She holds up paper that has been folded into accordion pleats.*) Indigo folded this square piece of paper. If you hold the bottom of the folds together and spread the top like this, (*She demonstrates.*) you have a fan. Wave it back and forth across your face, and it will blow the cooling wind against your skin.

ROSE (*Snatching fan; eagerly*): Let me try it! On a hot day like this I crave a little relief. (*She fans herself;*

happily) How delightful! How pleasant to feel such a welcome breeze! It actually is wind in a paper. When I made those two requests, I never believed you could truly achieve them. I am happy to welcome the two of you back as if you were my real daughters. You have passed the test, and very cleverly, too!

MOON BLOSSOM: Indigo did it all.

LOTUS FLOWER: Oh, yes. They were her ideas.

ROSE (*To* LONG FOO): When you marry, my son, I hope you choose a girl who has as much wit.

LONG FOO: I think I have already found my future wife, Mother. She has wit, and she is also beautiful. Indigo, will you join our humble family as my bride?

INDIGO (*Embarrassed*): I am only a poor orphan—and I have no dowry.

LONG FOO: But as my mother so wisely observed, you have riches more valuable than money. You have shown that you can use your wits.

ROSE: We can provide for you, child. A person's worth does not depend upon material possessions. Those with money and no intelligence soon lose their money. (*Smiling*) But you must have some finer name when you join our family. What would you like to be called?

MOON BLOSSOM: How about Wealth of Wit and Wisdom?

LOTUS FLOWER: Or Lustrous Pearl?

INDIGO: What do you think, Long Foo?

LONG FOO (*Smiling*): I am sure that someone as wise as you could choose a suitable name. What pleases you best?

INDIGO: Secretly, I have always wanted to be called Rising Sun. When I see the sun come up over the fields, I am filled with wonder and happiness. (*All smile and clap hands in delight.*)

ROSE: An excellent choice! Rising Sun you shall be named. And now, Long Foo, you must bring out fresh tea and serve us.

LONG FOO (*Amazed*): You want *me* to fetch the tea? Your daughters-in-law have returned—why not ask them? It is the custom!

ROSE (*Smiling*): Every rule has exceptions, my son, and a woman my age knows when to change the rules. So hurry, now, and bring out our best tea! (LONG FOO *smiles good-naturedly, shakes his head in resignation, and exits.*) Now, my daughters, sit beside me and we shall all enjoy fanning ourselves. Do you have more paper fans?

LOTUS FLOWER: Oh, yes, we brought others with us. (*They seat themselves on rug at* ROSE's *right, and each one takes out a paper fan from a pocket. They all fan themselves and smile at each other as the curtain falls.*)

THE END

(*Production Notes on page 312*)

The Mice That Ate Money

An Indian folktale

by Beatrice S. Smith

Characters

BANKER
SON
SERVANT
YOUNG MAN

TIME: *Long ago.*
SETTING: *A garden in ancient India. There are several potted plants left and right. Couch with colorful coverlet stands center.*
AT RISE: BANKER *lies on couch.* SON *plays with ball as* SERVANT *enters, carrying large umbrella.*
SERVANT (*Holding out umbrella*): Did you ask for this, Master?
BANKER: Yes. Open it and hold it high, so the sun does not shine in my eyes. I wish to take a nap. (SERVANT *raises umbrella over* BANKER.)
SERVANT: May I remind you, Master, that you awoke only an hour ago?

BANKER (*Angrily*): What does that matter! Rich people
   may sleep whenever they choose!

SERVANT (*Bowing*): Yes, Master.

BANKER: Do you know how rich I am?

SERVANT: No, Master, how rich are you?

BANKER (*Smugly*): Very rich. I have more bags of silver
   coins than I can count.

SERVANT: I see. Earned, no doubt, by the sweat of your
   brow?

BANKER (*Snorting*): No, indeed! Sweat is not for bank-
   ers. A fool gave me my money.

SERVANT: A fool?

BANKER: Yes. A stupid young man went off to find work
   in another land and gave me his coins for safekeeping. (*Rubs hands gleefully*) Now I am rich.

SERVANT: But, Master, they are not yours to keep.
   Won't this young man want his coins returned?

BANKER: Of course he will. (*With villainous laugh*) But
   wanting is not having.

SERVANT: What will you tell him?

BANKER (*Shrugging*): Whatever comes into my head.
   He is stupid. He will believe anything I tell him.
   (*Frowns*) And you're stupid, too! Why do you hold
   that umbrella? It isn't raining, or even cloudy. (SER-
   VANT *closes umbrella and tucks it under arm.*) Be
   gone now, and let me rest. (SON *is now bouncing ball
   against couch.*)

SERVANT: Yes, Master. Shall I take your son away so he
   won't disturb you?

BANKER: No. He is my favorite child. He may stay. But
   see to it that no one else disturbs me. Do you understand?

SERVANT (*Bowing*): Yes, Master. (*Exits*)

BANKER: Miserable wretch! (*Puts head back and
   snores;* SON *bounces ball against couch. After a mo-*

ment, SERVANT *reenters.* SON *bounces ball against* SERVANT'*s legs.* SERVANT *makes threatening gesture.*)

SON: Miserable wretch! Touch me and you will regret it.

SERVANT (*Shaking head in disgust*): You are already much like your father.

BANKER (*Blinking, sitting up, scowling at* SERVANT): I told you I did not want to be disturbed!

SERVANT: I apologize, Master, but there is a young man outside who insists upon seeing you.

BANKER (*Yawning, grumbling*): Oh, very well. Let him come in. (SERVANT *bows, exits.* BANKER *gazes at* SON *and smiles, as* SON *continues to bounce ball against couch.*) Come here, my son. (SON *bounces ball once again, then comes slowly to* BANKER'*s side.*) What do you wish to be when you grow up, child?

SON: Rich. With many servants to do as I command.

BANKER (*Nodding, smiling*): So you shall be.

SON: But, Papa, where will I get the money? For I also want a throne of gold and a crown made of diamonds.

BANKER: Never fear, my son. I have more bags of coins than I can count.

SON: Where did you get them, Papa?

BANKER: From a stupid young man who gave me his coins for safekeeping. (*Glances at* SERVANT, *who reenters with* YOUNG MAN) And here is the simpleton now. (*To* SON) Leave us, my son. (SON *goes to side of stage and continues to bounce ball.*)

SERVANT: Master, here is the young man who insisted upon seeing you.

BANKER (*Looking at* YOUNG MAN, *then nodding curtly to* SERVANT): You may go. (SERVANT *exits.* BANKER *turns to* YOUNG MAN.) Yes? What is it?

YOUNG MAN: Good morning, sir. Isn't it a beautiful day?

BANKER (*Shrugging*): I hadn't noticed.

YOUNG MAN (*Trying to be polite*): Your garden is beautiful, too.

BANKER (*Shrugging*): I suppose so.

YOUNG MAN (*Gesturing toward* SON): Surely you consider that child beautiful.

BANKER (*Beaming happily*): Ah, yes. My favorite son is indeed beautiful. (*Smiles*) Have you come here to admire my garden?

YOUNG MAN: Ah—not exactly, sir. (*Hesitates*) You know who I am, do you not?

BANKER (*Pretending surprise*): Should I?

YOUNG MAN: Yes, sir. A long time ago I gave you my savings for safekeeping.

BANKER (*Impatiently*): I do not remember.

YOUNG MAN: But you must. There were bags and bags of silver coins, more than I could count.

BANKER: Silver coins? You are greatly mistaken, young man. I have none of your money.

YOUNG MAN: But you have, sir. (*Reaches into pocket and pulls out a small piece of brown paper*) When I gave you the coins, you gave me this piece of paper as a receipt.

BANKER: What paper?

YOUNG MAN: This paper, sir. (*Hands* BANKER *paper*)

BANKER (*Tearing it into many pieces, and flinging pieces over his shoulder*): What paper? I see no paper.

YOUNG MAN (*Staring at bits of paper, then, firmly*): Sir, the paper does not matter. I have a witness who saw me give you the coins.

BANKER (*Standing*): And who would that be?

YOUNG MAN: I will fetch him, sir. (*Exits*)

BANKER (*Sneering*): A witness, indeed! The young fool!

(YOUNG MAN *reenters with* SERVANT.)

YOUNG MAN: Here is my witness, sir.

BANKER: My servant is your witness?

YOUNG MAN: Yes, sir. He saw me give you the coins for safekeeping.

SERVANT: It is so, Master. I did, and I will swear to it.

BANKER: Miserable wretch! Do you think a judge will believe the likes of you?

SERVANT: Yes, Master, I am sure of it. I have always been an honest man.

BANKER (*Glaring at* SERVANT, *then suddenly smiling gleefully*): You may have seen this young man give me bagfuls of silver coins for safekeeping. But alas— (*Sighs*) that was long ago. (*Sighs again*) They are gone now.

YOUNG MAN (*Shouting*): Gone! (*Agitated*) Then I am penniless!

SERVANT: Gone? But Master, you have more sacks of coins than you can count. You said so yourself only moments ago.

BANKER: True. But all silver coins look alike. The coins I have belong to a poor widow. They do not belong to this young man. (*Pauses*) Would you tell me different—and so cheat the poor old widow?

SERVANT: No, Master! I would cheat no one.

BANKER (*To* SERVANT): Miserable wretch! Be gone! (SERVANT *looks helplessly at* YOUNG MAN *and exits.* BANKER *speaks to* YOUNG MAN.) You heard what I said. The coins I have are not yours. Now, be off. I wish to take a nap.

YOUNG MAN (*Humbly*): If you please, sir—you say that the coins you have belong to a widow. Would you kindly tell me what happened to my coins?

BANKER (*Yawning*): They are gone.

YOUNG MAN: Gone? Where?

BANKER (*Pretending regret*): Alas! I am sorry to say that your coins were eaten by mice.

YOUNG MAN (*In disbelief*): Mice? Did you say mice?

BANKER (*Nodding*): Yes, I said mice. Mice ate your coins.

YOUNG MAN: You must be dreaming, sir. Mice do not eat coins.

BANKER: These mice did. I speak of what I have seen with my own eyes. Mice ate your coins, I say.

YOUNG MAN (*Frowning*): Mice. Hm-m. Who would believe it? (*Shakes head, glances about, sees* SON, *who is still bouncing ball*) Please, sir, I have traveled far. Would you be so kind as to give me a drink of water before I go?

BANKER: Indeed. (*Smiles*) I will fetch it myself from yonder brook. (*Exits. As soon as* BANKER *exits,* YOUNG MAN *hurries toward* SON.)

SON (*In unpleasant tone*): What do you want, simpleton?

YOUNG MAN: Would you like to play a trick?

SON (*Eagerly*): I like tricks. What must I do?

YOUNG MAN: Give a loud shout, then hide nearby, and stay there until I call.

SON: My father will be upset when he does not see me.

YOUNG MAN: I know. That is the trick.

SON (*Laughing*): What a fine trick! (*Gives loud shout and runs offstage, just before* BANKER *enters*)

BANKER: Here you are. (*Hands jug of water to* YOUNG MAN) Drink your fill. (*Looks around*) What was that noise I heard just now?

YOUNG MAN: Noise? (*Cocks head*) Did you say you heard a noise?

BANKER: I did. It sounded like a braying donkey.

YOUNG MAN: A braying donkey? You call your son a braying donkey?

BANKER (*Whirling round and round, looking for* SON): My son! Was that noise made by my son?

YOUNG MAN: It was indeed. (*Takes a sip of water in unconcerned manner*)

BANKER (*Shaking* YOUNG MAN's *arm*): What happened?

YOUNG MAN (*Shrugging*): Your son is gone.

BANKER (*Shouting*): Gone? Where did he go?

YOUNG MAN (*Sighing, pretending regret*): I'm sorry to say that a hawk swooped down from the sky and carried him off.

BANKER (*Shocked*): That's impossible!

YOUNG MAN: No, it is true. I speak of what I have seen with my own eyes. A hawk about this big (*Measures long distance with his hands*) swooped down and carried him off.

BANKER (*Enraged*): Don't be an idiot! How could a hawk carry off a boy?

YOUNG MAN (*Speaking slowly*): If my silver coins could be eaten by mice, a hawk easily might carry off a boy. (*Cocks head*) Don't you agree?

BANKER (*Glaring at* YOUNG MAN, *then slumping on couch, and putting head in hands*): Oh, my son—in the clutches of a hawk. (*Moans*)

YOUNG MAN: Perhaps we can make a deal.

BANKER: What kind of a deal?

YOUNG MAN: If you can find the mice who ate my coins and persuade them to cough up every one, I will find the hawk and persuade him to release your son from his clutches. Will you agree?

BANKER (*Jumping up, nodding and smiling*): Yes. Yes, indeed! (*Claps hands, shouts to* SERVANT *offstage*) Servant! Go to the money room and pack the sacks of coins in a cart for this young man. Be quick!

SERVANT (*From offstage*): Yes, Master.

BANKER (*To* YOUNG MAN): It is done.

YOUNG MAN (*Satisfied*): Very well. (*Claps hands and*

shouts to SON *offstage*) Boy! Come back! (*Sound of footsteps*)

BANKER: Now, we both shall live happily ever after, eh?

YOUNG MAN: Well, I don't know about that. But we both shall get what we deserve. (*Smiles as* SON *comes bounding in and throws himself into* BANKER's *arms. Curtain*)

THE END

(*Production Notes on page 312*)

Baron Barnaby's Box

A Welsh folktale

by J. G. Colson

Characters

WILL GOODWIN
BESS GOODWIN
NICHOLAS NOODLE
THOMAS TINHEAD
MATTIE MEDDLER
BARBARA BUSYBODY
SIMON SNAFFLE
SALLY SNAFFLE
BARON BARNABY

TIME: *Early one summer evening.*

SETTING: *The village green in the tiny village of Barnaby Turf, Wales.*

AT RISE: WILL GOODWIN, *an old man, enters down left, followed by his wife,* BESS, *who is obviously very tired.*

WILL: Come, Bess, come. Keep a stout heart.

BESS: My heart's stout enough, Will, but my legs—they just won't go.

WILL: We must go on.

BESS (*Seeing a log and sitting on it*): That's better. It's shady here, and it's so hot on the road.

WILL: The hottest day this summer, I'll be bound. But we can't tarry, Bess. 'Tis evening already, and we've many a mile to walk yet.

BESS (*Wearily*): My poor legs! Can't we stay at an inn for the night?

WILL: No, my dear.

BESS: Why not, Will?

WILL: You know why not. (*Reaches into his pocket and takes out two pennies*) Look! Only two pennies.

BESS: Is that all we have?

WILL (*Sighing*): That is all. Not enough for a night's lodging. (*Puts pennies back into his pocket*)

BESS: But my legs will never carry me to Cousin John's. The village of Appleby is miles off yet.

WILL: You'll feel better when you've rested. Don't worry.

BESS: But I *am* worried. We shall have to walk all night. We should have stopped that coach when it passed us. Perhaps we could have begged a ride for part of the way.

WILL: The coach wouldn't stop for the likes of us! Didn't you notice that fine lord sitting inside?

BESS: He had a kind face. (*Sighs*) Of course, we look poor.

WILL: We *are* poor. But cheer up, Bess, there's plenty of work waiting for us at Cousin John's.

BESS: If we ever get there, Will. Why, oh, why did we leave Wyberton?

WILL: You know in your heart that we would have starved in Wyberton. There's no more life in the ground. Nothing would grow any more.

BESS (*Rising*): Let's move on, Will.

WILL: Lean on my shoulder, Bess. You'll feel better soon.

BESS: Ay, but oh, my legs ache so! (*They start left, as voices are heard off right.*)

WILL: Listen!

BESS: People. They sound upset, too.

WILL: Something's the matter! Look over there! (*He points right.*) Can't you see them?

BESS: Ay, proper excited they are, too.

WILL (*Nervously*): They're coming this way. (MATTIE MEDDLER *enters right, carrying medium-sized wooden box, which is tied shut. She is followed by* BARBARA BUSYBODY. WILL *and* BESS, *who move upstage, are unobserved by the villagers.*)

MATTIE: I've got it! I've got it! Here it is. (*She puts box down.*) Come and see!

BARBARA: Just in time, Mattie. That Simon Snaffle would have run off with it.

MATTIE: Ay, Barbara, we got rid of him, we did. (NICHOLAS NOODLE *and* THOMAS TINHEAD, *two old men, enter, followed shortly by* SIMON SNAFFLE *and his wife,* SALLY, *who hurry in.*)

THOMAS: What's all this shouting for, Mattie Meddler?

MATTIE: I'll tell ye, Thomas Tinhead.

NICHOLAS: Go on, we're waiting.

MATTIE: Barbara Busybody and I saw Simon Snaffle there (*She points to him.*) pick up this box on the roadside. . .

SIMON: I was only going to show it to my wife.

MATTIE: A likely tale that is, Simon Snaffle.

SALLY: Don't you go saying things about my husband, Mattie Meddler!

NICHOLAS: Now, now! Don't squabble. This is a fine

box, for sure. But how did it come to be on the side of the road?

SIMON: I don't know.

BARBARA: Well, now that we've brought this box to the village green, what are we going to do with it?

THOMAS (*Nervously*): Don't open it. There might be something queer inside.

SALLY: There might be money in it.

SIMON: Ay, money—silver money.

NICHOLAS: Silver! I haven't seen any silver since grandfather showed me his silver fourpenny.

THOMAS: Throw it in the river, I say. Might be spirits inside. (*They all crowd round.*)

SALLY: No. Take it to my house.

THOMAS: Give me a hand, Nicholas. Let's dump it in the river.

SIMON: No! (*There is a slight scuffle around box.* WILL *and* BESS *move downstage.*)

WILL (*To* BESS): What simple folk!

BESS: Quite foolish, I think.

WILL: We had better go over to see what is happening. Perhaps we can help. (WILL *and* BESS *walk to crowd.*) Good evening, good people. (*Villagers stare at them.*)

SIMON (*Boldly*): Who are you?

BARBARA: What are you doing in Barnaby Turf?

SALLY: Where do you come from?

WILL (*Holding up his hand*): All in good time. All in good time. I'm Will Goodwin. (*Pointing*) Bess my good wife, here, and I have come from Wyberton.

THOMAS: From Wyberton! All that way!

NICHOLAS: And where be you going?

BESS: To Appleby to work with my cousin John.

THOMAS: I've heard tell that folk from Wyberton be wise.

NICHOLAS: Ay, that be true. Wyberton folk be the wisest in the world.

SIMON: Just the man we need. (*To* WILL) Tell us what to do with this box.

WILL: Let me look at it first.

SIMON: Ay, do, but don't interfere with it.

WILL (*Looking at box*): The lock's broken.

SALLY: We know that—but the cord looks strong.

WILL: Carefully knotted.

SIMON: I'll cut it with my knife.

NICHOLAS: No, you won't. Let the wise man decide.

SALLY: Let's take it to my house, stranger. That's what we ought to do.

WILL: All in good time, mistress. I must think. (*He examines box more closely.*) Ha! Now I can see some writing on it.

NICHOLAS: Writing! Writing! What's that?

THOMAS: Letters, you fool. Didn't you ever go to school?

NICHOLAS: School! If there's a school in Barnaby Turf, nobody told me about it.

BARBARA: Tell us what those letters say, Master Goodwin.

WILL (*Peering*): It's a long time since I learned my alphabet. Come, Bess, you're cleverer than I am. Read the words for us.

BESS (*Looking at box*): It says "Baron Barnaby, his box."

SIMON: Baron Barnaby!

WILL: Baron Barnaby! Who is he?

BARBARA: The richest man for many a mile.

MATTIE: He owns all the land as far as you can see.

NICHOLAS: Lord of the Manor, he is called.

BESS: Then this must be his chest.

SALLY: It's ours! Simon found it!

SIMON: That's true. I found it. It's mine.

WILL: But it belongs to the Baron.

SALLY: The Baron's rich enough. He won't miss one box.

WILL: Take my advice, good villagers of Barnaby Turf. Take the box to the Baron.

BARBARA: But it might be full of silver.

NICHOLAS: Silver!

SIMON: I'll take it home.

MATTIE: No, you won't! We'll divide the silver among us. Cut that cord with your knife, Simon Snaffle.

SIMON: I'd rather take the box home.

BESS: But that would be stealing!

WILL: Ay, it's wrong to steal.

NICHOLAS: Stealing! What does that mean?

THOMAS: Bet you don't come from Wyberton, do you, Nicholas?

WILL (*Firmly*): Listen, good folk, this box might be a trap.

NICHOLAS: Ay, it might be, wise man.

WILL: I've heard of queer things before, especially in chests like this. Harmful things.

SIMON: Have you now! Perhaps I'd better not touch it.

BARBARA: Harmful or not, I'd like to see what's inside. Go on, Simon, cut that cord. Baron Barnaby wouldn't put anything dangerous in his own box.

NICHOLAS (*To* WILL): Dare you open it, Master Goodwin?

WILL: 'Tis not mine to open. Besides, I suspect that someone has set a snare for you.

SALLY: Nonsense! We've fooled about long enough.

BARBARA: Ay, open it, Simon. (SIMON *does not move.*)

SALLY: Don't listen to this nonsense, Simon. Open it.

SIMON: Oh, very well—since you all wish it. (*Takes knife from pocket, moves slowly to box, cuts cord, and cautiously throws back lid, revealing a quantity of golden coins)*

NICHOLAS: Yellow money!

THOMAS: Yellow coins! Hundreds of 'em. (*Villagers start toward box.*)

WILL (*Loudly*): Keep back! Don't touch those coins. (*He waves them away from box.*) They're dangerous. It's a trap!

NICHOLAS: I can't see any trap—though those coins are a funny color.

WILL: Of course they are. That's the trick. I'll show you. Look! (*He pretends to pick one up, then draws his hand back, as he touches it.*) Oh! (*Puts his fingers into his mouth*)

NICHOLAS: Now what's the matter?

WILL: As I thought. They're burning hot! Those coins are on fire. (*Shakes finger as if to cool it*) I touched just one of them. If I'd picked it up, it would have burned my fingers off. (*Steps back*) Feel for yourselves. (*Villagers shrink back.*)

THOMAS: Not I.

WILL: You, Simon, come and feel.

SIMON (*Moving away*): No—no. I believe you, Master Goodwin.

NICHOLAS: It's a good thing you came along, Master Goodwin.

WILL: I'll close the lid now, while we're all safe. (*He closes lid on box.*) Those coins were burning. That's what made them a golden color. I've seen that sort of red-hot silver before.

THOMAS: We might have lost our fingers.

WILL: You might have, Thomas.

BARBARA: Now we're back where we started.

NICHOLAS: It could have been worse if we'd been burned.

WILL: Good folk, I know you're disappointed. But, here, take these. (*He pulls two pennies out of his pocket.*) Spend them at the inn.

SALLY: Two pennies! (*Villagers crowd round.*)

MATTIE: Ay, we'll spend them, Master Goodwin.

SIMON: Give me them!

MATTIE: No, me!

WILL: Patience! Patience! (*They crowd round him. He throws pennies off right. They rush out after coins,* THOMAS *and* NICHOLAS *at rear.* NICHOLAS *turns at exit.*)

NICHOLAS (*Shaking his head*): Throwing your money about! Even if you do come from Wyberton, Master Goodwin, you are a fool.

THOMAS: Come on, Nicholas. Let's be off to the inn. (*Exits*)

NICHOLAS (*To* WILL *and* BESS): Good day to you both. Take care of that box. (*Exits*)

WILL: Poor simple folk!

BESS: You worked that very well, Will. You're cleverer than I knew.

WILL: I had an inspiration. But do you know, Bess, I've never seen so many golden crowns in my life.

BESS: It's a good thing those villagers had never seen gold before. (*She walks across to box.*) Enough here to make us rich for life.

WILL: But it's not ours.

BESS (*Sighing*): No . . . And you've thrown away your last pennies.

WILL: No use crying over that, Bess. (*He moves over to box.*) Help me hide this chest. Those villagers might come back. We'll put it behind the bushes over there. (*Points left*)

BESS: You know best, Will. (*They carry box to one side.*)

WILL: Now, sit on that log and rest your legs a while.

Keep an eye on the box while I go off to find this Baron Barnaby. (BARON BARNABY *enters up left.*)

BARNABY: There is no need to look farther. He is here.

BESS: You, sir?

BARNABY: Yes, Madam. I am Baron Barnaby.

WILL (*Pointing to chest*): Tell me, sir, is that your box?

BARNABY: It is. It fell off my coach.

BESS: Ah, then you must have passed us along the way.

BARNABY: As a matter of fact, I did.

WILL: Those villagers brought your chest here.

BESS: And would have stolen your gold.

BARNABY: I know. But Will, my good fellow, your cleverness saved it. I was behind those bushes (*He points up left*) and heard everything. I was curious, so I didn't interfere. Believe me, I'm grateful. You shall both be well rewarded.

BESS (*Gratefully*): Oh, thank you, sir. (BARON BARNABY *goes to box and takes out handful of gold coins.*)

BARNABY: Take these. You have earned them. (*He gives each several gold coins.*)

BESS *and* WILL (*Ad lib*): Oh, thank you, sir. You are very kind. (*Etc.*)

BARNABY: Don't thank me. It is I who should thank you. Now, where are you going?

BESS: To work at Appleby where my Cousin John lives.

BARNABY: Appleby! That's a long way from here. How do you propose to reach there?

BESS: On foot, sir.

BARNABY: Oh, no, you will ride in my coach.

WILL: You are very kind. The gold you've given us is enough to start a farm. (*To* BESS) Come, Bess, our fortune is made, our future happiness assured. (WILL *and* BESS *start off, as curtain falls.*)

THE END

(*Production Notes on page 312*)

The King and the Bee

An Israeli folktale

by Virginia Payne Whitworth

Characters

LORD CHAMBERLAIN
KING SOLOMON
BEE
KEEPER OF THE ROYAL OINTMENT
PAGE
QUEEN OF SHEBA

TIME: *Many years ago.*
SETTING: *King Solomon's garden. Low wall and bushes enclose garden. Ornamental vases stand at right. Bench with cushions stands left.*
AT RISE: *Soft, appropriate music is heard, then fades, as* LORD CHAMBERLAIN *enters.*
CHAMBERLAIN (*Pounding on floor with staff, and intoning*): Make way for His Majesty, the King! Make way for King Solomon. (KING SOLOMON *enters.*)
SOLOMON: Peace, Lord Chamberlain! The garden is

quite deserted. You may go. I wish to be left alone, to think—maybe to sleep a little.

CHAMBERLAIN: To sleep—here—in the garden, sire?

SOLOMON: Yes, to sleep, and perhaps to dream of the coming of the beautiful queen from the land of Sheba.

CHAMBERLAIN (*Bowing*): I go, sire, but I shall be not far off, should you require me. (*Exits*)

SOLOMON: Very well, Lord Chamberlain. (*Yawning*) This heat makes me drowsy. (*Stretching out on bench*) The quiet is good. I can almost hear the flowers growing. Even the bees buzz only faintly in the distance. This crown is too heavy for a hot day. (*He takes off crown and lays it on the ground.*) That's better. (*As he closes his eyes, music of "Flight of the Bumblebee" begins softly.* BEE *enters, moving about in an aimless kind of dance. Music grows louder.*)

BEE: This must be the king's garden. I've never seen so many flowers. (*Bends over flowers, as if gathering nectar*) Mm-m-m! This is very good nectar. (*She suddenly sees* SOLOMON.) A man! I wonder if he is asleep. (*She peers into his face, and as she bends over him, her wings touch his face. He wakes and waves his hand to brush her away. Frightened, she strikes out with her stinger, and pricks his nose.*) Oh! What have I done? I fear I have pricked his nose! (*She runs back from bench.*)

SOLOMON (*Putting his hand to his nose and looking around*): Oh, my nose! What has hurt me? Who's here?

BEE: Oh, dear, oh, dear! I'm so frightened! (*Looks at stinger*) I've broken the point of my stinger! (*Hides behind bush*)

SOLOMON: Who speaks? I hear a little voice crying that she is frightened.

BEE (*Amazed*): He understands me! No human being has ever understood me before. It must be the great and wise King Solomon!

SOLOMON: Step forth, creature. Name yourself.

BEE (*Coming forward timidly*): It is only I, sire. One of the humblest of the Lord's creatures—a honeybee.

SOLOMON: Do not be afraid. Only tell me why you struck me just now. (*Holds her arm*)

BEE: Please do not kill me, sire. I did not mean any harm. I was curious to see whether you were asleep, and as I bent over to look, you woke very suddenly with a jump. When I am frightened or startled I always strike out with my little stinger—and so I did this time, touching your royal nose. Forgive me, Your Majesty.

SOLOMON: How do you know that I am king? I wear no crown.

BEE: No, but you understood my language. No one but the wisest of the wise may do that.

SOLOMON: I was dreaming of the lovely Queen of Sheba, and you disturbed me.

BEE: I am sorry, sire. Please, sire, let me go free!

SOLOMON: What if I do?

BEE: Maybe sometime I can show my gratitude. Maybe I can be of service to you, who knows?

SOLOMON (*Laughing*): That is very kind of you, little creature! Service to me, eh? Well, as you say, who knows? (*Feeling his nose*) Who knows—hm-m-m! Very well, you may go. (*Releasing her arm*) Remember your promise! (*Laughing*)

BEE: Yes, sire. I thank you! You may count on me. (*She exits over wall.*)

SOLOMON (*Clapping his hands*): Lord Chamberlain! (LORD CHAMBERLAIN *runs in.*)

CHAMBERLAIN: Your Majesty! Has anything harmed

you? Where is your crown? Oh, here it is upon the ground! (*Staring*) Your nose! Sire!

SOLOMON (*Feeling it*): Is it that bad?

CHAMBERLAIN: Your Majesty! What has befallen you?

SOLOMON: A little creature in gauze and velvet, and carrying a small dagger, has just been interfering with the royal rest. (*Laughing*)

CHAMBERLAIN: May I not call in the doctors, Your Majesty? Truly, your nose is becoming—shall I say—

SOLOMON: It is, indeed, Lord Chamberlain, but a bit of ointment will fix it. Please send for some.

CHAMBERLAIN (*Calling very loudly*): Keeper of the Royal Ointment! Come into the king's garden!

SOLOMON: I hope I shall not frighten the Queen of Sheba.

CHAMBERLAIN (*Announcing*): The Keeper of the Royal Ointment. (KEEPER, *carrying many boxes and jars on a tray, enters and bows.*)

KEEPER (*Standing before* KING): I am the Keeper of the Royal Ointment, Your Majesty.

SOLOMON: Well, you should have something there that would soothe my swollen nose.

KEEPER (*Taking out large magnifying glass*): May I examine Your Majesty's royal nose?

SOLOMON: Do, please.

KEEPER (*Studying nose*): Ah, yes, just as I feared, bad swelling . . . a nasty bee sting! You will need a poultice to ease your pain. (*Places poultice on* KING's *nose*)

CHAMBERLAIN (*Taking out bright silk scarf*): Here is His Majesty's silk kerchief to hold it in place.

KEEPER: Tie it firmly in the back. (CHAMBERLAIN *does so.*)

SOLOMON: How does it look? (*Takes up mirror*) Dear me, what a strange sight I am!

CHAMBERLAIN (*Placing crown on* SOLOMON's *head*): Your Majesty's crown.

SOLOMON: I don't think that helps much, do you, Keeper?

KEEPER (*Bowing*): Your Majesty, you must leave the poultice on until two suns have set.

SOLOMON: I believe the village children know more about bee stings than you do. They simply put wet mud or clay on the spot, and in an hour or so the whole matter is forgotten. (*Sound of gong or trumpet*)

CHAMBERLAIN (*Looking off*): The Queen of Sheba approaches! (QUEEN *enters, preceded by* PAGE, *who carries two enormous bouquets of flowers.* CHAMBERLAIN *and* KEEPER *kneel.* SOLOMON *bows.* QUEEN *curtsies.*)

QUEEN: Hail, O King! Your Majesty, I, the Queen of Sheba, have journeyed for many days over seas and deserts to see the great and wise Solomon.

SOLOMON: I, Solomon, am deeply honored, lovely queen!

QUEEN (*Looking curiously at* SOLOMON's *bandaged nose*): Pardon the question, Mighty King, but is Your Majesty the victim of some illness?

SOLOMON (*Touching the bandage*): You mean my nose? Nay, I am the victim of my friend, the Keeper of the Royal Ointment. He insists that I keep this stupid poultice on until two suns have set. I have received a very slight injury.

QUEEN: I see. As you have been told, I come here to test the great wisdom of Solomon. I have heard it said that Solomon can always give the correct answer to whatever question is asked him.

SOLOMON: It has been my good fortune to be able to solve some of the problems puzzling my people.

QUEEN: Do you draw these answers all from the greatness of your own brain?

SOLOMON: I am always helped by divine guidance and the world around me, Sheba. What is your question, gracious queen?

QUEEN (*Gesturing to* PAGE): You see here two bouquets of flowers, both colorful, both fragrant—but only one of them is real. The other is the work of one of my most skillful artisans. Can you tell me without touching them, which one is real?

CHAMBERLAIN: How beautiful they both are!

KEEPER: No one could tell the difference!

QUEEN: Look well, O King. Use all the wisdom in your power. Call on all your senses save those of taste and touch. (SOLOMON *examines bouquets closely.*)

SOLOMON (*Bending over to smell flowers*): They are both perfect in fragrance, too.

QUEEN: Yes, but only one is the work of God.

SOLOMON: Here, Lord Chamberlain, I command you to untie this scarf. I care not if the Queen *does* gaze upon my nose. I must test the fragrance of these flowers. (CHAMBERLAIN *unties it.*)

KEEPER: Alas! I fear the worst!

SOLOMON: You are always fearing the worst, Keeper. Why not try to expect the best?

QUEEN: Solomon is as handsome as the world has reported him.

SOLOMON (*Bowing*): Sheba is as gracious as she is beautiful. Come, Page, let me smell these flowers properly. (*Inhales deeply*) Hm! Quite marvelous! Both have the fragrance of a thousand gardens, and the colors are nature's own!

CHAMBERLAIN (*Aside*): The King's wisdom will fail him. (*Buzzing grows loud.*)

SOLOMON: Hush! What is that I hear? (BEE *enters. Others do not notice her.*) I thought I heard you, little friend. What? Where are you going? (BEE *circles around the two bouquets, finally pausing at one and burying her face deep in the flowers to draw out nectar.*) I see! I see! The little creature keeps her promise! Thank you, little friend! (BEE *dances away;* SOLOMON *points to one bouquet.*) This, O Queen, is the real bouquet, the honey-laden flowers of nature. The others, beautiful as they are, never grew in the earth, but came from the hand of man.

CHAMBERLAIN: Great King Solomon!

KEEPER (*Astonished*): How did he guess?

SHEBA (*Impressed*): Wise he is, indeed!

SOLOMON (*Leading* QUEEN *to window*): Look among my garden flowers, O Sheba. There you will see the little creature who wounded me earlier. Now she makes amends by solving your riddle.

QUEEN: Ah, yes, I see! The little bee flying from flower to flower. You are wise in your friendship with all the earth's creatures, for even the tiniest can serve you.

SOLOMON: Now may I lead you to the feast that is prepared for Solomon's royal guest?

CHAMBERLAIN (*Pounding floor with staff and intoning*): Make way, make way, for the Queen of Sheba, the royal guest of His Majesty, King Solomon, the wise! Make way! (CHAMBERLAIN *exits, followed by* SOLOMON *and* QUEEN. PAGE *places bouquets into large vases and exits, followed by* KEEPER. BEE *reenters, music grows louder. She dances around flowers, hovers over real ones, as curtain falls.*)

THE END

(*Production Notes on page 313*)

The Hodja Speaks

A Turkish folktale

by Barbara Winther

FIRST TALE: *Feeding the Donkey*

Characters

NARRATOR, *offstage voice*
THE HODJA
WIFE
THIEF
MUSTAFA

BEFORE RISE: *Music. Lights are dimmed.*

NARRATOR (*From offstage, on microphone*): For hundreds of years in the country of Turkey, tales have been told about Nasr-ed-Din Hodja, a legendary character. Although he was not always as wise as he thought, neither was he the fool that many considered him. But whether wise or foolish, he always had something to say that was amusing and thought-provoking, as in this tale about feeding the donkey. (*Turkish music is heard as curtain opens, and lights come up.*)

* * * * *

SETTING: *Inside the Hodja's house in a Turkish village.*
Low table with brass vase on it is center; two large
pillows are on floor nearby. Up right is trunk with
valuables inside. Right exit is to kitchen; left exit to
street.

AT RISE: *Stage is empty. Music fades as* HODJA, *wearing*
large turban, and WIFE *enter right.*

THE HODJA: Every day I go outside (*Pointing left*) to
feed the donkey. It is time you did it.

WIFE (*Shocked*): That is a man's job.

HODJA: Where is it written a wife should not feed a
donkey?

WIFE: How should I know? *You* are the learned hodja.

HODJA: Then I say that somewhere it must be written,
"Men or women may feed donkeys."

WIFE (*Indignantly*): But I have other things to do.
Besides, when have you cooked the meals (*Indicating*
right) or cleaned the house?

HODJA (*Calmly*): I cannot remember.

WIFE: Because never have you done so.

HODJA: Well, neither has the donkey.

WIFE: Of course not!

HODJA: Then, since neither I nor the donkey does
housework, yet you feed me, why should you not also
feed the donkey?

WIFE (*Exasperated*): But, I—you—(*Throws up arms*) I
will not be tricked by you.

HODJA: Excellent! I would not want a wife who could be
tricked, even by her husband. (*Pauses as he pulls on*
beard, deep in thought, then smiles and claps hands)
I have the solution.

WIFE (*Warily*): Tell me what it is.

HODJA: We will have a contest—a silence contest.
Whoever speaks first will have to feed the donkey.

WIFE (*Considering*): You are rarely silent. I do not

believe you could keep quiet, unless you decide to take a nap.

HODJA (*Smiling slyly*): When value is to be gained, I have much determination.

WIFE: We shall see.

HODJA: The contest will start at the count of three.

WIFE: All right.

HODJA: One, two, three. (*They sit on pillows. After a moment,* HODJA *points in amazement at someone in the audience.* WIFE *follows his stare, shrugs, and just as she opens her mouth to question him, she claps hand over mouth. Next,* HODJA *points to imaginary bug crawling on floor.* WIFE *examines closely, but sees nothing. She starts to speak, then claps hand over mouth.* HODJA *leaps up, looks at ceiling in terror.* WIFE *follows his gaze. He holds hands over head and cringes.* WIFE *starts to speak, claps hand over mouth, shakes her finger angrily at him, and exits left.* HODJA *yawns and rubs eyes. He carries pillow upstage, stretches, lies down and falls asleep.* THIEF, *carrying sack over shoulder, enters left, stealthily, not seeing* HODJA.)

THIEF: Nobody is home. This is a good time for me to steal whatever is in that trunk. (*Tiptoes over to trunk, opens it, and begins to load contents into sack, looking warily at doors from time to time. He notices vase on table.*) That is a fine vase. I shall take it also. (*Picks up vase, accidentally drops it. At sound,* HODJA *awakens, jumps up in alarm, but does not speak.* THIEF *drops sack and sinks to knees, bowing head to floor.*) Oh-h-h, it is the Hodja, the wise and powerful one. I did not know you lived here. Please forgive me. I will replace everything I have stolen. Forgive me, and I will leave your house with a changed heart, never to steal again. (HODJA *opens mouth to speak, claps hand over it, shakes head, and returns to sit on pillow.* THIEF, *surprised, rises.*) Do you not forgive me? (*Pause. Looks at audience and shrugs. Aside*) The Hodja appears to have lost his voice. (*Crosses to* HODJA *and waves hand before his eyes*) You say nothing, and you do nothing. Perhaps you have suddenly turned into a statue. Hm-m-m. Since you have no objection to your treasures being stolen, I shall also steal your handsome kavuk, symbol of wisdom. (*Removes* HODJA's *turban and places it on his own head. Then, throwing sack over shoulder, he quickly exits left.* HODJA, *feeling his head, jumps up angrily.* MUSTAFA *enters, carrying dish.*)

MUSTAFA: Good day to you, Nasr-ed-Din Hodja. My father sends this plate of delicious pilaf for you to eat. (HODJA *rushes to him, gesturing wildly and pointing left.*) Is something wrong, Hodja? (HODJA *runs to trunk and points inside.* MUSTAFA *looks.*) Yes, that is a trunk. (HODJA *jumps inside trunk and waves his arms about.*) What are you doing in the trunk? (HODJA *leaps out and runs to table, pointing to it.* MUSTAFA *looks confused.*) Yes, that is a table. (HODJA *jumps on table.*) What are you doing on the table? (HODJA *runs to doorway and points to it.*) Yes, that is a doorway. I, Mustafa, came through your doorway. (HODJA *runs back to trunk and points furiously.*) No, I do not wish to get into your trunk. (HODJA *points to table.*) No, I do not want to stand on your table. I came to make you a present of this pilaf. (HODJA *shakes fists in frustration.*) Hodja, do not be angry with me. Have you lost your voice? (HODJA *sadly shakes head.*) Has it been stolen? (HODJA *nods emphatically, with great relief.*) Stolen, you say? (*Aside to audience, as* HODJA *points to top of his head*) Is this what comes from being a learned man?

(*To* HODJA) I must go home now. Please tell me where you want me to put the pilaf. (HODJA *continues to point at his head.*) You want it on your head? (HODJA *nods.*) Oh, well (*Shrugs*), if that is what you wish. (*Pours pilaf on* HODJA's *head and runs out left, calling*) Father, the Hodja thinks his mouth is on top of his head. (MUSTAFA *exits.* WIFE *enters, horrified at sight of* HODJA *and ransacked trunk.*)

WIFE: Husband, what has happened? (HODJA *shouts with delight.*)

HODJA: I won! I won the contest! You spoke—you will have to feed the donkey.

WIFE: But our treasures have been stolen, your kavuk is gone, and there is pilaf all over your head.

HODJA: If you had fed my donkey in the first place, this would not have happened.

WIFE: That is true.

HODJA: But now that I have won the contest, not only have you *one* silly, old donkey to feed (*Pointing off left*), you have *two.* (*Meekly points to self.* WIFE *bursts into laughter. Curtain closes as Turkish music plays.*)

* * * * *

SECOND TALE: *The Warmth of a Flame*

Characters

NARRATOR
THE HODJA
WIFE
JAMAL
MUSTAFA, *his son*

BEFORE RISE: *Lights are dimmed. Music fades.*

NARRATOR (*From offstage, on microphone*): Here is another tale in which Nasr-ed-Din Hodja has much to say, this time concerning the warmth of a flame. (*Music up and out as curtain opens and lights go up*)

* * * * *

SETTING: *Same as Scene 1. Pillows on floor are right and left of table, trunk is closed, and vase replaced on table.*

AT RISE: HODJA, *wearing kavuk, and* JAMAL *are seated on pillows, each drinking a glass of hot tea.*

JAMAL: This hot tea warms my stomach. It is so cold tonight.

HODJA: Indeed! Jamal, my friend, I wish to thank you for catching the thief who stole my kavuk. (*Points to turban*) Without it my head would be cold and my mind frozen.

JAMAL: It was my eldest son, Mustafa, who pointed out the wicked man. When he saw your kavuk on the thief's head, he cried out to me, "That is the Hodja's kavuk."

HODJA (*Smiling and nodding*): To show my appreciation for what you have done, I would enjoy coming to your house for dinner.

JAMAL (*Startled*): To *my* house for dinner? I should be invited to *your* house for dinner.

HODJA (*Rising*): No, no, no. I would not appreciate that.

JAMAL (*Rising*): But I would.

HODJA: You are not the one to show appreciation. I am.

JAMAL: But I—But you—(*Throwing up arms*) I will not be tricked by you.

HODJA: Excellent! (WIFE *enters with teapot.*) I would not want a friend who could be tricked, even by his best friend.

WIFE (*Chuckling*): Nor would you want a wife who could be tricked. (*She refills glasses with tea.*)

HODJA (*Clapping hands*): I have the solution.

JAMAL (*Warily*): What is it?

HODJA: We will have a contest.

WIFE: The last contest was a losing one for everybody, including you.

HODJA (*Stroking beard*): You are right, wife. Jamal, it would be better if we were to make a bet. The loser will have to make dinner for the winner. (JAMAL *thinks for a moment, then smiles.*)

JAMAL (*Aside to audience*): I know a bet I can surely win. (*To* HODJA) I wager you cannot stand out in the cold street all night, without warming yourself at a fire.

HODJA: When value is to be gained, I have much determination. I shall go out now and prove I can remain in the street all night. (*Exits left*)

WIFE (*Shaking head*): Why do learned men so often suffer?

JAMAL: Possibly because they have the burden of knowledge to carry around, whereas mere cleverness is as light as a leaf. (*Chuckles*) I shall return in the morning to see how you fared. (*Exits left, as lights dim.* WIFE *exits right, carrying teapot and glasses. Brief musical interlude to indicate passage of time. Lights go up and music fades out, as* HODJA *reenters, shivering.*)

HODJA (*Calling*): Wife, wife, I am nearly dead with the cold. (WIFE *enters, carrying blanket and glass of hot tea.*)

WIFE: Here. Wrap this blanket around you. (HODJA *wraps blanket around himself.*) I cannot imagine anything important enough to freeze to death for.

(JAMAL *enters.* HODJA *sits on pillow and sips tea.*)

JAMAL: Good morning, my friend. You are still alive, I see.

HODJA: Yes, Jamal. And I am proud to say I stood in the street all night, though an icicle formed upon my nose, and my beard froze stiffer than the knees of an ancient camel.

JAMAL (*Surprised*): Surely you warmed yourself beside a fire.

HODJA: Upon my honor as a hodja, I did not.

JAMAL: Not even once?

HODJA: The only flame I ever saw was a candle in a window. (JAMAL *raises arms as if in victory.*)

JAMAL: Aha, I knew it. I knew it!

HODJA (*Confused*): Knew what?

JAMAL: You warmed yourself by the flame of that candle.

HODJA: But it was inside a house down the street. I did not go near the candle.

JAMAL (*Gleefully*): The thought of the warmth of the candle kept you from freezing to death. I win the bet. (*Claps* HODJA *on shoulder*) Too bad, my friend. I shall return this evening for dinner, and with me will be my eldest son, Mustafa. (*Exits left, laughing and rubbing hands.* HODJA *glowers and strokes beard.*)

HODJA (*Thoughtfully*): Jamal is a clever man.

WIFE: What shall we have for dinner?

HODJA: Pilaf and eggplant. (*Rises*) That will be *our* dinner, eaten early. The dinner for Jamal and Mustafa will take more preparations. (*Crossing right*) Let us go to the kitchen and discuss the matter. (HODJA, *carrying blanket and glass, exits, followed by* WIFE. *Music fades in and lights dim. A moment*

later lights go up and music fades out as HODJA
enters. He peers off left, then runs right, shouting.)
They are coming, wife. Is the fire still on under the
kettle?

WIFE (*Calling from off*): It is.

HODJA (*Calling*): Then, I shall take care of the dinner
for them. Rest yourself.

WIFE (*Calling*): That I shall gladly do. (HODJA *crosses
left and bows as* JAMAL *and* MUSTAFA *enter.)*

HODJA: Welcome to my humble house. Please be seated
on these pillows by the table. (*They sit.*) My wife and
I have eaten earlier so that we may better attend to
serving you.

JAMAL: For one who has lost a bet, you are most gracious, my friend. (HODJA *bows head in acknowledge-
ment.*)

HODJA: I shall see how dinner is coming along. (*Exits
right*)

JAMAL: Let this be a lesson to you, Mustafa. Win or
lose, accept the results with grace.

MUSTAFA: Yes, Father. Nasr-ed-Din Hodja appears to
be as happy about losing as he would be about win-
ning. (HODJA *reenters.*)

HODJA: The food is not quite ready, but it will not be
long.

JAMAL: What are we having for dinner?

HODJA: A very special lamb stew with pine nuts and
currants. It has been cooking all day.

JAMAL: Then surely it is ready. Let us eat it now.

HODJA: Of course. I shall bring it in at once. (*Bows and
exits right*)

JAMAL: Good. I am nearly starved.

MUSTAFA: So am I. I have not eaten all day. (HODJA
enters, seemingly upset.)

JAMAL: What is wrong? Where is this special lamb stew?

HODJA: The meat does not seem to be cooked.

JAMAL: Perhaps the fire beneath the kettle is not large enough.

HODJA: That could not be.

MUSTAFA (*Rising*): I will see what the problem is. (*Exits right, returning almost immediately*) Father, The Hodja has only a candle burning under the kettle.

JAMAL (*Jumping to feet*): What? Only a candle to cook a stew?

HODJA (*Innocently*): But the candle is right next to the kettle.

JAMAL (*With disgust*): That makes no difference and no sense. A tiny flame would not even heat the kettle.

HODJA (*Feigning surprise*): Oh, really? Then, tell me, Jamal, how could a candle in a window down the street keep me warm on a freezing night? (JAMAL *looks shocked, and* MUSTAFA *bursts into laughter, but* JAMAL *gives him a warning glance, and he stops.*)

MUSTAFA: Sorry, Father, but I do see the Hodja's point.

JAMAL (*Striding left*): You win the bet, Hodja. (*Angrily*) Come along, Mustafa, there will be no dinner here tonight. (*Exits left*)

HODJA: Let this be a lesson to you, Mustafa. Win or lose, accept the result with grace. (*Sits on pillow, as* MUSTAFA *starts to exit left*) However, it *is* more satisfying to win, especially when it is by cleverness. Just ask your father, and I believe he will agree. (MUSTAFA *bows to* HODJA *and exits right. Music fades in as lights fade out and curtain closes.*)

THE END

(*Production Notes on page 313*)

The Bremen Town Musicians

A German folktale

by Mildred Hark McQueen

Characters

DONKEY
HOUND
CAT
COCK
CAPTAIN OF ROBBERS
THREE ROBBERS

SCENE 1

SETTING: *A country road in old Germany. Scene may be played before curtain.*

AT RISE: DONKEY *enters left, carrying a lute. A kettledrum and drumsticks hang from a cord around his neck.* HOUND *enters right. He lies down, puffing.*

DONKEY: My, my, you poor old hound. What are you puffing about? Have you run a long way?

HOUND: I have indeed. I am quite old, and I have grown weak. I can no longer hunt for my master, so he planned to get rid of me.

DONKEY: Then you and I are in the same situation. My master was ungrateful, too. For years and years I carried his corn sacks to the mill, but now I am too old for such heavy work; he did not want to feed me, so I ran away.

HOUND (*Anxiously*): But now that we are on our own, how are we to eat?

DONKEY: Come along with me. I am on my way to Bremen to be a town musician. We can play sweet music in the town square. I will strum the lute, and you shall beat the kettledrum.

HOUND (*Sitting up slowly*): I am not sure if I can.

DONKEY: Of course you can. (*Hands him drum and drumsticks*) Here, beat a few measures on this drum. (*Unnoticed by* DONKEY *and* HOUND, CAT *enters right and sits down wearily.* HOUND *beats drum, at first half-heartedly and then louder.*)

HOUND (*Looking happier*): How is that?

DONKEY: Splendid, splendid, my friend! You will make a fine Bremen Town musician. Let's be on our way! (*They start right and see* CAT. *They stop and stare at* CAT.)

CAT (*Mournfully*): Meow! Meow!

DONKEY: Now, then, Cat, what is wrong with you?

HOUND: I never saw such a sad cat.

CAT: How can I be merry when my life is in danger? I am getting old, and my teeth are worn, so I can no longer hunt mice.

DONKEY: I suppose your mistress was going to drown you?

CAT: How did you know? No mistress is as ungrateful as mine. Now that I prefer to sit by the fire and snooze, rather than catch mice, she will have none of me. So I ran away.

HOUND: Good for you.

CAT: It may not be so good. Now what shall I do?

HOUND: The Donkey here can tell you what to do.

DONKEY: Indeed, yes. Come with us to Bremen, and be a town musician. You understand night music.

CAT (*Rising with more spirit*): Night music, ah yes. All cats understand night music. Do you need a singer?

DONKEY: What is a band without a singer? Can you hit a high note?

CAT: Very high, very high, indeed. (CAT *tries.*) Meow-w-w!

HOUND: That's very nice, but I prefer a lower tone—a bark.

DONKEY: All hounds do, but a fine high note is much appreciated in musical circles. (*To* CAT) Come on. We'll go along together. (*As they start right,* COCK *enters and begins to crow with all his might.*)

COCK: Cock-a-doodle-doo! Cock-a-doodle-doo! Cock-a-doodle-doo! (*They all stop and stare at* COCK.)

DONKEY: Gracious me! Your crowing goes right through me. What is the matter?

COCK: I have been foretelling fine weather. But now guests are coming for Sunday dinner, and the cook has no pity on me.

CAT: She plans to serve you for Sunday dinner?

COCK: Yes, she wants to make me into soup. (*He crows again very loudly.*) Cock-a-doodle-doo! Now, I am crowing as loud as I possibly can.

DONKEY: But, Sir Cock, you need not go back to the cook. We are going to Bremen to be town musicians. Come with us. You have a fine voice.

CAT: Yes, a wonderful pitch. You and I will sing a duet.

HOUND: We will all make music together. (*He bangs on drum, and* DONKEY *strums lute.*)

CAT *and* COCK (*In unison*): Meow-w-w! Cock-a-doodle-doo!

DONKEY (*Nodding*): Cat and Cock, you sing a fine duet. Splendid, splendid. Let's go on.

HOUND (*Looking up*): You know, it is growing dark.

CAT: I see very well in the dark.

COCK: But I do not.

DONKEY: Nor I. We shall never reach Bremen this evening. We shall have to spend the night in the forest.

CAT: I see a good place just ahead. There is a very large tree.

DONKEY: Fine. We shall all be comfortable under the big tree for the night.

COCK: I shall fly to the top and rest in the branches.

CAT: I shall climb up.

HOUND: I shall lie down underneath the tree.

DONKEY: Come on, then, let's get a good night's rest. (*All exit. Curtain*)

* * * * *

SCENE 2

SETTING: *Downstage right is a large tree with over-hanging branches. Upstage left is the front of a house, with a door and window. A light shines from window. There may be a backdrop of a forest.*

AT RISE: HOUND *and* DONKEY *are stretched out under the tree.* COCK *is behind the tree.* CAT *comes from back of tree.* DONKEY *is snoring loudly.*

CAT: Well, well, you all are snoozing pretty soundly. I did not like it up in the tree, after all. Perhaps I will prowl a little.

DONKEY (*Raising head*): Be quiet, please. I was having a nice dream.

CAT: But it was *your* snoring that woke me. . .

COCK (*Coming from behind tree*): I flew way to the top

of the tree. I looked around on all four sides, and then I saw a little spark burning. Look there's a light.

DONKEY (*Looking left*): If there's a light, there must be a house.

HOUND (*Looking left*): There *is* a house.

DONKEY: If so, we had better get up and be on our way. (*Getting up*) I think I heard some thunder, and the shelter here is poor.

CAT: Perhaps there is someone in the house who will give us something to eat.

HOUND (*Getting up*): I need a bone with some meat on it. Let's go.

DONKEY (*Starting left, as others follow*): Look, the light is growing brighter.

COCK: And larger. There's the house. (*They are almost upon it.*)

CAT: We had better look in the window before we knock. You're the biggest, Sir Donkey. See who's in there.

DONKEY (*Going to window and peering in*): The window is open. Aha, we were clever to look.

COCK: What do you see?

DONKEY: I see a table covered with good things to eat and drink.

HOUND: Is there a juicy bone?

DONKEY: There is a fine roast of beef, and four robbers are sitting around the table enjoying themselves.

COCK: Robbers! They have no right to be there. That is just the sort of meal we need.

DONKEY: Yes, and how I wish we were inside instead of outside.

CAT: We should be able to drive away those robbers.

DONKEY: But we must be careful. (*Looks in window*) They look very fierce. They have big black beards.

CAT: How can we frighten them away? (*Thinks*) Why don't we rehearse our music?

HOUND: A fine idea. That should scare them!

COCK (*Preening*): I'll crow with all my might.

DONKEY: I'll press against the window. Then you jump on my back, Hound, and you come next, Cat. Climb on the hound here. Then you, Sir Cock, perch on Cat.

HOUND: Very good. (DONKEY *presses against window.* HOUND *places paws on back of* DONKEY, CAT *on back of* HOUND, *and* COCK *comes last.*)

DONKEY: At a given signal, we'll start our music. I'll bray as loud as I can and strum my lute.

HOUND: I'll bark and beat my drum.

CAT: I'll meow and wail.

COCK: And I'll crow, louder than ever before.

DONKEY: Then we'll burst in through the window with a great crash.

DONKEY: Now, I'll count to three. One, two, three . . . Go! (DONKEY *brays and strums the lute,* CAT *meows,* HOUND *barks and beats the drum, and* COCK *crows.*)

COCK: They're frightened to death! They're running out the back door.

DONKEY: Yes, yes, they're running for their lives. We must get inside before they see us. (DONKEY, HOUND, CAT, *and* COCK *exit into house through window.* CAPTAIN OF ROBBERS *and* THREE ROBBERS *enter left, carrying bags of money, and walk to center stage.*)

CAPTAIN: Phew-w-w, that was a close call. What on earth caused that terrible noise?

1ST ROBBER: Ghosts, horrible ghosts.

2ND ROBBER: There must have been several of them.

3RD ROBBER: We must run away deep into the forest before they come after us.

CAPTAIN: Be quick. Our lives are at stake. (*They all run off right. After a pause,* DONKEY, HOUND, CAT, *and* COCK *come slowly around house.* DONKEY *carries a large carrot,* COCK *has an ear of corn,* HOUND *has a large bone with meat, and* CAT *has a smaller bone.*)

DONKEY (*Pointing off*): They're running away.

COCK: We frightened them, all right.

HOUND: Now, we can go back and feast to our hearts' content.

DONKEY (*Happily*): And then go to sleep. I think I may sleep in the yard on a nice bit of straw.

HOUND: I'd like to sleep behind the door.

CAT: I'll curl up on the hearth near the warm fire.

COCK: I'll perch on a beam up high.

CAT: I think someone should stand guard while we sleep. The robbers may come back after they get over their fright.

HOUND: Let us take turns, then. Why don't you watch first, Donkey? You are sleeping outside, anyway.

DONKEY: Very well. I shall try to stay awake, but I am very tired.

CAT: After I have a short snooze by the fire, I'll go on guard. Then you can snore away, Donkey. (*Yawns loudly*) It's well past midnight. Time for bed. (CAT, HOUND, *and* COCK *enter house.* DONKEY *lies down at left. The light goes out. After a pause,* CAPTAIN *and* THREE ROBBERS *enter right, walking stealthily.*)

CAPTAIN (*With bravado*): There, you see, the light is out.

1ST ROBBER: The house seems quiet.

CAPTAIN: We shouldn't have let ourselves be so frightened.

2ND ROBBER: Perhaps there was no one in the house. We may have imagined the whole thing.

3RD ROBBER: It may just have been the wind blowing hard.

CAPTAIN: If there was someone in the house, he's not there now. But we must make sure. Someone should check the house before we go back.

1ST ROBBER: And you, Captain, should do it, as our leader.

CAPTAIN: Not I. You shall be the messenger.

1ST ROBBER (*Frightened*): I? Not I.

CAPTAIN: Yes, you. I order you to. . .

1ST ROBBER (*Sighing*): Very well. (*He walks stealthily to door of house and goes in. Other* ROBBERS *wait watchfully. Suddenly, a great commotion is heard from inside the house.*)

CAT (*Offstage, meowing angrily*): Meow-w-w!

HOUND (*Barking off*): Bow-wow-wow. Woof! Woof!

COCK (*Offstage, very loudly*): Cock-a-doodle-doo! (1ST ROBBER *runs in from behind house.*)

1ST ROBBER: Help! Help! (*As he passes* DONKEY, DONKEY *reaches out and grabs his leg.*) Ouch! Ouch! Help! (*Runs to other* ROBBERS, *clearly terrified*)

CAPTAIN: What happened to you?

1ST ROBBER: I went into the kitchen to light a candle. All seemed to be still, but as I bent near the hearth, I saw what looked like glistening, fiery eyes. I took them for live coals. But suddenly, someone seemed to fly at me. I tell you, there is a horrible witch sitting in there by the fire. She scratched my face with her long claws.

3RD ROBBER: You're lucky you escaped.

1ST ROBBER: Yes, I ran for the back door, but there stood a man with a loud growling voice. The next thing I knew I felt a terrible pain in my leg, as if someone had bitten me.

3RD ROBBER: He must have stabbed you with a knife.

1ST ROBBER: But what was worse was the black monster at the side of the house, who beat me with a wooden club. And most frightening of all, somewhere up on the roof sat a judge, who called out, "Bring the rogue to me. Bring the rogue to me." I got away as fast as I could!

CAPTAIN: We must all get away, and never return to that house again.

1ST ROBBER: Not for all the gold in the world. Let's go.

2ND ROBBER: There's no time to lose.

3RD ROBBER: Run for your lives! (*Robbers run off. After a pause,* DONKEY *comes from side of house, and* CAT, HOUND, *and* COCK *come from inside house. They are all laughing.*)

CAT: Ha, ha. So I'm a horrible witch.

HOUND: And I'm a man with a growling voice and a knife. Ha, ha.

DONKEY: And I'm a big black monster. He-haw! He-haw!

COCK: And I'm no less than a judge. "Bring the rogue to me." Cock-a-doodle-doo!

DONKEY: Did you hear them say they would never come back to this house again?

HOUND: This house suits me very well.

CAT: I'd like to live here for the rest of my days.

COCK: I would, too.

DONKEY: Fine. We four friends will live here together. After a good night's sleep, we'll go to Bremen and hire ourselves out as musicians.

HOUND: And now, we can go to sleep.

CAT: After all this excitement I'm wide awake. Let's play some music together before we go to sleep.

DONKEY (*Holding lute*): Good idea! One, two, three—go! DONKEY *brays and strums lute;* HOUND *barks and beats drum;* CAT *meows;* COCK *crows. There is a merry din as the curtain falls.*)

THE END

(*Production Notes on page 313*)

The Snow Witch

A Russian folktale

by Dorothy Dixon

Characters

MARINA, *peasant grandmother*
KATYA, *little girl*
SNOW WITCH
PRINCESS VALESKA
DRIVER
IVAN, *young soldier*
VERA, *dancer*
DANCERS

SCENE 1

TIME: *A cold winter evening in old Russia.*
SETTING: *Simple peasant kitchen, with fireplace down right, table and two stools up right with shelf for cups behind table. Window with "snow" is in rear wall, door to outside left, rocker between window and door.*
AT RISE: MARINA *is looking out window;* KATYA *is setting table.*
MARINA: It is a fine night, Katya, but cold. My, how the stars are shining! They are as white as the snow that

covers the steppes. And the snow—how it whirls wherever the wind passes. Now it looks like a shawl streaming in the wind—now like a woman with a crown of frost leaves. (*Looks off left*) There are the lights in the village, and the boys and girls are dancing. (*Wistfully*) Dancing . . . (*Tries a few steps*) No, no, Marina, your feet are too old for that. (*Looks out window again*) Ah, something is moving out there.

KATYA (*Crossing to window*): Where, Babushka?

MARINA: Why, it's the Snow Witch who goes abroad before the flakes come flying. I wonder why she was at my window? (*There is a knock at door.*)

SNOW WITCH (*Calling; offstage*): Marina, Marina, let me come in.

KATYA (*Frightened*): Oo-oh!

MARINA: The Snow Witch is calling me!

KATYA: I'm afraid, Baba. Don't open the door. (*Huddles in rocker*)

MARINA: Don't worry, child. All the Snow Witch does is wander about before a storm. I'll let her in. (*Opens door. SNOW WITCH whirls in and around stage, then stops in front of KATYA.*)

SNOW WITCH (*Kindly*): Child, there is no need to be frightened. I am a good witch. I use my powers to shelter the animals of the forest and to help honest villagers. I warn people when a storm is coming. Sometimes I follow the roads; sometimes I stop at the doors of people's houses. (*Turns, to MARINA*) Tonight I saw the friendly gleam from your window, and I said to myself, "Marina will make me welcome." (*Whirls around stage*)

MARINA: Will there be a storm tonight?

SNOW WITCH: No, the night is bright and clear, but tomorrow clouds will gather and the flakes will fly.

MARINA: You must see strange sights on your travels.

SNOW WITCH (*Moving about as she speaks*): I see great white wastelands where never a person stirs. I see forests black against the stars. I see fields where the drifts lie deep and the lone wolf is swift as a moving shadow. (*Looks around*) You must be very happy in this little house of yours, Marina.

MARINA: Happy? All my good years are behind me, and no joy to come. If only I were young now like the girls dancing in the village, or rich like the Princess Valeska—then I would be truly happy.

SNOW WITCH: Would you like to change, Marina, to be young again?

MARINA: Change? (*Excitedly*) Have you the magic power to let me change, Snow Witch?

SNOW WITCH: Just lay your hand in the hand of the person you would like to be, and you will change places. (MARINA *looks at* SNOW WITCH *in disbelief.*) I see you do not believe me, Marina. Look into my eyes and do not doubt me.

MARINA (*Looking into* SNOW WITCH's *eyes*): There *is* magic in your eyes, Snow Witch.

SNOW WITCH: Now you can change your lot, if you will. That is my magic gift to you.

MARINA (*Joyfully*): Is it really true? Oh, to think I don't have to be old Marina any longer! (*Curtsies in front of* SNOW WITCH) Thank you, thank you.

SNOW WITCH: I must go now, but when I return I will see what you have done with your gift. Choose wisely, Marina. (*Glides out.* KATYA *rises, shuts door.*)

MARINA: Choose! I have the whole village to choose from. I can be whatever I like. (*During following speech,* MARINA *stands center, acting out parts as she speaks.* KATYA *mimics her behind her back.*) Why, I can change places with a handsome soldier with a sword, or a driver on a painted sleigh with three beautiful horses—(*Breaks off, laughs*) How the soldier will rage to find himself in petticoats, knitting, instead of marching along to music!

KATYA (*Laughing*): Oh, Babushka, you are so funny!

MARINA (*Thinking*): No, after all, it is better to stay a woman. Let me see, shall I be Maria Toplova? No, her nose is too long. Anna Paloska? No, she is too poor. To be happy one must be rich and noble. (*Sound of sleigh bells is heard.*) Hark! Sleigh bells. I wonder who can be passing.

KATYA (*At window*): Baba, it is a beautiful sleigh with three white horses! (*Knocking is heard.* MARINA *opens door.*)

DRIVER (*Entering*): Do you have a fire here and shelter for the Princess Valeska?

MARINA: Oh, my, the Princess! Yes, yes. Come in, Your Highness. (PRINCESS *enters.*) All I have is at your service. (*Curtsies*)

PRINCESS (*To* DRIVER): Wait for me outside. (DRIVER *bows, exits.* PRINCESS *sweeps over to fireplace; to* KATYA) Here, child, warm my cloak. (*Tosses cloak to* KATYA, *who holds it close and strokes the fur*)

MARINA: How may I serve Your Highness?

PRINCESS: The warmth of your fire is what I need. Soon I must go on, but I am so cold.

MARINA: Will Your Highness have some tea? It is all I have to offer.

PRINCESS: No, no. I want only the heat and light. I am afraid of the night.

MARINA: You fear the night?

PRINCESS: Yes, the night and the robbers.

MARINA *and* KATYA: Robbers!

PRINCESS: They are after my gold and jewels. The robbers follow me everywhere and gallop after my sleigh to the very doors of my castle.

MARINA: I should die of terror!

PRINCESS: Even in my dreams I see their greedy cruel eyes. Do you ever have such dreams, good woman?

MARINA: Oh, no! I am happy to live quietly here with Katya.

PRINCESS: I see peace dwells beneath your roof. A princess must travel about, but a peasant is safe from danger. (*Looks about, sighs*) You may kiss my hand. (*Holds out hand*)

MARINA (*Drawing back*): No, no! I mean—I shall not touch your snowy white hand with mine.

PRINCESS (*To* KATYA): Call my driver, please, child. (MARINA *takes cloak from* KATYA, *wraps it around* PRINCESS.)

KATYA (*Opening door and calling*): Driver, the Princess is ready to leave.

MARINA: Godspeed to Your Highness and a safe journey! (*Curtsies*)

DRIVER (*At door*): Your Highness, the sleigh is ready. (PRINCESS *and* DRIVER *exit.* MARINA *and* KATYA *watch at window. Sound of sleigh bells fades, then the two women cross center.*)

MARINA (*Shuddering*): I shiver to think of what would have happened if I had put my hand in hers! Darkness and robbers! (*Firmly*) I would not be the Princess for a thousand rubles.

KATYA: Nor I, Babushka. (*Clings to* MARINA) To have robbers chasing me . . . oh, no!

MARINA (*Thoughtfully*): It is bad luck to be a woman. If I were a man, now, with the world before me—like Ivan, the soldier, so strong and handsome. . . . He'd be a match for a dozen robbers. (*Knock on door.* IVAN *bursts in.*) Ivan, how you startled me! (KATYA *goes to*

IVAN, *smiling.*)

IVAN: The world is full of surprises, Marina. (*Twirls* KATYA *around*)

MARINA: It is, indeed. What would you say if you suddenly found yourself turned into an old woman knitting by the fire?

IVAN (*Laughing and going to fireplace to warm his hands*): And what would you say if you found yourself a soldier? You think it would be wonderful with a cloak and clanking sword, but you should see us on the road with our shoes frozen to our feet, and nothing to eat but crusts and snow, no roof over our heads at night, marching, marching, marching. (*Shakes his head*) You would not envy us then, I give you my hand on it. (*Extends his hand to* MARINA)

MARINA (*Stepping back*): No, no, don't give me your hand. I'll take your word for it. I didn't realize what it was like to be a soldier. (*Dance music is heard.*) Listen, there's music, Ivan. The dancers must be coming from the village. (*Voices and humming are heard offstage.* MARINA *and* KATYA *look out window.*)

KATYA: Yes, they are here! (*Opens door.* VERA *and* DANCERS *enter.*)

MARINA: Welcome, pretty ones. Come in, come in. Will you dance for us here? (*Moves rocker up left, sits, and watches*)

VERA: Good evening, Marina and Katya, and to you, Ivan. (*All ad lib greetings.*) We'd like to dance for you. (*Folk music is heard.* DANCERS *take positions and dance. At the end of dance,* MARINA, KATYA, *and* IVAN *applaud.*)

MARINA (*Approaching* VERA): Ah, to dance like that again, as I did when I was young! Vera, there's no one as beautiful and light of foot as you. Will you take a step or two with an old woman? (*Holds out hand. Suddenly, sound of wolf howl is heard in distance.*)

VERA: Hush, what was that?

IVAN (*Joking*): The werewolf is calling you, Vera.

MARINA (*Pulling hand back*): Heavens, you can't mean that, Ivan. Have the evil powers cast a spell over her?

VERA: He is only joking. Come, Marina, take my hand, the music is calling.

MARINA (*Nervously*): No, no. I was joking, too. My feet are too old for dancing now. Dance and be happy while you can.

VERA: Well, then, goodbye to you. Come, folks. (VERA *and* DANCERS *dance out.*)

MARINA: Ivan, you were joking, weren't you? It's not true that there's a spell on Vera.

IVAN (*Seriously*): You can't tell about another's life, good neighbor. There are dark spells woven in the sun, and bright ones in the shadow. No life is all shadow or all sun. Good night to you both. (*Twirls* KATYA *again and exits.* KATYA *shuts door and goes to look out window.*)

MARINA: I don't know whether he jokes or not, but I'm sure of one thing now. I would not change places with anyone. The princess is always in terror, Ivan suffers when he marches, and Vera—was it true about the werewolf, I wonder?

KATYA: I hope not, Baba. She is so beautiful.

MARINA: Anyway, I am glad I didn't take her hand. No, it's better just to be myself, with my own troubles.

SNOW WITCH (*Entering swiftly and quietly*): Well spoken, Marina. I see you have learned wisdom. Look, the fire has burned low and the charm has ended. You may lay your hand in mine without fear. (*Takes* MARINA's *hand, leaving gold ring in it*) Look again into my eyes. (MARINA *does so.*) May you live in peace, Marina. Goodbye. (*Floats softly out door and shuts it*)

MARINA: Look, Katya, she gave me a ring! It's beautiful! And there's writing on it.

KATYA: What does it say, Babushka?

MARINA (*Reading slowly*): "Choose not another's life or wealth. Happiness lies within thyself." (*Thoughtfully*) Yes, the Snow Witch speaks truly. (*Curtain*)

THE END

(*Production Notes on page 314*)

The White Spider's Gift

A South American folktale

by Jamie Turner

Characters

WHITE SPIDER, *offstage voice*
KUMA, *Guarani boy*
OLD WOMAN
PIKI, *Guarani boy*
MOTHER, *Piki's mother*
TUKIRA, *Chieftain's daughter*
TWO WOMEN
CHIEFTAIN
MESSENGER
GIRL
DIKA
DABU
KINTA } *Guarani boys*
MUNGA
CHILDREN
VILLAGERS } *extras*

SCENE 1

TIME: *Long ago.*

SETTING: *Forest of Paraguay. Played before curtain. Murals on walls flanking stage depict trees and undergrowth. One large bush, displayed on right wall outside curtain, represents spider's home. Bush must be visible throughout the play. A large spider's web of white yarn covers most of the bush.*

BEFORE RISE: KUMA *enters left and runs toward spider's web.*

SPIDER (*From offstage*): Help me! Please, I am over here in the spring!

KUMA (*Stopping; irritably*): What? Who are you? (*Peers over stage apron*)

SPIDER: Please, will you bend down here and lift me out? I have fallen into the spring.

KUMA: What? Help a spider? I cannot stop for such a small matter. I must go find tea leaves for my father. I have already wasted much time, and he will be angry.

SPIDER (*Pleading*): Oh, please. I would not trouble you if I were not so tired. The water bubbles up so, and I cannot reach the edge.

KUMA (*Looking up at the sky*): I must hurry. Father is waiting. (*Runs out.* OLD WOMAN *enters, using a cane. She approaches spider web, dragging a burlap sack behind her.*)

SPIDER (*Calling*): Kind woman! Please help me! (OLD WOMAN *cocks head, puts hand to ear.*)

OLD WOMAN: What is it that I hear?

SPIDER: It is I, the little white spider who lives in the *yerba* bush beside the spring.

OLD WOMAN (*Looking up at web*): Eh? Who? Where?

SPIDER: No, no, not in the web. I am down here in the

water! I fell from my web and cannot get out. Please help me!

OLD WOMAN (*Looking over edge of stage; shaking head, sadly*): Ah, yes, life is full of trouble, little spider. And the older one gets, the more burdened with care he becomes.

SPIDER: But will you not help me, Guarani woman? Will you not hold your stick down and let me crawl upon it so that you may lift me out?

OLD WOMAN: I am old, little spider. I must help myself. I must look for twigs so that I may have a fire tonight. (*Exits, mumbling*) Trouble, trouble. Life is full of trouble. (PIKI *and* MOTHER *enter, carrying large earthen jars. They walk across stage.*)

SPIDER: Help! Oh, please! I am growing weak! Please help me!

PIKI: Do you hear a cry for help, Mother?

MOTHER: Yes, Piki, I do. (*Calls*) Who is calling? Where are you?

SPIDER: It is I, the white spider. Here in the spring! (*Voice grows fainter.*) I cannot swim any longer. My legs are . . .

PIKI (*Dropping to knees and looking over edge of stage*): Oh, Mother, it *is* a spider. She is sinking! (*Reaches down. "Spider"* [*see Production Notes*] *may be concealed in* PIKI'S *hand when he first enters or hidden on ledge near spring.*)

MOTHER: Can you reach her, Piki?

PIKI (*Rising, cupping hand gently*): Yes. Oh, I hope she's still alive!

MOTHER: Oh, Piki, see—she opens her eyes!

PIKI (*Patting inside hand with finger*): Little spider, are you really alive? I am so happy I could catch you before the water pulled you down.

MOTHER: Is this the little white spider who lives in the *yerba* bush there beside the spring? (*Looks up at web*)

PIKI: Yes. I see her each day when I come to fill the water jars. She lives so quietly and peacefully, spinning her beautiful web of silk.

SPIDER (*Weakly*): Thank you, kind Piki. You are a good, strong young Guarani.

PIKI: Strong? But it does not take strength to lift a small spider.

SPIDER: No, it does not take a strong body, Piki, but it takes a strong heart. A selfless heart is the strongest of all. Will you please place me back in my web so that I may rest?

PIKI: Certainly. (*Places* SPIDER *in center of web*) Rest quietly, little friend. I will visit you tomorrow to see if you are well. Goodbye.

SPIDER: Goodbye, Piki. Someday I shall help you as you have helped me this day. (PIKI *stoops, as if filling jar with water.* MOTHER *takes it from him and gives him another to fill.* TUKIRA *enters at side, pretending to gather berries, placing them into basket.* PIKI *looks up and sees her; he stands slowly, gazing in wonder.* TUKIRA *sees him, looks down quickly, turns and runs off.*)

PIKI: Mother! Who is she?

MOTHER: She is Tukira, the chieftain's daughter.

PIKI: But why have I never seen her before?

MOTHER: When Tukira was a small child, her mother died, and the chieftain sent her to live with an aunt in a distant village. She is sixteen now and has come back to our village to live. The chieftain will soon choose a husband for her.

PIKI: How will he do that?

MOTHER: Tomorrow he will assemble the young men from our village and announce his plan. You will be among them.

PIKI (*Lifting jar to his shoulder*): Tukira . . . what a beautiful name.

MOTHER (*Lifting other jar*): Yes. A beautiful name for a beautiful princess. Let us start home now, Piki. It is growing late. (*They exit.*)

* * * * *

SCENE 2

TIME: *The next day.*

SETTING: *Chieftain's home. Cloth-covered wooden frame center has leafy branches laid across the top. Large earthen jars, weaving frame, and wood for fire are on either side. Background mural shows forest.*

AT RISE: CHIEFTAIN *sits on floor beneath frame.* 1ST WOMAN *pretends to cook over open fire.* CHILDREN *run across, laughing as they play tag.* 2ND WOMAN *pretends to weave on loom.* MESSENGER *enters and bows before* CHIEFTAIN.

CHIEFTAIN: Have the six youths received my message to come today?

MESSENGER (*Bowing*): Yes, Chieftain. They come now. (PIKI, DIKA, DABU, KINTA, MUNGA, *and* KUMA *enter, carrying bows and arrows. All but* CHIEFTAIN, MESSENGER, *and youths exit. Youths stand on either side of* CHIEFTAIN, *their backs to audience.*)

CHIEFTAIN: The winner of the contests I have arranged may have the hand of my daughter Tukira in marriage and perhaps may rule our village when I grow old. (*Speaks to each of six in turn*) You, Kuma, are tall and strong. Dika, you swim and fish with the skill of your father. With your swift arrows, Dabu, you have fed your family well. You, Kinta, have the wisdom of your ancestors. Munga, you are brave in times of war. And you, Piki, are kind and generous. Today you will compete in running, shooting, and wrestling. First there is the foot race. The course is clearly marked through the forest and back to our village. My messenger will signal the start. (MESSENGER *sits, beats on small drum. Youths lay down bows and arrows.*)

KUMA (*Boastfully*): I shall surely win the race, for I am the oldest.

DABU: You may be the oldest, but I have seen young Piki run—and he is very fast. He saves his energy by running steadily, and then his feet seem to grow wings as he nears the end of a race.

KUMA: He will not pass me. You will see. (*They line up in front of* MESSENGER, *facing left. Drum grows louder.* MESSENGER *shouts, and race begins. They run offstage through audience, with* KUMA *in the lead and* PIKI *right behind.* KUMA *returns to stage slightly ahead of others, glances back and deliberately trips* PIKI. CHIEFTAIN *seems not to see the incident.* PIKI *rises, brushes off knees and hands.* KUMA *looks exultant. Other contestants return to stage, panting.*)

CHIEFTAIN: You all ran well, but you, Kuma, finished first. Next is the shooting contest. (*Points off left*) Do you see the red feather on the trunk of the old tree beside the river? (*They nod.*) The one whose arrow pierces the tip of the feather will be the winner. (MESSENGER *stands far left, announcing results of each shot.*) Munga, you may try first. (*One at a time each one stands, faces left, raises bow, and aims an arrow.*)

MUNGA (*Shooting*): How close is it?

MESSENGER: It is very close, only a hand's length from the feather's tip. (MUNGA *runs out left.* KINTA *shoots next and runs out left.*) That was a good shot, but the first arrow is still closer.

DABU: Surely I can shoot closer. I will pretend the feather is the forehead of a wild boar. (*Shoots*)

MESSENGER: Dabu's arrow is only a finger's width from the tip of the feather! (DABU *shouts joyfully, exits.*)

DIKA: Save your joy, Dabu. There are three more of us to try. (*Shoots*)

MESSENGER: Your arrow did not fly true, Dika. It fell far beneath the feather. (DIKA, *disappointed, exits.*)

KUMA (*Boastfully*): With my new bow I can easily win. Watch how straight my arrow will fly! (*Shoots*) I won, did I not?

MESSENGER: No, Kuma, your arrow flew beyond the feather. Now, Piki, it is your turn. (KUMA *sits, sulking.* MESSENGER *exits.*)

KUMA: *You* will never win, Piki. You are the youngest of us. Have you ever even held a bow before?

PIKI: I have held a bow for many years, Kuma. This was my father's bow, and it has never failed me. (*Shoots. All reenter, shouting excitedly.* MESSENGER *holds feather aloft. Feather is large and may be made out of red construction paper, cut partway down the middle as if split by the arrow.*)

MESSENGER: Piki, your arrow pierced the feather's tip, dividing it exactly in half. You are the winner! (KUMA *scowls angrily.*)

CHIEFTAIN: Kuma has won the foot race, and Piki has won the shooting contest. Now you will all wrestle. (MESSENGER *hands* CHIEFTAIN *a stick.*) You will hold this stick between you, and you must keep both hands on the stick at all times. You may not move your feet once the contest begins. The one who can force the other to lose his balance will win. Kuma and Dika will fight first. (KUMA *and* DIKA *grasp stick with both hands, their feet planted firmly.*)

MESSENGER: Begin. (KUMA *and* DIKA *begin their "fight." After brief struggle,* DIKA *loses balance, and* KUMA *wins. Next,* DABU *and* KINTA *fight, and* DABU *wins. Then* MUNGA *and* PIKI *fight, and* PIKI *wins.*)

CHIEFTAIN: Now the three winners will fight. First, Piki and Dabu. (PIKI *and* DABU *face each other and begin. Others form semicircle behind them, upstage, facing audience, but* KUMA *stands in back of others, drops to ground, takes tube out of his waistband, and aims at* PIKI'*s ankle as if blowing stone or dart.* PIKI *winces and grabs his ankle, losing his balance. No one else appears to see what* KUMA *did.*) Dabu has won. Now, Dabu, you and Kuma will fight. (DABU *and* KUMA *fight, and* DABU *wins.*)

KUMA (*Throwing stick down angrily*): That was not fair! I was not ready to start!

CHIEFTAIN: Dabu is the winner. (*Looks around*) You have all done well today, but only three have won. Kuma, Piki, and Dabu will now compete in a final contest. The winner will marry my daughter Tukira. (DIKA, KINTA, *and* MUNGA *exit;* CHIEFTAIN *addresses remaining three.*) Each of you must find a beautiful gift to present to my daughter. Return in three days with your gifts, and she will choose the best. Go now and may your search be rewarded. (*Drum beats as* KUMA, DABU, *and* PIKI *exit. Curtain*)

* * * * *

SCENE 3

TIME: *Two days later.*

SETTING: *The forest; before curtain.*

BEFORE RISE: PIKI *enters, carrying jar. He approaches spring, kneels down as if to fill jar, then sets jar beside him and sits, looking sad.*

SPIDER (*From offstage*): Piki, Piki, why do you look so sad?

PIKI (*Looking up at bush in surprise*): Oh, it is you, little spider. (*Sighs*) My heart is heavy because I shall not win the beautiful Tukira for my wife. I ran well, I shot well, and I fought well. But now I have no hope. Tukira will surely become the wife of Kuma or Dabu.

SPIDER: I can help you can win the final contest.

PIKI: Do you know of the contest?

SPIDER: Yes. I listen as I sit quietly in my *yerba* bush spinning my web. The women talk as they come to fill their water jars. I heard them speak of the gifts you must bring to the lovely princess.

PIKI: Yes, the lovely princess . . . but she will never be mine. Tomorrow we must present our gifts. It is said that Dabu will bring a headdress woven of colorful feathers from rare birds. And Kuma boasts openly of his gift, a necklace of gold, encrusted with the lovely topaz stones of the highlands. But I . . . I have nothing. My mother and I are poor, unlike the families of Dabu and Kuma.

SPIDER: Piki, did you not hear me? I shall help you win Tukira's hand.

PIKI: But how can you help, little spider?

SPIDER: Go home to your mother, Piki, but return to the spring at sunrise. Your special gift for Tukira will be ready. Be joyful, Piki, for the morning will dawn bright.

PIKI (*Puzzled yet hopeful*): I shall do as you say, little friend. You give me hope. (*Starts to exit*)

SPIDER: Piki, I promised to repay you for saving me, and I will. (PIKI *exits. Lights dim and music plays softly, indicating night.*) I will spin my most delicate thread and sprinkle it with moon dust. In the center I will form the beautiful *guava* flower . . . the loveliest I have ever spun. And then, rare orchids of many designs. Then I shall spin stars to twinkle around the edges, and then I shall weave all the designs together with a fine, intricate lace. Now I will begin my work, for I must finish before the sun reaches the horizon. (*Music continues for 30 seconds, with lights gradually coming up. Music stops.*)

PIKI (*Entering left, approaching bush*): The new day has dawned, and I have returned as you said, friend.

SPIDER: Look beneath the bush, Piki. I have finished your gift.

PIKI (*Removing lace mantle from bush; holding it up*): Oh, it is beautiful! Never have I seen such delicate lace! It is fit for a princess.

SPIDER: It will be Tukira's bridal veil. Take it to the chieftain at the appointed time.

PIKI: How can I thank you, White Spider? (*Gently folds lace and turns to exit, but* KUMA *enters, blocks his way.* PIKI *hides lace behind his back.*)

KUMA: Piki, what makes you rise so early? Surely you are not still searching the forest for a gift worthy of the princess? (*Laughs*)

PIKI: No, Kuma, I am no longer searching. But I cannot talk; I must go now. (PIKI *starts to move on, but* KUMA *stops him roughly.*)

KUMA: The women of the village say you have no gift to bring. (*Laughs rudely*) I have fashioned gold into a necklace for Tukira.

PIKI: Yes, Kamu, I have heard of it. The whole village has heard.

KUMA (*Taunting him*): And soon Tukira will wear my necklace and become my bride. What will you bring, Piki? Perhaps a bowl of tea leaves? (*Laughs*) Or a dish of berries?

PIKI: I must go now, Kuma. (*Exits, followed by* KUMA, *laughing. Curtain rises.*)

* * * * *

TIME: *Later that morning.*

SETTING: *Chieftain's home.*

AT RISE: CHIEFTAIN *and* TUKIRA *sit side by side.* GIRL *combs and arranges flowers in* TUKIRA's *hair.* MESSENGER *sits behind them, tapping a drum as they talk.*

CHIEFTAIN: The morning has come, daughter. Soon the three young braves will hear the drum and arrive to present their gifts.

TUKIRA: Father, what if I cannot decide which is the most beautiful gift?

CHIEFTAIN: You will know. Your heart will tell you. Stand, now. Here come the youths. (CHIEFTAIN *and* TUKIRA *stand as* DUBA, KUMA, *and* PIKI *enter, carrying gifts behind their backs.* MESSENGER *stops beating drum, and* VILLAGERS *enter, gather around.*) The three days have ended, and now Tukira will choose among you. Present your gift first, Duba. (DUBA *steps forward, kneels, holds out feathered headdress.*)

TUKIRA (*Taking headdress; with admiration*): It is lovely. Such rare feathers and such brilliant colors!

Thank you, Dabu. (TUKIRA *hands headdress to* GIRL. DABU *rises and moves back.*)

CHIEFTAIN: Now your gift, Kuma. (KUMA *steps forward, kneels, presents necklace to* TUKIRA. KUMA *glances back at* PIKI *scornfully.*)

TUKIRA (*In admiring tone*): What fine gold! And such glowing topaz stones! Thank you, Kuma. (TUKIRA *hands necklace to* GIRL.)

KUMA (*Pompously*): The topaz stones do not compare to the beauty of your eyes, lovely princess. (TUKIRA *lowers her eyes, and* CHIEFTAIN *motions* KUMA *back.*)

CHIEFTAIN: Piki, you may present your gift now. (PIKI *steps forward, kneels, and presents lace mantle.* VILLAGERS *gasp, reach forward to touch it, murmuring loudly at its beauty.* TUKIRA *takes mantle, unfolds it, studies it silently.*)

TUKIRA (*After a moment*): Never have I held such beautiful lace. It is clearly a miracle, for no hands could spin such glistening threads and intricate patterns—so delicate yet so strong. I choose Piki's lace mantle as the best gift, Father. (PIKI *bows head gratefully, rises, steps back.* KUMA *scowls angrily.*)

CHIEFTAIN: You have chosen well, daughter. (*To* PIKI) You have competed with honor and have won the hand of my daughter. Let us make ready for the ceremony tonight.

TUKIRA: And I shall wear the lovely lace mantle for my veil.

PIKI: Yes, you shall. Just as my friend said you would. (PIKI *gently places mantle over* TUKIRA's *head as curtain falls.*)

THE END

(Production Notes on page 314)

The King's Dreams

A Russian folktale

by Lenore Blumenfeld

Characters

KING
QUEEN
SASHA
MISHA } *King's advisers*
ROSHINSKY
IVAN, *a peasant*
SERPENT

SCENE 1

SETTING: *A palace in old Russia. Colorful towers are seen in background.*

AT RISE: KING *enters, sleepwalking. He wears crown and nightshirt, and carries pillow and blanket. He lies down on floor, covers himself, and snores.*

KING (*Suddenly crying out*): Oh! Oh, no! Go away— (QUEEN, *in crown, nightgown, and old bathrobe, rushes in.*)

QUEEN: Husband, Your Highness, what's wrong? Shall I call a doctor?

KING (*Awakening*): Where am I? (*Gets to his feet*) Oh, dear wife, what a terrifying dream! There was a fox with a bushy tail, evil eyes, and pointed fangs, and he was about to attack me!

QUEEN: Calm yourself, husband. It was only a dream.

KING: Don't you know that dreams have secret meanings?

QUEEN: Then call your advisers. Perhaps they can interpret the message hidden in that terrible nightmare.

KING: Yes, my advisers have explanations for everything. (*Bellowing*) Sasha! Misha! Roshinsky! (SASHA, MISHA, *and* ROSHINSKY *leap onstage like Cossack dancers. They bow to* KING.)

QUEEN: My goodness! How did you get here so soon?

SASHA: Simple.

MISHA: Easy.

ROSHINSKY: We were listening at the keyhole.

KING (*To* QUEEN): They were eavesdropping!

QUEEN (*To* KING): They were spying!

KING: Writing down my every word in secret code—

QUEEN: Which they can transmit to the enemy!

KING (*Bursting into tears*): Oo-o-oh, Sasha, Misha, Roshinsky—how could you betray me this way? (SASHA, MISHA *and* ROSHINSKY *whip out handkerchiefs to dry* KING's *tears.*)

SASHA: Don't cry, Your Majesty.

MISHA: We can explain everything. (*Nudging* ROSHINSKY *with elbow*) Explain!

ROSHINSKY: Er—yes—well—Your Majesty, we weren't really spying. We stationed ourselves at your keyhole so that we would be close by in case you had a dream that needed to be interpreted.

QUEEN: What excellent advisers. So thoughtful and loyal.

KING: Wife, what can we give these fellows as suitable rewards for thoughtfulness and loyalty?

QUEEN: I have just the thing. (*She pulls comb, stocking, ribbon, apple, scissors, harmonica, red rose out of her bathrobe pockets. Finally she holds up a cluster of medals.*) Look, gentlemen, medals engraved with my husband's profile. (SASHA, MISHA, *and* ROSHINSKY *grab medals.*)

SASHA: How pretty!

MISHA (*Peering closely at medal*): Remarkable likeness!

ROSHINSKY (*Biting medal*): Real gold!

KING: Stop chewing those medals and tell me the meaning of my dream.

SASHA: Why, it's very clear.

MISHA: To dream about a fox simply means (*Nudging* ROSHINSKY)—explain!

ROSHINSKY: Ahem—yes—well—since the fox had a bushy tail, it obviously means the King should give the Queen a new fur coat.

QUEEN: Obviously.

KING: Ridiculous! She already has a new fur coat.

SASHA: In that case, the dream means the King is going to meet a red-haired woman.

KING: Aha!

QUEEN: Impossible! My husband never looks at other women.

KING (*Sighing*): Of course not.

MISHA: I have it! Everyone knows foxes come out at night and steal chickens. Therefore, the King's dream means he is going to have chicken for dinner tonight.

QUEEN: Wrong again! We had chicken last night. You foolish advisers don't know anything about dreams. Be gone! Out! (*They exit.*)

KING: Wife, you shouldn't have chased them. Now we'll never find out the meaning of my dream.

QUEEN: Dear husband, if you want to know the truth, don't consult your advisers, for they will only tell you what you want to hear. For an honest answer, you must go directly to the people.

KING: Very well. We'll put on our sturdy leather boots and roam the countryside in search of a simple peasant. (*He gathers up pillow and blanket. They walk off, arm in arm. Curtain*)

* * * * *

SCENE 2

SETTING: *A field. Tall grain is growing.*

AT RISE: IVAN, *a simple peasant, is hoeing. He pauses to mop his brow.*

IVAN: How harsh is the lot of a simple peasant! All day I work in the burning sun, and what is my reward? Nothing—for I must give my entire harvest to the King, who will use the grain for white bread, which he will eat from a gold-rimmed plate, while I stand in the field (*Taking out chunk of black bread*), gnawing at a crust of dry pumpernickel. (SERPENT *enters.*)

SERPENT: Ivan, I'm so hungry. Please let me have a bit of your pumpernickel.

IVAN: A serpent! (*Brandishing hoe*) Shoo! Go away! Out!

SERPENT (*Dodging blows*): Don't be so quick to chase me, Ivan. I came to tell you that the King just had a dream in which he was attacked by a bushy-tailed, evil-eyed, sharp-fanged fox.

IVAN (*Covering ears*): Not another word, Serpent. I'm not interested in having palace gossip hissed into my ear by a talking snake.

SERPENT (*Shouting so* IVAN *will hear*): Ivan, listen—the King will soon be in this very field looking for someone to interpret his dream.

IVAN: There's no one here who's clever enough.

SERPENT (*Shouting*): You, Ivan, you!

IVAN: I? (*Lowering voice*) Serpent, how can I, a simple peasant, interpret the dream of a king?

SERPENT: Ivan, if you promise to bring me a bit of the King's white bread when he invites you to dinner, I will tell you the meaning of his dream.

IVAN (*Eagerly*): Dear Serpent, I'll bring you a whole slice. Now tell me. (SERPENT *hisses in* IVAN's *ear.*) Aha! So that's what it means!

SERPENT (*Slithering away*): Don't forget my white bread, Ivan.

IVAN: Trust me, Serpent. (SERPENT *leaves.* IVAN *resumes hoeing.* KING *and* QUEEN *enter. Both wear boots.* KING *carries pillow and blanket.*)

QUEEN: Ah, this fresh country air! How nice it would be to live as a simple peasant, working all day in the bright sunshine and stopping now and then to nibble at a piece of crusty pumpernickel.

KING (*To* IVAN): You there!

IVAN: The King! (He *bows. Meanwhile,* SASHA, MISHA, *and* ROSHINSKY *sneak in, carrying daggers, and stand behind* KING *with daggers poised.* IVAN *sees them and is speechless with terror. He tries to warn* KING *by pointing frantically, but* KING *thinks* IVAN *is merely waving, and waves back.* QUEEN *waves, too.*)

KING: Peasant, do you happen to know the meaning of a dream about a fox?

IVAN: Of course, sire. The fox represents deceit and treachery. Therefore, your dream means (*Raising his voice as he sees* SASHA, MISHA, *and* ROSHINSKY *about to plunge their daggers into* KING)—that your own advisers are standing behind you, about to assassinate you! (KING *and* QUEEN, *turning their heads, discover the would-be assassins.*)

QUEEN: Help! Save us!

KING: Traitors! (IVAN *uses his hoe to duel with advisers.*)

IVAN: Ha-ha, you villains. Do not underestimate the powers of a simple peasant. (*He lunges. They flee and exit.*)

KING: Peasant, you have saved my life. How can I reward you?

IVAN: Sire, all I want is rest from work and something good to eat.

QUEEN: Then put down your hoe, and be at the palace at eight tonight, and I myself, Ivan, will serve you white bread on a gold-rimmed plate.

IVAN (*Bowing*): Your Majesty!

KING (*Offering* QUEEN *his arm*): Come, my dear. It's time for my afternoon nap.

QUEEN: Tonight at eight, Ivan. (*She takes* KING'S *arm, and they exit.* SERPENT *enters.*)

SERPENT: Ivan, make sure you bring me some of the King's white bread.

IVAN (*Sneering*): White bread is too high-class for a simple serpent.

SERPENT: Ivan—you promised!

IVAN (*Covering ears*): Please! A man on his way to eat white bread at the palace doesn't wish to be bothered by a slithering snake.

SERPENT: Very well, Ivan. I won't bother you. I'll leave forever. And I won't be here to help you when the King asks you the meaning of his new dream— which is about buttons.

IVAN (*Uncovering ears*): Buttons?

SERPENT: At this very moment, Ivan, the King is

dreaming he is surrounded by buttons—lines and rows, parades and processions, of gold buttons—gleaming, glittering, glinting, glowing, glowering, glaring gold buttons (SERPENT *moves closer.*)—approaching, encircling, advancing, closer and closer, until the King cries out in terror! (*Hissing*) What does it mean, Ivan? What? What?

IVAN: I don't know. Do you? (SERPENT *nods, then slithers off.* IVAN *scratches head.* QUEEN *enters.*)

QUEEN: Ivan, the King just awakened from his nap crying out in terror because he dreamed he was surrounded by buttons. Ivan, what does it mean? What? What?

IVAN: Ah—well—uh—please, Your Majesty, tonight at dinner I'll be happy to interpret the King's new dream.

QUEEN: Until tonight, then, Ivan. (*Exits*)

IVAN (*Calling out*): Serpent, where are you? Serpent, dear Serpent, graceful, soft-spoken Serpent, please come back. (SERPENT *slithers in.*)

SERPENT: What do you want, you liar, you traitor, you promise-breaker?

IVAN: Serpent, everything you say about me is true. I was dishonest and nasty, and I humbly apologize.

SERPENT: Hm-mm-mph.

IVAN: Well, now that I have apologized, Serpent, please, will you tell me the meaning of the King's dream about buttons? Will you, please? (SERPENT *shakes head.* IVAN *kneels.*) Please, Serpent, tell me, I beg you. (SERPENT *shakes head.* IVAN *shrugs, stands up, and looks nonchalant.*) All right. You don't want to help me? Then don't.

SERPENT (*Startled by* IVAN's *change of mood*): All right, I won't.

IVAN: All right. Then go home.

SERPENT: All right. I will. (*Starts to exit*)

IVAN (*Calling after* SERPENT): But wherever you live, Serpent, I hope you have a strong door.

SERPENT: I live in the grass, Ivan. I do not have a door.

IVAN: Good. Then the secret police will find you easily when they come to arrest you.

SERPENT: Why should the police arrest me? I've committed no crime.

IVAN: My dear Serpent, don't you know it is a crime to withhold information from the state?

SERPENT: I'm a simple serpent, Ivan. What do I know about affairs of state?

IVAN (*Sternly*): Don't try to play innocent with me, Serpent. You know well that the King is the head of state—and yet you deliberately refuse to tell me the meaning of his dream! That is a crime against the state! Serpent, you are guilty of treason, and the secret police will show no mercy when they find you!

SERPENT: I don't care. Let them beat me, throw me in prison, exile me to a rocky island populated only by seagulls. I will not interpret the King's dream unless I get a fair share of his white bread.

IVAN: Well, then, tell me the meaning of his dream. I will tell him, he will reward me with a fine dinner, and I will save you some bread.

SERPENT: Promise?

IVAN: Trust me, Serpent.

SERPENT: All right, Ivan. Now listen carefully. A dream about buttons—gleaming, glittering, glinting, glowing, glaring gold buttons, coming closer and closer, means that an enemy army in full uniform is about to attack!

IVAN: Then we will soon be at war! Fighting. Shooting. Standing in line for potatoes. How terrible!

SERPENT: Not so terrible, Ivan. For when you tell the

King the meaning of his dream, he can secretly prepare our troops in advance. Then, when the enemy strikes, we will win a swift victory. And then, Ivan, parades, bells ringing. (IVAN *strikes* SERPENT *with his hoe.* SERPENT *falls, writhing and gasping in agony.*) Ivan, Ivan, why did you strike me?

IVAN: Serpent, only you and I know that our nation is about to make secret plans for war. Now, I myself, Serpent, am very good at keeping secrets—but I'm afraid that you will gossip to the enemy. Therefore, I must silence you. (*He swats at* SERPENT *several times.*)

SERPENT: Oh—help! Murder! So this is the reward I get for saving the state from destruction.

IVAN: Serpent, don't you know it is a great privilege to suffer for one's country? (*He strikes* SERPENT *several times.* SERPENT *crawls offstage.* KING *enters, carrying pillow and blanket, followed by* QUEEN.)

KING: Ivan—Ivan—

IVAN (*Bowing*): Your Majesty!

KING: Ivan, have you found out the meaning of my dream about buttons?

IVAN: Alas, sire—it means we will soon be at war.

KING: War! Then there's not a moment to spare. I must take drastic measures to meet this national emergency.

IVAN: Will you call out the army, load the cannons, and tell people to stand in line for potatoes?

KING: No, no, no. I'm going to lie down right here in the field and cover myself with my blanket until peace is declared. (*He lies down.*)

IVAN (*To* QUEEN): Your Majesty, with the King asleep, who will lead us to victory?

QUEEN: Simple peasant, don't you know that making peace is woman's work? (*Pulls trumpet out of pocket, blows it, shouts offstage)* Attention! Soldiers and citizens, prepare for attack. Shoulder arms (IVAN *shoulders hoe.*), start marching (IVAN *marches.*), and make sure there is no lint on your uniforms. (IVAN *picks speck off sleeve, marches offstage.* QUEEN *marches after him.*) Onward to victory! (KING *snores. Curtain*)

* * * * *

SCENE 3

SETTING: *Same as Scene 2.*

AT RISE: IVAN *marches in, shouldering hoe.* QUEEN *enters from opposite side, blowing trumpet.*

IVAN: Greetings, Your Majesty. What's the latest news about the war?

QUEEN: Ivan, thanks to your brilliant interpretation of the King's dream about buttons, we were able to make advance preparations for the enemy's attack, and easily vanquished them.

IVAN (*Jubilantly waving hoe*): The war is over! We won! Our citizens can put down their weapons (*Throws down hoe*) and lead normal lives once more. And I, a simple peasant, can join you for white bread at eight tonight.

QUEEN: Look here, Ivan, when you arrive at the palace, kindly be prepared to interpret the frightening dream the King had while he was waiting for the war to end.

IVAN: Another dream! (*He sighs and shrugs.*) What was this one about?

QUEEN: This time, Ivan, the King dreamed he was outside the window of a humble cottage. There he saw a little old lady with a flowered babushka sitting near the hearth, weeping and wailing, moaning and groaning, sighing and sobbing until her tears formed a foaming, churning stream which flooded the fire in the fireplace and rose so high that it flowed through the window and carried the King himself out to sea!

IVAN: What a strange dream!

QUEEN: Yes, but I'm sure you'll be ready to explain it when you come to dinner. (*Exits*)

IVAN (*Hitting his forehead*): Ivan, you dolt! Why, oh, why, did you beat that poor Serpent? Without its help, how can you—a simple peasant—interpret the King's dream? Fool! Dunce! Peasant! (SERPENT *slithers on*.)

SERPENT: Good afternoon, Ivan.

IVAN (*Startled*): Serpent, I beat you to a pulp—but there's not a scratch on you!

SERPENT: Don't you know, Ivan, that serpents can shed their skins?

IVAN: Aha! Well—since you're not harmed by my beating, we're still friends. Now surely, friend, you'll tell me the meaning of the King's latest dream?

SERPENT: No.

IVAN (*Shaking head*): No?

SERPENT (*Nodding head*): No.

IVAN: Serpent, how can you be so heartless and cold-blooded?

SERPENT: Ivan, how can you cheat me and beat me—and still expect me to be your friend?

IVAN: Come now, just because I did something wrong in the past, you shouldn't hold it against me forever.

SERPENT: Very well, Ivan. I'll give you one more chance. Just let me hold your hoe so you can't beat me, and I'll tell you the meaning of the King's new dream.

IVAN (*Handing him hoe*): Here, Serpent, you are a true friend.

SERPENT: The King's dream means, Ivan (*Seizing hoe and raising voice*)—that in a humble cottage sits your own mother, weeping her eyes out because her son turned out to be a promise-breaker and serpent-beater who deserves to be beaten with his own hoe! (*Hits him with hoe*)

IVAN: Oh, no, don't! Oh! (KING *and* QUEEN *enter.* KING *carries pillow and blanket.*)

KING: Here, here, stop that!

IVAN *and* SERPENT (*Bowing*): Your Majesties.

QUEEN (*To* SERPENT): Who are you?

SERPENT: A serpent.

KING (*Draping blanket over himself*): A serpent! Oo-o-o-h!

SERPENT: Don't worry, sire. I'm non-poisonous.

QUEEN: Serpent, were you or were you not beating this simple peasant with his own hoe?

SERPENT: I was.

KING (*Flinging off blanket*): That's treason! Serpent, you've committed a crime against the state. I'll have you thrown into prison, and after a fair trial I'll send you to a rocky island populated only by seagulls.

SERPENT: Sire, I'm a simple serpent. What do I know about treason, trials, and seagulls?

KING: Don't give me that innocent look. Don't you realize that anyone who beats Ivan endangers the safety of the entire state? (IVAN *nods vigorously.*)

QUEEN: Serpent, Ivan is the one who interprets the King's dreams, thereby warning us of attacks by assassins and other enemies. Without Ivan, our state is lost. (IVAN *puffs out chest with pride.*)

SERPENT: Your Majesties, didn't you ever wonder how a

simple peasant could interpret a king's dreams without help? (IVAN *frowns.*)

KING: Are you suggesting Ivan gets his information from someone else? (IVAN *looks alarmed.*)

SERPENT: Exactly.

QUEEN: I wonder who that unknown someone can be?

SERPENT: Me. (IVAN *hunches shoulders and tries to look small.*)

KING: You? (SERPENT *nods.*) *Not* Ivan? (SERPENT *shakes head.*)

QUEEN (*Pointing an accusing finger at* IVAN): Ivan, you deceived us.

KING: You took credit for information hissed into your ear by a simple serpent. (IVAN *looks away sheepishly, picks up his hoe, and tries to back offstage.*)

KING: Why are you sneaking away, Ivan?

IVAN: Oh, Your Majesty, everything you accuse me of is true and I deserve to be punished, so I am going to visit my weeping mother in her humble cottage where I will ask her to beat me with my own hoe. (*He backs out.*)

KING: Well, Serpent, since you are the only one who knows the meaning of my dreams, I hereby cancel your banishment to a rocky island populated only by seagulls.

SERPENT: Oh, thank you, Your Majesty.

KING: Instead, you may live in my garden, where you will serve the state as Royal Dream Interpreter.

SERPENT (*Bowing*): Your Majesty, what an honor.

QUEEN: And every night, Serpent, you may dine with us at the palace, where I personally will serve you white bread on a gold-rimmed plate.

SERPENT: A royal treat, Your Majesty.

QUEEN: Come along, then. It's almost dinnertime.

(KING *puts pillow on ground, lies down, covers him-self with blanket.*) Husband, aren't you coming?

KING: I'll be there later. First I'm taking a short nap so I can dream a new dream for the Serpent to interpret. (*He snores.*)

QUEEN *and* SERPENT: Sh-h-h-h! (QUEEN *and* SERPENT *tiptoe out.* KING *snores. Curtain*)

THE END

(*Production Notes on page 315*)

The Strange and Wonderful Object

A Chinese folktale

by Gillian L. Plescia

Characters

NARRATOR
CHANG, *a young man*
SING-HI, *his wife*
MAN
WOMAN } *his neighbors*
NEIGHBORS, *men and women, extras*
OLD PRIEST
SERVANT
WILLOW TREE
PEACH TREE
MUSICIANS, *the orchestra*

SETTING: *Ancient China. An archway stands on raised platform up center. At front of platform is a large Chinese vase. There is a bench in front of stage or at one side.*
AT RISE: MUSICIANS, *dressed in black, enter carrying*

126

*gong, wind chimes, triangle, jingle bells, wooden xy-
lophone, etc. They sit on bench. Gong sounds. With
small shuffling steps,* NARRATOR, *also in black, enters, crosses to archway, and bows to audience.*

NARRATOR: Honorable ladies and gentlemen, welcome
to our play. I am the Narrator, and it has fallen to me
to explain to you some of the customs of our Chinese
theater. As you see, my friends (*Gestures to* MUSI-
CIANS) and I are dressed in black. This black costume
means that we are invisible to you. So, when I have
finished talking, you will please take no further
notice of us. Now, this archway (*Points*) behind me is
the entrance to the house where Chang lives with
his wife, Sing-Hi. Later it will become the entrance
to the Temple. Along this winding path (*Moves
downstage in zigzag as if following winding path*)
Chang goes to work each day, always stopping to
greet the Willow Tree (*He stops, as* WILLOW TREE
*enters and takes place on one side, to accompaniment
of wind chimes.*) and the Peach Tree. (PEACH TREE
*enters and moves into place on opposite side to ac-
companiment of jingling bells.* NARRATOR *continues
to zigzag, then takes small mirror from sleeve.*) And
this, ladies and gentlemen, is the strange and wonderful object Chang finds lying in his path one day
that sets in motion the events that will now take
place before your eyes. (*He puts mirror down on
path, then bows.*) Honorable ladies and gentlemen,
our play! (*Gong sounds.* NARRATOR *exits.* CHANG *and*
SING-HI *enter through archway.*)

SING-HI (*Bowing*): Farewell, dear husband. May your
day be tranquil.

CHANG (*Bowing*): May your day also be tranquil, dear-
est wife. Farewell. (*Starts down winding path, to
accompaniment of xylophone*)

SING-HI: Farewell. (*She exits through archway.* CHANG *continues, then stops at* WILLOW TREE.)

CHANG (*Bowing*): Good morning, Willow Tree. (WILLOW TREE *shakes branches to accompaniment of wind chimes.*) It is a fine morning, is it not? (WILLOW TREE *shakes branches.* CHANG *bows, then continues down path. He stops at* PEACH TREE *and bows.*) Good morning, Peach Tree. (PEACH TREE *shakes branches to accompaniment of jingling bells.*) Your blossoms are beautiful today. (PEACH TREE *shakes branches.* CHANG *bows, continues on his way, sees mirror lying in path and stops.*) What is this? (*Bends down to look at mirror.*) A shining object lying in the road. Someone must have dropped it. (*Picks it up, looks at it, and gasps*) Why, it is a picture of my honored father, who went to live with his ancestors many seasons ago! But why is this picture lying here? (*He ponders. Suddenly*) It is a sign sent to me by my ancestors, revealing that I have found favor in their sight. (*Smiling*) Ah, how fortunate I am to receive this precious gift! I must take it home and hide it in a safe place, somewhere my wife Sing-Hi will not find it. It is my own special treasure. (*He tucks mirror inside sleeve and hurries back along path toward house, nodding to* TREES, *which bow to audience and exit.* CHANG *glances around.*) Now, where shall I hide my treasure where Sing-Hi will not find it? I hear her coming. I must be quick! (*Looking around*) I'll hide it in this vase for now. (*Carefully puts mirror in vase, as* SING-HI *enters*)

SING-HI: Why, Chang, my husband. You have returned so soon. You are not sick, I hope.

CHANG: No, no. I—I forgot something!

SING-HI: Oh? What did you forget?

CHANG: I—well, to speak the truth, I have forgotten

what I forgot!

SING-HI: How strangely you are acting!

CHANG (*Trying to be casual*): Not at all. We are all forgetful at times. Now I must hurry to work, or I shall be late. (*Starts off*)

SING-HI: No, wait. (CHANG *stops.*) There *is* a strangeness about you. What were you doing when I came out? (*Looks around and sees vase*) Something with this vase. (*Looks inside vase*) Ah! I see you were hiding something in here. Something shiny. (*Happily*) A surprise for me!

CHANG: No! I mean—that is to say . . . (SING-HI *takes mirror out of vase, looks at it, and cries out.*)

SING-HI: Oh! Oh! Cruel, unfaithful husband! It is not a surprise for me. It is the portrait of a beautiful young lady. How could you! We have been married only six months, and you no longer love me! My heart is broken! (*She begins to sob loudly.* CHANG *goes to her and takes mirror.*)

CHANG (*Angrily*): What foolishness is this? It is a picture of my honored father, sent to me by my ancestors as a sign of favor. How can you say it is a beautiful young lady?

SING-HI (*Taking mirror and looking at it again*): But it is a beautiful young lady.

CHANG: *My father!* (*They stare at each other angrily, turn their backs to each other,* SING-HI *holding mirror. To accompaniment of triangle,* MAN *and* WOMAN *enter with other* NEIGHBORS, *men from one side, who stand on* CHANG'S *side, women from the other, who stand on* SING-HI'S.)

WOMAN: Dear Sing-Hi. We heard your husband shouting so loudly that we came to see if you needed assistance.

MAN: Chang, good friend. We heard your wife's voice

raised in anger and we came to see if you needed our support.

CHANG: Oh, it is nothing of importance. (*With the wave of his hand*) A trivial disagreement. But you can indeed help to solve it. I found this object (*Holds out hand to* SING-HI, *who hesitates, then hands him mirror*) on the path. Look at it closely, and you will see it is my honored father, sent to me by my ancestors as a sign of favor. (*Hands mirror to* MAN, *who looks at it carefully*)

MAN: Yes, it is indeed a man, and may well be a portrait of your father, whom it was never my honor to know, but it also reminds me somewhat of my own father. (*He passes mirror down line of men. They nod and ad lib agreement.* MAN *returns it to* CHANG.) We are all agreed. It is the portrait of a man. What, then, was the cause of the dispute? (SING-HI, *furious, snatches mirror from* CHANG.)

SING-HI: How can you say that it is the portrait of a man when it is plain to any eye that it is the portrait of a woman, a beautiful young lady, and my cruel husband was hiding it from me in a vase! (*She shows mirror to* WOMAN.)

WOMAN (*Examining it closely*): It is indeed the portrait of a woman. (*Glares at* CHANG) Such deceit! (*She passes mirror to women, who nod in agreement. They glare at* CHANG *and men.* WOMAN *returns mirror to* SING-HI.) We are agreed. It is the portrait of a woman.

CHANG (*Snatching mirror*): Indeed it is not! It is a man.

MEN: Yes, most certainly. It is a man.

SING-HI (*Snatching it back*): Ridiculous! It is a woman. (*Groups stare furiously at each other.*)

WOMAN: Neighbors, since we cannot agree, let us take

our dispute to the Temple and consult the Old Priest. He will know the answer to this puzzle.

CHANG: You are right. He will know the answer—and my wife will not presume to argue with him!

SING-HI: Let us go to him, then, for my husband will surely accept *his* decision! (CHANG *and* SING-HI *lead way down path, to accompaniment of music.* NEIGHBORS *form double column and move downstage.* NARRATOR *enters and turns archway around, so it becomes entrance to the Temple, then exits, taking vase with him.* CHANG *"knocks" on Temple door. Temple* SERVANT *enters through archway and bows.*)

SERVANT: What is your wish?

CHANG (*Bowing back*): We wish to consult the Old Priest.

SERVANT: I will tell him. Wait here. (*He bows and exists. Gong sounds and* OLD PRIEST *enters, followed by* SERVANT.)

PRIEST: Do you wish to consult me? Please tell me your problem.

CHANG: My wife—

SING-HI: My husband—(PRIEST *holds up hands, and both fall silent.*)

PRIEST: Let the wife speak first. (CHANG *looks indignant,* SING-HI *triumphant.*)

SING-HI: My husband, O Honorable One, brought home this object and hid it in a vase. (*Holds up mirror*)—As you can see, it is the picture of a beautiful young woman. And we have been married only six months! (*Starts to weep*)

PRIEST (*To* CHANG, *sharply*): And what does the husband have to say?

CHANG (*Taking mirror*): My wife is mistaken. I found this object as I journeyed to work. It is the portrait of my honored father, sent to me by my ancestors. Such a great treasure I hid in the vase until I could find a safer place for it. (MEN *nod in agreement.* PRIEST *takes mirror and studies it carefully.*)

PRIEST (*Stroking beard thoughtfully*): Hm-m-m. (*Looks up, decisively*) You are both wrong! (*All gasp. He turns to* SING-HI.) It is not the portrait of a beautiful young lady (*Turning to* CHANG), nor is it the portrait of your honored father. You were right to bring it to me, however, for it is, in fact, the portrait of an old and holy man, a sage, and must be kept in the Temple with all the other sacred objects. I will place it there, and you may come and view it on holy days. But for the present (*Touches* CHANG *and* SING-HI *on shoulder*), make up your quarrel, and henceforth live in peace. (*Gong sounds.* PRIEST, *followed by* SER-VANT, *goes into Temple. All look at each other sheepishly.* MAN *and* WOMAN *move toward each other, bow and shuffle off together, followed by* NEIGHBORS. CHANG *and* SING-HI, *left alone, look at each other shyly, then hold hands, move downstage, bow to audience, and exit.* MUSICIANS *rise, bow, and exit, as curtain falls.*)

THE END

(*Production Notes on page 315*)

The Miller's Guest

A folktale based on an old English ballad

by Margaret Hall

Characters

MILLER
HUNTER
MILLER'S WIFE
RICHARD, *the Miller's son*
MARGERY ⎫ *Miller's daughters*
DORA ⎭
TWO COURTIERS

SCENE 1

SETTING: *A footpath near the King's forest. Scene may be played before curtain.*

AT RISE: MILLER *enters left, carrying heavy sack of flour over one shoulder. He stoops under the heavy burden.*

MILLER (*Groaning*): Why is it that the longer you carry a sack, the heavier it grows? I'll try slinging it over to my other shoulder. (*He does so.*) There! I think that will feel better for a while. I should be thankful, I suppose, for carrying these heavy sacks every day keeps me strong. (*Sound of hunting horn is heard*

from offstage.) That's a hunter's horn. (*Fearfully*)
The royal archers must be in the forest, chasing the
King's deer. My son is out hunting for deer now, too! I
pray he stays out of the archers' way, for he'll pay
dearly if caught poaching in the King's forest!
(HUNTER *enters right, carrying bow in one hand and
horn in the other. A quiver with arrows is strapped
over one shoulder. He stops at center stage and blows
horn.* MILLER *puts both hands over his ears.*) A-h-h!
Why are you blowing your horn, sir?

HUNTER: I have lost my way in this forest, and
darkness is falling. A group of us was out hunting,
but I rode ahead in the chase and now I can't find my
companions. (*He steps back to examine* MILLER.)
That sack must be heavy, my good man. My guess is
it must be filled with flour, and you, therefore, must
be a miller.

MILLER (*Impressed*): Your deduction is keen, sir. I am a
miller by trade. (*He drops sack and rubs his shoulder in pain.*) Perhaps I can help you find your
friends—(*Hastily assuring* HUNTER) though I have
seen no one hunting the King's forests today! (*He
looks about apprehensively.*)

HUNTER: You may indeed help me, Miller, if you will be
so kind as to tell me the way to Nottingham.

MILLER: Nottingham? Why would you be going there?
The King and his court are in Nottingham just now.
All the lodging places will be filled, and besides, it is
not a town where a hunter should go. (*Laughs*) Unless you are hunting a place at court!

HUNTER: In a sense I am hunting such a place, good
miller. I'll wager that the King himself is no better
man than I am. However, I must sleep somewhere
tonight. Would you happen to have a room in your
own house where I might have shelter for the night?

MILLER (*Eyeing him suspiciously*): I have no way of knowing if you are an honest man or a thief. Many dishonest men wear fine clothes. You might rob us.

HUNTER (*Stepping closer; in amusement*): I am harmless enough. Will you refuse lodging to a stranger in need? I will pay for my room, of course.

MILLER: My wife and I do have room in our hut for a lodger. (*Doubtfully*) But how do I know that you have even a penny in your purse?

HUNTER (*Tapping his pocket*): I have at least forty pence in gold here. If you ask no more than that, I can pay it. And I'll not rob you. Search me if you like. (MILLER *runs his hands up and down* HUNTER'S *clothing. He takes a small pouch from* HUNTER'S *pocket and steps back.*)

MILLER: Very well. You seem to be speaking the truth, so you shall have the room, as we need the money. (*Shaking his head*) This has been a bad year for crops.

HUNTER: Then it's settled. Here is my hand to seal our agreement. (*He holds out his hand.* MILLER *backs away.*)

MILLER: Nay, not so fast, Hunter. I must know you better before I shake hands. I take none but an honest man's hand.

HUNTER (*Bemused*): You are a hard man to convince! (*Determined*) Well, I hope to take your hand someday. Lead on, my stout miller, and I shall follow.

MILLER (*Gesturing left*): My cottage is over this way. (*He picks up sack, throws it over shoulder, and leads* HUNTER *off left.*)

* * * * *

SCENE 2

TIME: *Immediately following.*

SETTING: *Inside Miller's cottage.*

AT RISE: MILLER'S WIFE *stands cooking at stove, rear.* MILLER *enters left, followed by* HUNTER.

MILLER: Wife, I have brought a lodger home to supper. He is a stranger, but I like his face well. He may stay with us tonight, may he not?

MILLER'S WIFE (*Studying* HUNTER): You are a handsome young man, but it is best not to trust anyone too soon. You may be a thief in disguise.

MILLER: He has paid gold in advance.

MILLER'S WIFE: Where is it? (MILLER *hands her the purse.*) I suppose it is all right. Show us your traveling papers, and we shall believe you.

HUNTER (*Bowing courteously*): Good dame, I do not carry any credentials, and I was never any man's servant, unless I might be called a servant of the people of this kingdom. I am a humble courtier who asks only for a night's lodging.

MILLER'S WIFE (*Considering for a moment*): You do have good manners. (*Decisively*) We would not turn you out in the dark.

MILLER: If you are a courtier, then you are used to much finer surroundings than our humble cottage. (*Simply*) We are plain and poor people.

HUNTER: I would never look down on anyone simply because he had less than I. In fact, I vow you are a better man than I, for you work with your hands to earn an honest living, while mine remain idle in my work. (RICHARD *runs in right.*)

RICHARD (*Out of breath*): Good evening, Father, Mother. I got a fine buck today. I have left it outside the door. (*He runs off left, as* MILLER *looks at* WIFE *in panic.*)

HUNTER (*Bewildered*): That lad passed through as quickly as a hurricane! What was that he said—something about a fine—

MILLER'S WIFE (*Cutting him off*): Luck! He said he had fine *luck* today . . . er, in keeping the crows out of the wheat fields. (*She looks to* MILLER *for agreement.*) Isn't that right?

MILLER (*Stammering*): Th-that's it, sir. Our son, Richard, had good luck in the fields and he left it outside the door so it would be there for him tomorrow! (*Smiles nervously; aside to* WIFE) If he finds we have been poaching in the King's forest, he's sure to report it. (WIFE *nods.*)

MILLER'S WIFE (*To* HUNTER; *cordially*): Supper is ready, good sir. You are welcome to our plain fare, and you shall have a clean bed with good, flaxen sheets.

HUNTER (*Bowing*): The King himself will sleep on nothing finer tonight.

MILLER: What is keeping Richard and the girls? They are never far off when food is on the table. (*Calling*) Richard! Margery! Come to supper! Come, Dora. (MARGERY *and* DORA *enter left.*)

MARGERY: Richard is washing up, Father. He is plenty filthy after a day in the forest hunting for—

MILLER'S WIFE (*Interrupting*): See what I have made for supper, Margery . . . There's pudding and cider—

DORA (*Crossing to stove*): And a nice stew! (RICHARD *reenters, left, rubbing his hands.*)

RICHARD (*Laughing*): Stew! After today we will be able to have roast every day! (*Seeing* HUNTER) Oh, I did not see that we had a guest. (MARGERY *and* DORA *notice* HUNTER.)

MILLER (*To* HUNTER): These are our children, sir— Richard, (*Claps him on the back*) Dora, and Margery. Richard, will you bring over the other chair for our guest? (HUNTER *bows to them. Girls curtsy.* RICHARD *bows, then brings extra chair to table.* WIFE *serves food and they begin to eat.*)

HUNTER (*Enthusiastically*): I have never tasted a more delicious stew! I am sure the King is eating no finer meal.

RICHARD (*Curiously*): You are dressed in clothes that might be worn at court. Do you know the King, sir?

HUNTER: I have never seen the King's face.

DORA: He must be a very grand person!

HUNTER: I expect he is just a man like most others, with arms and legs, the usual number of features, and some hair on his head.

MILLER'S WIFE: I feel ashamed at having no better food to offer you, but the grain crop did not do well this year, so there is only this dark bread. But the butter is fresh—I churned it just this morning.

HUNTER: What could be better than fresh bread and butter? And this stew is delicious. It must have a very special meat in it.

MILLER'S WIFE (*Nervously*): Oh, no, there is nothing special about it.

HUNTER (*Tasting stew*): Of course! It is venison. I have hunted enough deer myself to recognize the taste.

DORA: You guessed right; it is venison. It is wrong to shoot the deer, I suppose, but we would starve if we didn't.

MILLER'S WIFE: Quiet, Dora! You and Margery don't have to tell a stranger all you know, just to prove that you can talk. You make us sound like lawless poachers.

MILLER (*To* HUNTER): Life is not easy for serfs like us. We depend on our crops for food, and our overlord never allows us any meat. This year we had no rain, and my crops failed. So I was forced to hunt in the

King's forest to find enough food for my family. Sometimes we find a deer, or it may be a game bird. But I would not have the King hear of my hunting.

HUNTER: I can keep a secret. The King shall never know more about this than he does at present. (*Furrowing his brow*) So, all the working families have too little to eat, eh? (*Emphatically*) The King should spend time talking with his subjects, and learn more about their problems!

RICHARD: You are right, sir, he should! The farmers and millers must give all their best corn, wheat, and vegetables to the land owners.

MILLER'S WIFE (*Shrugging her shoulders*): We are allowed to raise poultry, but we can't eat the birds ourselves. Just as a blacksmith must make all the armor that the knights may need, but he may not even have shoes for his own horse!

MILLER: It would help me to have a bigger field of my own, so I could raise more grain.

HUNTER: I did not realize that things were so bad! There should be some solution. (*With determination*) You shall have your larger field, Miller. I can promise you that and more. (*Loud knocking is heard at door, left.*)

MILLER (*Startled*): Who is there?

1ST COURTIER (*From offstage*): We are from the royal court. We seek our King.

MARGERY (*In awe*): The King!

DORA: Who would come here to look for the King?

MILLER'S WIFE (*Calling*): There is no king here. Go and look for him at the palace!

HUNTER: It is all right, my friends. (HUNTER *rises, walks to door and opens it.* TWO COURTIERS *enter, with swords drawn.*)

1ST COURTIER (*Bowing, to* HUNTER): We heard your

horn blowing from this direction, Your Majesty. (*He drops down on one knee.*)

2ND COURTIER: Pardon us for losing sight of you, Your Majesty. (*He also kneels.*)

MILLER'S WIFE (*As others rise, trembling*): It is the King himself! And I served him venison taken from his own forests.

MILLER (*Stricken*): And I doubted his honesty. Oh, I am done for!

MARGERY: We treated him like any common peasant.

RICHARD: I shouted out about the buck I had shot.

MILLER: Besides that, I even refused to shake hands with him. (*To* HUNTER) Your Majesty, I fear you will never forgive us.

HUNTER: Don't be so hasty! You did me a service to open my eyes to the sad conditions in my kingdom. (*To* 1ST COURTIER) Hand me your sword, Geoffrey. (*Sword is handed to him.*) Now then, will you kneel down, Miller?

MILLER (*In terror*): Please don't cut my head off! I do most humbly implore your forgiveness. I did what I had to keep my family from starving.

HUNTER: Nay, I must repay your kind courtesy. Will you tell me your given name?

MILLER (*Kneeling*): It is John, Your Majesty.

HUNTER: John, I dub thee knight. (*He taps* MILLER *on shoulder with sword.*) Rise up, Sir John of Mansfield. From now on you will be master over others, and I know you will treat them justly, for you know their troubles.

COURTIERS (*Together*): Well done, sire!

MILLER (*Slowly rising*): Your Majesty, I promise my family and I will devote our lives to your welfare.

MILLER'S WIFE: For many a day hereafter we shall tell

of the night the King spent with us.

HUNTER (*Smiling*): And I also shall tell of the time I was taken for a thief and ate of my own deer in your house! (*Quick curtain*)

THE END

(*Production Notes on page 315*)

Cap o' Rushes

An English folktale

by Jean Feather

Characters

BARON FORESTER
ALICIA
LOUISA
CATHERINE (CAP
  o' RUSHES) } *his daughters*
NANNY, *his cook*
MARY ANN, *his housemaid*
DUKE OF DONCASTER
DUCHESS OF DONCASTER
ROBERT, *the Duke's son*
TILLY, *a kitchen maid*
THOMAS, *Robert's servant*
COOK
FOOTMAN
LADY WARCUM
JANE, *her daughter*

SCENE 1

TIME: *Long ago.*
SETTING: *Dining room of Baron Forester's home.*

AT RISE: NANNY *is seated behind table.* CATHERINE *enters right, carrying a plate which she places in front of* NANNY. MARY ANN *stands just inside the door.*

CATHERINE: Here is your dinner, Nanny.

NANNY: Thank you, Catherine.

CATHERINE: Oh, I do hope it's all right.

NANNY: Why shouldn't it be? You know how to cook by now, surely. You've been under my feet in the kitchen ever since you could walk.

CATHERINE: Yes, but it's the first time I've ever cooked a dinner all by myself.

NANNY: Well, let's see. (*Tastes it*) Ugh!

CATHERINE: What's wrong?

NANNY: Taste it and see for yourself.

CATHERINE: But I did everything the way you do. (*Tastes it*) Oh, no! I forgot the salt! (NANNY *and* MARY ANN *laugh.*) Oh, Nanny, how could I?

MARY ANN: I tried to tell you, Miss Catherine, but you wouldn't listen.

CATHERINE: I know. I wanted to do it without any help.

NANNY: And I'm sure you can, Catherine. Anyone might forget salt.

CATHERINE: For want of a shake of salt, the meat is ruined. It tastes terrible. (ALICIA *and* LOUISA *enter left.* MARY ANN *notices them and exits right.*)

NANNY: Never mind. We'll just. . . .

ALICIA (*Interrupting*): Well, it seems the servants have taken over the house!

NANNY (*Rising*): We're just preparing dinner, Miss Alicia. (*She exits right with plate.*)

CATHERINE: Alicia, that's no way to speak to Nanny!

ALICIA: She's the cook, and her place is in the kitchen.

LOUISA: Catherine, aren't you going to change before Father comes?

CATHERINE: Oh, my goodness, yes. (*She rushes off left.*)

ALICIA: That Catherine. She spends all day with the servants in the kitchen.

LOUISA (*Nastily*): Father doesn't care as long as his little pet is here when he comes in. Oh, Alicia, you're wearing Mother's pearls again. You wore them yesterday.

ALICIA: What if I did? I'm the oldest. They ought to be mine.

LOUISA: Father said we were to take turns.

ALICIA: You can have them for the next two days, then. I promise. (*Sighs*) I wish Father would let us wear all of Mother's jewels—her diamond necklace and earrings, and her ruby ring. . . .

LOUISA: He'd give the best to Catherine. Anyway, we never have a chance to wear fine clothes and jewels.

ALICIA: No. We just sit here and listen to Father talk about tenants and crops and hunting, till I could scream.

LOUISA: He won't even take us to the Duke of Doncaster's ball tomorrow night. And they say the Duke's son is ready to choose a wife.

ALICIA: Everyone will be there except us!

LOUISA: Let's ask Catherine to coax Father. He'll do anything for her. (CATHERINE *enters, wearing a bright, silk dress.*) Catherine, dear, we think Father ought to take us to the Duke's ball tomorrow night. What do you think?

CATHERINE: You know Father would rather stay home managing the accounts or visiting the tenants.

ALICIA: He can spare a few hours for us. How are we ever going to get husbands if we never go anywhere?

LOUISA: You might like to spend the rest of your life here with Father, but we wouldn't.

ALICIA (*Cajoling*): Please, Catherine, ask him.

BARON (*Entering*): Well, have my daughters had a busy, happy day?

ALICIA *and* LOUISA: Yes, Father.

CATHERINE: Did you have a good day, Father? (*She holds a chair for him.*)

BARON (*Sitting*): Yes, my dear. I've been riding around my property, visiting my tenants. Do you know what I was wondering?

CATHERINE: What, Father?

BARON: I was wondering whether their children love them as much as my daughters love their old father.

ALICIA: What made you think of that?

BARON: I don't know. But, tell me, Alicia, how much do you love me?

ALICIA: Why, Father, I love you more than hundreds of beautiful dresses, and boxes of sparkling jewels, and thousands of invitations to wonderful parties.

BARON: That was a good answer, my dear. Now you, Louisa.

LOUISA (*Kneeling beside him*): Dear Father, I love you as I love my life.

BARON: There, my child, get up. You're a good girl. And now my youngest, my little Catherine, how much do you love me?

CATHERINE (*With a half-laugh*): Oh, Father, you know I can't make fancy speeches.

BARON: Answer me, Catherine.

CATHERINE: Let's say I love you as fresh meat loves salt.

BARON (*Sternly*): Don't joke, Catherine.

CATHERINE (*Seriously*): Father, you know whether or not I love you.

BARON (*Irritated*): Then answer the question.

CATHERINE (*Simply*): I've answered it. I love you as fresh meat loves salt.

BARON (*Furiously*): Ungrateful girl! You have nothing to add to this foolish answer? (CATHERINE *shakes her head*.) Leave my house! Now! At once!

CATHERINE: But, Father. . . .

BARON: Silence! How dare you call me Father, you unnatural child. Go! Leave my house, and never show your face here again. (*Turns to exit*) Alicia! Louisa! Come. (*He exits left.* ALICIA *and* LOUISA *follow him off, looking back at* CATHERINE, *who sinks to a chair, sobbing.* MARY ANN *enters right.*)

MARY ANN: Oh, Miss Catherine! We heard your father. . . .

CATHERINE: Mary Ann, what should I do? Where can I go?

MARY ANN: Nanny says you should go to the Duke of Doncaster's castle. You'll likely get work in the kitchen there. But you'll have to cover that dress—here, take my cloak. (*Gives her cloak*) There, let me see you. (CATHERINE *stands.*) Oh, your hair! Take my cap. (*Gives her cap*)

CATHERINE: I can't take your things, Mary Ann.

MARY ANN: Yes, you must. The cap's a poor thing I wove of rushes, but it will cover up your lovely hair. (*Leads* CATHERINE *off left*) Come on, now, I'll walk a little way with you. Remember, don't tell them who you are. (*They exit, as curtain falls.*)

* * * * *

SCENE 2

BEFORE RISE: TILLY *and* CATHERINE *enter in front of curtain.*

TILLY: Listen, you can hear the music from the Duke's ball. Come on, Cap o' Rushes. The housekeeper said we could go in and watch the dancing as soon as we finished the pots and pans.

CATHERINE: Oh, Tilly, I'm so tired. I walked a long way this morning before I started work here at the Duke's castle.

TILLY: But you can sit down and watch the fine ladies and gentlemen dancing. All the other servants are there already.

CATHERINE: No, Tilly, you go in. I ought to go to bed.

TILLY: All right. I'll tell you all about it tomorrow. (*She exits left.*)

CATHERINE (*Deep in thought*): How I'd love to go to the ball, but not as a servant. (*Pauses*) My dress! Why not? No one will know who I am. I'll go back through the kitchen, take off my old cloak and my cap o' rushes, and then I'll run around to the main entrance and go to the ball! (*She runs off right.* LADY WARCUM *enters left, followed by* JANE.)

LADY WARCUM: Jane, I could box your ears, you stupid girl. Stand up straight. (JANE *straightens, sulking.*) And smile, girl! (JANE *grimaces.*) The duke's son has danced with everyone of rank except you. I think you hide when you see him coming.

JANE: Oh, Mother, Lord Robert is not going to dance with me.

LADY WARCUM: Of course he's not, if you hang your head and scowl. Now stand up straight. And smile!

JANE: Yes, Mother.

LADY WARCUM (*Looking off left*): Who's that girl the duke's son is dancing with now?

JANE: Let me see. (*Looking off left*) I don't think I've ever seen her before.

LADY WARCUM: No matter. We'll go back in, and when this dance is over, you look at Lord Robert and smile. You hear me?

JANE: Yes, Mother.

LADY WARCUM: Come, then! (*They exit. After a moment,* LORD ROBERT *and* CATHERINE *enter.*)

ROBERT: Good! This room is empty. We can talk here. Have I ever seen you before?

CATHERINE: No, milord.

ROBERT: Do you live nearby?

CATHERINE: Yes, I do now.

ROBERT: And are you really all alone, Catherine?

CATHERINE: I'm alone, milord.

ROBERT: I call you Catherine. You must call me Robert. (*She nods.*) But how will I find you after tonight if I don't know your last name?

CATHERINE: I don't know.

ROBERT: Catherine, I can't let you disappear. I must see you again.

CATHERINE: Oh, you'll see me. But I'm not sure that you'll know me.

ROBERT: Not know you! I feel as if I've known you all my life. (*Pause*) What do you mean, I may not know you?

CATHERINE: Oh, just a joke, Robert.

ROBERT: You puzzle me, Catherine. Here, take this ring. If I should not know you, then show me the ring.

CATHERINE: Oh, Robert, I can't.

ROBERT: Yes, take it. (*She takes ring.*)

CATHERINE: Thank you, Robert.

ROBERT: Come, Catherine. (*They exit.*)

* * * * *

TIME: *A year later.*

SETTING: *The Duke's dining room.* (*It is the same set as in* SCENE 1.)

AT RISE: CATHERINE *and* TILLY *are setting table.*

TILLY: Cook said to set the table, but I don't know if anyone will eat.

CATHERINE: Is the duchess very upset?

TILLY: Yes, and the duke, too. You'd think they'd be so happy, their son coming home after a whole year away. Instead they're heartbroken.

CATHERINE: Is he really dying, Tilly?

TILLY: Lord Robert? I don't know. Thomas says he is, and Thomas has been with him all the time, searching the world for this lady. But how can you find someone if you don't know her last name?

CATHERINE (*Sighing*): He may never find her.

TILLY: It's strange. Lord Robert just saw this lady once, at the ball the day you came here, Cap o' Rushes. He's grieving his heart out because he can't find her again. Do you know what they're cooking in the kitchen for him? Gruel! Thomas says that's all he'll eat—if he eats anything. How can anyone live on gruel? (*They exit right.* DUCHESS *enters left, followed by* DUKE.)

DUKE: Now, Charlotte, don't cry.

DUCHESS: Do you think our son is dying?

DUKE: Of course not! Young fool!

DUCHESS: He's sick with disappointment because he can't find that girl.

DUKE: Not at all proper. The girl came to our ball, wasn't introduced to us, and didn't even tell him her name.

DUCHESS: We must find her!

DUKE: Well, if she exists outside Robert's imagination, where is she?

DUCHESS: I don't know. It's strange no one knew her. I didn't even notice her. Ah, here's Robert now.

(ROBERT *and* THOMAS *enter.*) Come and sit at the table, my son. (FOOTMAN *brings in dinner and* THOMAS *helps him serve.*)

DUKE (*Being served*): Are you rested, my son?

ROBERT: Yes, thank you, Father. (FOOTMAN *exits.* THOMAS *stands near* ROBERT'*s chair.*)

DUCHESS: Thomas suggested the gruel. But if you'd rather have a slice of mutton. . . .

ROBERT (*Uninterestedly; stirring his broth*): No, this is fine. (*He finds the ring in it.*) What is this? My ring! The ring I gave Catherine! Where did it come from? (*Jumps up*)

DUCHESS: I don't know. Thomas, please tell the cook to come here. (THOMAS *exits right.*)

ROBERT (*Excitedly*): I gave this ring to Catherine a year ago at the ball. I told her to keep it. How did it get into the bowl of gruel?

COOK (*Entering, curtsying*): You sent for me, Your Grace?

DUCHESS: Yes, Cook. Who made the gruel?

COOK: Why, I made it myself, ma'am, for Lord Robert.

ROBERT: Did anyone help you?

COOK: Well, young Cap o' Rushes stirred it a bit. Why, ma'am, is there . . .

DUCHESS: Send her in at once, please. (COOK *exits.*)

ROBERT: Mother, who is Cap o' Rushes?

DUCHESS: She's the kitchen maid. A pleasant, well-spoken girl.

ROBERT: How long has she been here?

DUCHESS: Oh, about a year, I think. (CATHERINE *enters and curtsies.*)

ROBERT (*Looking at her closely*): Are you Cap o' Rushes? (*She nods.*) Where did you get this ring?

CATHERINE: From the man that gave it to me.

ROBERT: Catherine! Catherine, take off that cap. (*She*

does so.) It is you! Here in my home all the time. Oh, Catherine, I've searched the world for you.

DUKE: What is this? Don't tell me, Robert, you're dying for love of a scullery maid.

ROBERT: I'm dying for love of Catherine, Father.

DUKE: What madness is this! My son must not marry a common servant.

ROBERT: Please, Father, don't say I can't marry Catherine. I love her.

DUKE (*Angrily*): It's out of the question.

CATHERINE: May I make a request, Your Grace?

DUKE: Well, girl, what is it?

CATHERINE: Do you know Baron Forester?

DUKE: Yes, I know him.

CATHERINE: Then before you make up your mind about your son's marriage, would you invite Baron Forester to dinner?

DUKE: But . . . but . . .

DUCHESS: I'm sure we can do that.

CATHERINE: Thank you, Your Grace. But please do not say anything to him about me beforehand. (Curtain)

* * * * *

SCENE 3

TIME: *A few days later.*

SETTING: *The same as Scene 2.*

AT RISE: DUKE, DUCHESS, ROBERT, *and* BARON FORESTER *are seated at table.*

DUKE: Well, Baron, we had a good day's hunting.

BARON: Yes, indeed. A very pleasant day. (THOMAS *and* FOOTMAN *enter right with trays and begin serving.*) (*To* ROBERT) I thought you were still traveling, milord.

ROBERT: I came home three days ago, Baron Forester.

BARON: And will you stay for a while now? (FOOTMAN *exits right.* THOMAS *stands near* ROBERT'S *chair.*)

ROBERT: I think so.

DUKE (*Tasting his dinner*): What! My dear Charlotte, what is this dreadful dish?

DUCHESS (*Tasting*): Inedible! The cook must have taken leave of her senses. Not a pinch of salt in that meat. (BARON FORESTER, *visibly affected, bows his head.*)

DUKE: Thomas, summon the cook.

THOMAS: Yes, Your Grace. (*He exits right.*)

DUKE (*Noticing* BARON): Why, Baron, are you ill?

BARON: No, Your Grace. Excuse me. It's just that tasting meat without salt reminded me again of . . . of someone.

DUCHESS: Of whom, Baron?

BARON: My daughter, ma'am. My youngest and best beloved. Foolish old man that I was, I asked my daughters to tell me how much they loved me. Two of them told me what they knew I wanted to hear, but my youngest, my little Catherine. . . .

ROBERT: Catherine!

BARON (*Continuing*): She said she loved me as fresh meat loves salt. I thought she was making fun of me, so I drove her away from our home. I haven't seen her since, and I miss her sorely.

COOK (*Entering and curtsying*): You sent for me, Your Grace?

DUCHESS: Who cooked this meal?

COOK: I cooked most of it myself, ma'am. But Cap o' Rushes wanted especially to cook the meat, so I let her do it.

DUCHESS: Send her in, please. (COOK *exits.*) Tell me, Baron, how long has it been since your daughter left your home?

BARON: A year, ma'am. A year ago I turned her out of my house. I haven't known a moment's peace of mind since. If only I knew she were safe and happy. . . .

CATHERINE (*Entering and curtsying*): You sent for me, Your Grace?

BARON (*Stunned*): Catherine! It can't be! (*Extends his arm to her*)

CATHERINE (*Going to him; joyously*): Father!

BARON: Catherine, my dear child, can you ever forgive your foolish father?

CATHERINE: Father, dear Father, I'm so glad to see you. Of course, I forgive you.

BARON: But are you all right, Catherine? What are you doing here?

CATHERINE (*Simply*): I'm the kitchen maid.

ROBERT (*To* DUKE): Father. . . .

DUKE: In fact, Baron Forester, she's the girl our son intends to marry. With your permission, of course.

BARON: Marry? You would like to marry the Duke's son?

CATHERINE: Yes, Father, if you consent.

BARON: My dear daughter, if that's what you want, then of course I shall consent. But, first, you must come home with me again, Catherine. We must prepare for your wedding! (ROBERT *and* CATHERINE *embrace, as* BARON *beams.* DUKE *and* DUCHESS *rise to embrace the couple. Curtain*)

THE END

(*Production Notes on page 316*)

The Cobbler Who Became An Astrologer

A German folktale

by Joellen Bland

Characters

TITUS, *cobbler and astrologer*
WIFE, *a greedy woman*
ROYAL JEWELER
JEWELER'S WIFE
MAN
WOMAN
ROYAL ASTROLOGER
KING
KING'S SERVANT
TWO THIEVES

SCENE 1

TIME: *Many years ago.*
SETTING: *A faraway kingdom. Backdrop of city street.*
   Cobbler's house is at center. Door leads inside house;
   bench is beside the door.

AT RISE: TITUS *sits at bench, mending shoes. He hums to himself, contentedly.* WIFE *enters.*

WIFE (*Irritably*): There you are, my husband, still mending those wretched shoes!

TITUS (*Patiently*): And what else should I be doing, good wife? I'm a simple cobbler.

WIFE: You should be making us rich! You should become the Royal Astrologer!

TITUS (*Astonished*): The Royal Astrologer? My good wife, I know nothing about reading the stars. Why should I want to become an astrologer?

WIFE: Because I just saw the wife of the Royal Astrologer, wearing a magnificent silk robe and precious jewels. She was attended by three servants.

TITUS: My dear wife, you have no cause to envy that woman. We have enough to live on and be comfortable.

WIFE: I don't want to be comfortable! I want to be rich! (*Exits into house*)

TITUS (*Sighing*): What am I to do? How can I become an astrologer? (*Paces*) Let me think. What do astrologers do? They read the stars and learn answers to difficult questions. I recall seeing one who walked proudly about the streets, shouting, "Come, good people, come to me for answers to all your problems! (*As* TITUS *tries to imitate an astrologer,* ROYAL JEWELER *enters, looking very worried.* TITUS *continues, with gestures, raising his voice.*) I am a great astrologer! I can read the stars! The sun! The moon!"

JEWELER (*Rushing up to* TITUS): Did I hear you say that you are a great astrologer?

TITUS: Oh! Yes, I said that, but I was only—

JEWELER: I am the Royal Jeweler, and I am in terrible trouble! You must help me!

TITUS: Sir, I am only Titus the Cobbler. I can mend shoes, not troubles.

JEWELER: If you wish to pose as a cobbler, that is your business, but only your great powers can help me. Yesterday the crown jewels were entrusted to me for polishing. This morning I discovered that one of them was missing—a beautiful red ruby of great value! I have searched everywhere, but I cannot find it. If I do not return all of the crown jewels to the King today, I will lose my head!

TITUS: I am very sorry, but what can I do?

JEWELER: You must find the missing ruby for me!

TITUS (*Disturbed*): How can I find it?

JEWELER: When you do, I will give you two hundred pieces of gold. But if you do not, I shall see that you lose your head, too.

TITUS: Lose my head?

JEWELER: Use your great powers, and you will succeed! I will return within the hour. *(Exits)*

TITUS (*Shouting*): I have no great powers! And it is noon! There are no stars to consult! (*Begins to pace in front of house;* JEWELER'S WIFE *enters.* TITUS *shouts to the heavens.*) Oh, woman, woman, you are as poisonous to a man's happiness as a wicked serpent!

JEWELER'S WIFE (*Stopping, with a shriek*): I am discovered!

TITUS (*Turning, startled*): What?

JEWELER'S WIFE: You must be a magician, or a great astrologer to know my secret!

TITUS (*Puzzled*): Your secret?

JEWELER'S WIFE (*Falling to her knees*): Oh, Great One, be merciful! I am the Royal Jeweler's wife, and I have been very wicked. I beg of you, do not tell my husband what I have done! Spare me, and I will confess everything!

TITUS (*Amazed*): You will confess to me?

JEWELER'S WIFE: I crept into my husband's workroom in the middle of the night and stole the King's red ruby. It was so beautiful! I wanted it for myself. Although my husband is the Royal Jeweler, he never gives me any jewels. If you will keep my secret, I will do whatever you command me.

TITUS (*Sternly*): Very well! You must do exactly as I tell you. Find your husband at once and place the ruby in the pocket of his robe without letting him know it. Then go home and be content with what you have. Never steal again!

JEWELER'S WIFE: I promise! Thank you, thank you! (*Runs out*)

TITUS: Is this really happening? (*Sits on bench, wiping his brow*) One minute I am a simple cobbler with few cares, the next minute I am called something I am not and my life is threatened! Surely I am dreaming! (*JEWELER enters.*)

JEWELER (*Impatiently*): Well, have you found the missing ruby?

TITUS (*Solemnly*): Although you have given me very little time, sir, I have made my heavenly calculations. Look in the pocket of your robe, and you will find the King's ruby. (*Aside; crossing his fingers*) I hope!

JEWELER: My pocket? How could it possibly be in my— (*Reaches into pocket and finds ruby*) It's here! The King's ruby! I must have slipped it into my pocket without realizing it. I am saved! (*Claps TITUS on the back*) And you, Titus, Great Astrologer, have earned your two hundred pieces of gold! (*Hands him bag of coins*) I will spread word of your wonderful powers throughout the kingdom!

TITUS: Oh, no, please do not! I'd rather you didn't.

JEWELER: A modest astrologer? Whoever heard of such a thing? (*Hurries off, happily*) I'm saved! Titus the Great Astrologer has saved me!

TITUS (*Sighing in relief*): I am saved by the greatest chance! (*Looks in bag*) Real gold! (*Drops some coins onto bench, as* WIFE *enters*)

WIFE: Gold? Did you say gold?

TITUS: Yes, my reward for recovering a missing jewel for the King's Jeweler. Two hundred pieces of gold! Here, take them. Surely you will be satisfied now.

WIFE (*Greedily handling coins*): You have earned more in ten minutes than you earn in ten years as a cobbler! Soon your name will be known everywhere, and then you will be summoned by the King to be his Royal Astrologer.

TITUS: My dear wife, I have no wish to be an astrologer. A stroke of luck saved me this time, but I cannot depend on being so fortunate again.

WIFE: But two hundred pieces of gold aren't enough to make us rich forever! I want more. Much more!

TITUS: But, my dear wife, you may be sending me to my death!

WIFE: Nonsense! An astrologer can control his own fate.

TITUS: But, wife, I would have to study and become an apprentice to an astrologer for years to learn his art.

WIFE: There is no need for that! You did well enough with the King's Jeweler. Other people with problems will come to you!

TITUS (*To himself*): No one could have as terrible a problem as I have. (*Calling, softly*) I am an astrologer! I can see into the future.

WIFE: Call louder! No one will hear you!

TITUS (*Loudly*): I am Titus the Astrologer! By the power given to me by the sun, moon, and stars, I can tell anyone's fortune and solve anyone's problems!

WIFE: That's better. (*Exits into house;* MAN *rushes in, followed by* WOMAN.)

MAN: There he is, Titus the Astrologer! He's the one who helped the Jeweler find the King's lost ruby!

WOMAN: Are you really Titus, the Greatest of all Astrologers?

TITUS (*Bowing politely*): I am Titus—

WOMAN: Then you must help me! Yesterday I lost a valuable pearl necklace. I dare not tell my husband, because he gave me the necklace as a birthday gift. He will be very angry if he discovers I have lost it. Tell me where to find it, and I will give you three hundred pieces of gold. Fail to tell me, and I will see that you are whipped!

TITUS: Whipped? My dear lady, I must have time to consult the stars.

WOMAN: There is no time! I must have your answer at once. My husband will return home soon, and I must be there to greet him, wearing the pearl necklace.

TITUS: This is serious, indeed. (*Desperately*) As there are no stars, I must quickly consult with the sun. (*Looks up, shading his eyes with his hand*) It is very hot today. The sun seems to burn a hole in my hand.

WOMAN: Hole? Did you say hole?

TITUS: Yes.

WOMAN: Of course! The hole!

TITUS: The hole?

WOMAN: Now I remember! I put my pearl necklace into a hole in my chamber wall, to hide it from thieves. You are indeed a great astrologer! Here are your three hundred pieces of gold! (*Hands him money*)

You are the greatest astrologer in the kingdom! I shall tell everyone I see about you! (*Exits*)

MAN: You must go to the palace!

TITUS: The palace? Why?

MAN: To see the King. Surely you can help him recover his lost treasure! (WIFE *enters as he speaks.*)

WIFE: Did you say treasure?

TITUS: What treasure?

MAN: Forty chests of gold and jewels! The King's Treasury was robbed last night. The King is offering a great reward if the chests are recovered.

TITUS: Then the King should consult with his Royal Astrologer.

WIFE: No, *no! You* must recover the treasure and find the thieves!

ROYAL ASTROLOGER (*Entering; haughtily*): What is all this I hear about some pretender named Titus who claims to have greater powers than mine? I am the one and only Royal Astrologer!

WIFE (*Boldly*): My husband Titus *is* a great astrologer. His powers are unexcelled!

TITUS: Wife, be quiet, please!

ROYAL ASTROLOGER: No one has greater skills than I! (*Fearfully*) Does this—this Titus think he can recover the King's lost treasure?

WIFE: He *will* recover it!

ROYAL ASTROLOGER: Ha! Let him try! When he fails, I shall see him put in chains.

TITUS: I would not dream of taking that honor from you, sir.

ROYAL ASTROLOGER: What?

TITUS: I mean, *you* must recover the treasure. After all, you are the Royal Astrologer. (KING *enters with* SERVANT.)

KING: He will not be my Royal Astrologer for long if he fails to recover my treasure!

ROYAL ASTROLOGER: Your Majesty! (*Bows low*)

TITUS: The King! (*Falls to his knees*)

WIFE (*Eagerly*): The King! (TITUS *pulls her down on her knees.*)

MAN (*Bowing*): Here is Titus the Astrologer, Your Majesty! *He* will help you.

KING: Indeed? Rise, Titus. Now, can *you* tell me who stole my treasure? (TITUS *rises.*)

TITUS (*Trembling*): Not at the moment, Your Majesty. My calculations will require some time and careful consideration.

ROYAL ASTROLOGER: This man is a fraud, Your Majesty. Do not listen to him. *I* will recover your treasure.

KING: Then why haven't you done so?

ROYAL ASTROLOGER (*Nervously*): I, too, need time, Your Majesty. But I will not fail you.

TITUS (*Bravely*): I can tell you this much, Your Majesty. Not one, but forty thieves stole your treasure.

KING: Forty thieves? How do you know that?

TITUS: Could fewer than forty thieves have carried away forty heavy chests of gold and jewels?

KING: That is a very clever observation! But where are they? What have they done with my treasure?

TITUS: At the end of forty days I will tell you.

ROYAL ASTROLOGER (*Sneering*): Forty days! Ha!

KING: That is a reasonable time. I will grant both of you forty days to find the treasure and the thieves. If you cannot, then you will both be exiled! (*Exits with* SERVANT, MAN, *and* ROYAL ASTROLOGER)

TITUS: My good wife, I am afraid that your greed will cost me dearly in forty days. I answered bravely, but I cannot possibly recover the King's treasure.

WIFE: And why not? Use the same method by which you found the ruby and the pearl necklace.

TITUS: How can I? I was able to solve those two mysteries through sheer good luck. All I can do is count the days that are left to me. (*Crosses to bench*) I will put a nut in a bowl every day until there are forty. Then I will know when I must leave my beloved home.

WIFE: Foolish husband! I must have more jewels and more servants than the Royal Astrologer's wife! And you must get them for me. (*Exits into house*)

TITUS: I am the most miserable man in the kingdom! (1ST THIEF *creeps in and hides at the corner.* TITUS *takes a bowl from under bench and drops a nut into it.*) There is the first of the forty! (2ND THIEF *enters, stands down left.*)

1ST THIEF (*Startled; in fright*): He knows! (*As* TITUS *sits on bench, chin in hands, sighing,* 1ST THIEF *runs to* 2ND THIEF.) We are discovered!

2ND THIEF: What? That astrologer knows that we and our comrades stole the King's treasure?

1ST THIEF: Titus knows there are forty of us! I sneaked up to his house after we heard the rumor that he would recover the King's treasure. Although I was hiding, somehow he knew I was there! I heard him say quite clearly, "There is the first of the forty!"

2ND THIEF: Then we must bribe him not to turn us over to the King, or we are doomed! We will offer him as much of the treasure as he wants! Come. (TWO THIEVES *approach* TITUS *and bow before him.*)

1ST THIEF: Oh, great astrologer, we know you have found out who we are. Will you take two thousand pieces of gold to say nothing to the King?

TITUS (*Astonished*): Two thousand pieces of gold?

2ND THIEF: If that is not enough, we will give you three

thousand! Only have mercy on us, Great One! Spare our lives, and we and the thirty-eight other thieves will return the King's treasure!

TITUS (*Amazed*): What? (*Aside*) Did I hear right? (*Turns back to* THIEVES; *sternly*) Miserable thieves! How dare you try to bribe me! My skill penetrates the sun, moon, and stars! You could never escape from me. However, since you confess and promise to give back the King's treasure, I will try to intercede with him on your behalf.

THIEVES (*Together*): Oh, thank you!

TITUS: However, you must return all forty chests of gold and jewels, with nothing missing! Take them to the courtyard near the western wall of the palace by tomorrow at dawn. Make sure no one sees you.

1ST THIEF: We will do as you command!

2ND THIEF (*To* 1ST THIEF): Hurry! We must find the others! (THIEVES *exit*. WIFE *enters*.)

TITUS: It is a miracle! Again, I am saved by pure luck!

WIFE: Never mind how you did it, husband. You did it—and you will soon be the new Royal Astrologer, and I shall be rich, rich!

TITUS: Is that all you can think of? Isn't it enough that I won't be exiled and that the King's treasure has been found?

WIFE (*Dreamily*): Silks! Laces! Pearls! Servants! Everyone will admire me! Tomorrow all my dreams will come true! (*Curtain*)

* * * * *

SCENE 2

SETTING: *Throne Room at the Palace.*

AT RISE: KING *sits on his throne.* ROYAL ASTROLOGER

stands at one side, SERVANT *on the other.* TITUS *kneels before* KING.

KING: Titus, the forty days have not passed. Why have you come to see me?

ROYAL ASTROLOGER (*Scornfully*): You have come, of course, to tell His Majesty that you cannot accomplish the task, and that you leave it all to me!

TITUS: No. I have learned, Your Majesty, that you may have either the treasure or the thieves, but not both.

KING (*Sternly*): The thieves should be punished. But if it means I cannot recover my treasure, then let the villains go. I must have my treasure back, or my people will starve.

TITUS: Send your servants to the courtyard near the western palace wall, and they will find the forty chests of treasure.

KING (*To* SERVANT): See that this is done at once! (SERVANT *bows and exits.*) If this is true, Titus, you shall be my new Royal Astrologer. You shall have a fine house and servants, clothes, horses, jewels, anything you wish.

TITUS: Your Majesty is very generous, but I was quite happy in my old life. I would like to make and mend shoes again. This is work I understand.

KING: Whatever you wish, Titus. All I ask is that you serve me when I need you.

TITUS: Of course, Your Majesty. I will do my best. (SERVANT *enters.*)

SERVANT (*Bowing*): Your Majesty, the forty chests have been found in the courtyard, with seals unbroken. Everything is safe.

KING: Take the former Royal Astrologer to the outskirts of the kingdom. He is banished! (SERVANT *hustles the cowering* ASTROLOGER *off.*) Titus, what will you do with your reward?

TITUS: I will give my wife enough gold to buy everything she desires. Then I will insist that she travel around the world. (*Sighs*) I will go back to my own comfortable house and enjoy the peace and quiet. That is all the reward I require.

KING: You are indeed a wise man, Titus, whether a cobbler or an astrologer! (*Curtain*)

THE END

(*Production Notes on page 316*)

Dame Fortune and Don Money

A Spanish folktale

by Hazel W. Corson

Characters

DAME FORTUNE
DON MONEY
DON JOSÉ, *a rich man*
MANUEL, *a poor peasant*
ROSA, *the baker's wife*
MARIA, *the cloth merchant*
TWO THIEVES
SHERIFF
JUDGE
TWO WOMEN
BANKER
LAWYER
VILLAGERS

SCENE 1

SETTING: *The marketplace in a Spanish village. At rear, there are two cutaway stores—Maria's cloth store and*

Rosa's bakery. There are benches right and left. Table stands right.

AT RISE: DON JOSÉ *is sitting on bench right, reading document.* ROSA *and* MARIA *are busy in their stores.* DON MONEY *sits on bench, left, reading newspaper, and* DAME FORTUNE *sits beside him, knitting.*

DON MONEY (*Looking up from paper*): I tell you, Dame Fortune, money is more powerful than fortune.

DAME FORTUNE: You are wrong, Don Money. Good fortune is just as important. Money isn't everything.

DON MONEY: I never said that money was everything, but I do say, you won't get far without it.

DAME FORTUNE (*Pointing at* DON JOSÉ): Look at Don José there. He's the richest man in town; does his money bring him happiness? (MANUEL *enters left and approaches* DON JOSÉ.)

DON MONEY: Ah, but see that poor peasant there who works for Don José? He doesn't have a cent to his name, and he is certainly not happy.

MANUEL (*Timidly*): Good morning, Don José.

DON JOSÉ (*Looking up*): So it's you again, Manuel. Is anything wrong at the hacienda?

MANUEL: No, Don José.

DON JOSÉ (*Crossly*): Don't tell me something good has happened for a change. Perhaps someone wants to pay a good price for the wool from the sheep?

MANUEL: No, Don José.

DON JOSÉ (*Coldly*): Then I cannot imagine why you need to speak to me.

MANUEL: It's about my family, sir. My little ones are crying for bread. I have no money, and no way of getting any bread. I work hard for you, day after day. Can you give me some of my pay now?

DON JOSÉ: Pay! What pay? You have already eaten up

your pay for some time to come. I told you the last time you asked for money not to bother me again.

MANUEL: But my children, Don José!

DON JOSÉ: They are not my problem. I'm concerned about the fifty thousand pesetas I invested in a trading ship bound for India. (*Turning away annoyed*) Go back to your work. Do not speak to me again unless you have something important to say. (*Rolls up document, rises and exits right.* MANUEL *sinks down on bench, sighing in despair.*)

DON MONEY: You see, Dame Fortune, here is a man who is very poor, and very unfortunate. Watch and see how happy I can make him just by giving him a little money.

DAME FORTUNE: Very well! And when *you* have failed to help him, I will see what *I* can do, just by making him more fortunate.

DON MONEY: Agreed! (*Goes over to* MANUEL) Good day to you, my good man.

MANUEL: Good day to you, good sir.

DON MONEY: What is your name?

MANUEL: Manuel, sir.

DON MONEY: Tell me, Manuel, do you have any possessions?

MANUEL: I own very little, sir, and have a wife and six sons—all of them ragged and hungry. No matter how much I borrow or beg, I cannot afford to feed or clothe them.

DON MONEY: Borrow? Beg? Have you never thought of working?

MANUEL (*Sighing*): Indeed, I do work hard, sir, for Don José. But still I never seem to have enough money to feed my family.

DON MONEY: Why is that?

MANUEL: On payday I must give all my pay to my

master, Don José, for the hut he lets me and my family live in, and there is no money left to buy food. When I try to borrow from Don José, he always says that I owe him too much already.

DON MONEY: Well, Manuel, I'm going to improve your lot. (*Hands him money*) Here is a hundred-peseta note. May it bring you a new start in life.

MANUEL: Oh, thank you, gracious sir! A thousand blessings on you! I will go and buy bread for my family at once. (*Neither notices that the bill falls to ground by bench.*) How my wife and children will rejoice. Thank you! (*Runs to* ROSA's *bakery.* DON MONEY *returns to* DAME FORTUNE.)

DAME FORTUNE: Do you think that little bit of money will help him?

DON MONEY: It doesn't take much money to improve one's lot in life.

DAME FORTUNE (*Smugly*): We shall see. (*She continues to knit.* DON MONEY *sits down again to read newspaper.*)

MANUEL (*To* ROSA): What good fortune! I can hardly believe it. Give me two huge loaves of bread, good woman, and a cake, and some of those little pies.

ROSA (*Coldly*): Not so fast! Before I put so much as a crumb into your hand, I want to see your money.

MANUEL (*Cheerfully*): This time I have money. A kind gentleman just gave me one hundred pesetas. (*Reaches into pocket, turns it inside out, but finds it empty*)

ROSA: Ha! I knew you had no money.

MANUEL: It must be in my other pocket. (*Finds nothing*) Oh, unlucky me! Holes in both pockets. I must have dropped the note on my way here. I'll go look for it. (*Retraces his steps, looking for money*)

DON MONEY (*Looking up from paper*): Ah, Manuel!

How did your children enjoy the bread you bought?

MANUEL: Alas, I didn't buy any.

DON MONEY: Why not? What did you do with the money?

MANUEL (*Shamefaced*): I lost it before I could spend it.

DON MONEY: I don't understand. However, if I am to improve your lot, I can see that I must give you more. Here is a gold piece. (*Hands him money*) Do not lose this.

MANUEL (*Looking at gold piece in amazement*): Never fear! With this much money, I can buy cloth for clothes *and* food for my family. Oh, thank you! (*Runs to* MARIA'*s cloth store*)

DAME FORTUNE: The hundred pesetas didn't do much good.

DON MONEY (*Shaking his head*): He seems to be an unlucky man. (*Both rise and follow* MANUEL.)

DAME FORTUNE: But you said money would bring him good fortune.

DON MONEY: And so it will, Dame Fortune. See for yourself.

MANUEL (*To* MARIA): Good woman, I would like some nice, strong cloth to make clothes. Nothing too fine or fancy.

MARIA (*Scornfully*): You look as if you could use new clothes. And just how are you going to pay for my cloth?

MANUEL (*Holding up gold coin*): With this gold piece. (*Hands it to her*) And I'll have money left over.

MARIA: Ha! How did a sorry-looking man like you get a gold piece, I'd like to know?

MANUEL: It is mine, and just as good as any other gold piece.

MARIA (*Flinging gold piece on counter*): I doubt that! This coin does not ring true. I'm sure it is counterfeit. You are trying to cheat me. I will take this coin to the sheriff. Out of my shop! (MARIA *chases* MANUEL *off right.*)

DAME FORTUNE: Poor Manuel! Now he is not only dressed in rags and has no food, but he is going to get in trouble with the law.

DON MONEY (*Angrily*): That coin was not counterfeit! Maria is a fool. I *will* improve Manuel's lot. You'll see! I'll give him a great deal of money. (*Runs off after* MANUEL, *calling*) Wait! Manuel! Wait! (DAME FORTUNE *follows.*)

MANUEL (*Reentering right with both hands full of bills*): What a kind gentleman! All this money! I didn't know there was so much money in the world! (*Sits on bench, fingering bills*) What a beautiful sight! (TWO THIEVES *enter left, wearing kerchief masks.* 1ST THIEF *points to* MANUEL *and beckons to* 2ND THIEF, *as* DAME FORTUNE *and* DON MONEY *enter right and stand watching.*)

1ST THIEF: Look at him!

2ND THIEF: He's just asking to be robbed.

1ST THIEF: What are we waiting for? (1ST THIEF *pretends to hit* MANUEL *on the head, and he slumps down.* 2ND THIEF *grabs bills and stuffs money into sacks.*)

2ND THIEF: Let's get out of here. (*They run off left.* DAME FORTUNE *and* DON MONEY *go to* MANUEL.)

DAME FORTUNE (*Sarcastically, to* DON MONEY): Is this the happiness your money brings? (*Bends over* MANUEL) Are you going to help him any more, Don Money?

DON MONEY: It is plain to see that Manuel is unlucky. Nothing can help a truly unlucky man, not even money.

DAME FORTUNE: It is now my turn to see if I can bring

him happiness.

DON MONEY: Try if you will, but nothing can help. You'll see. (DAME FORTUNE *takes fan from her pocket and fans* MANUEL. *He moves and groans.*)

MANUEL (*Sitting up slowly, groaning with each movement*): What has happened? Oh, unlucky day! My money! Someone has taken my money!

DAME FORTUNE: Never mind the money. Take heart, Manuel. Things are going to be better for you.

MANUEL: I hope so. My life could hardly be worse. (*Getting up*) Now I must go home to my hungry wife and children.

DAME FORTUNE: Manuel, what is that by the bench?

MANUEL (*In surprise*): Why, it is a hundred-peseta note! (*Picking it up*) It is the same bill Don Money gave me this morning! I remember it, because it was torn just like this. (*Holds it up*) Now I can buy some bread for my family.

MARIA (*Entering from left*): So, Manuel, here you are at last! I have been looking for you everywhere!

MANUEL: I wish you had not found me. I have had enough bad luck for one day.

MARIA: No, no, my friend. I have done you a great wrong. When I took your gold coin to the sheriff, we found it to be real, not counterfeit at all. Here, it is yours. (*Hands coin to* MANUEL)

MANUEL (*Happily*): Wonderful. Now I can pay for cloth after all.

MARIA (*Apologetically*): I am ashamed of the way I treated you this morning. Come to my shop and tell me what cloth you want. I'm sure I have whatever you need. (MANUEL *and* MARIA *go to her shop.*)

DAME FORTUNE: Manuel does not seem so unlucky now. (DAME FORTUNE *and* DON MONEY *sit on bench. She knits.* MANUEL *selects cloth in* MARIA'S *shop, pays for it, then goes to baker's shop, where he buys a long loaf of bread from* ROSA. TWO WOMEN *enter left.*)

1ST WOMAN (*Excitedly*): I saw it myself. The sheriff has arrested two thieves, and they are to come before the judge here and now!

2ND WOMAN (*Pointing off right*): I see them coming now. (SHERIFF *enters right, leading* TWO THIEVES *and carrying their sacks. Some* VILLAGERS *enter behind them and join* TWO WOMEN, *all talking excitedly.* DAME FORTUNE *and* TWO WOMEN *look on with interest.* JUDGE *enters left and sits at table, right.* MANUEL *joins crowd, holding his cloth and bread.* ROSA *and* MARIA *leave their shops and come to watch.*)

JUDGE: Sheriff, how did you catch these men?

SHERIFF: I saw them running along the street, Your Honor. They wore masks, and kept looking back as if they were being followed, so I stopped them.

JUDGE: Did you search them?

SHERIFF: We didn't need to, Your Honor. They were carrying these sacks on their backs. (*Holds up sacks*) In the first sack, there were some jewels, probably taken from the count's palace. And in the second sack, a thousand pesetas. (*Shows sacks to* JUDGE)

MANUEL (*Excitedly*): Those must be the thieves who robbed me! That is my money!

JUDGE (*Looking at* MANUEL): You were robbed? When was this?

MANUEL (*Stepping forward*): Just today, Your Honor. This kind gentleman (*Points to* DON MONEY), who has been trying to help me, gave me one thousand pesetas. While I was sitting over there (*Points to bench*) counting it, someone hit me on the head. When I recovered, my money was gone.

JUDGE: Are these the men?

MANUEL: I didn't see the men, Your Honor, but I would recognize the money. It was new, and there were ten beautiful hundred-peseta notes.

DON MONEY (*Stepping forward*): That is true, Your Honor. I am Don Money, and I gave Manuel ten new hundred-peseta bills today.

JUDGE: How much money did you find, Sheriff?

SHERIFF: One thousand pesetas, Your Honor. (*He counts.*) Ten new hundred-peseta bills, as Manuel says.

JUDGE: Then the money is his. I see no reason why we should not return it to him at once. (SHERIFF *hands bills to* MANUEL.)

MANUEL: Oh, thank you, Your Honor! This started out to be the worst day of my life. Suddenly, everything has changed. This is the luckiest day of my life! (*Curtain*)

* * * * *

SCENE 2

TIME: *A year later.*

SETTING: *The same as Scene 1.*

AT RISE: DON JOSÉ *is sitting on bench, adding up figures in big ledger.* DAME FORTUNE *and* DON MONEY *are sitting on another bench. She is knitting, and he is reading a paper.* BANKER *enters right.*

BANKER: Good morning, Don José. I have good news for you.

DON JOSÉ: Ah, my banker! It's news about money, I hope?

BANKER: What could be better news? It is about the ship we sent out to trade in India last year. It is back after a successful voyage. Your share of the profit is ten thousand pesetas.

DON JOSÉ (*Incredulously*): Only ten thousand pesetas? I invested fifty thousand pesetas in that ship, and you dare to return to me a miserable sixty thousand? Do not think you can cheat Don José so easily!

BANKER (*Coldly*): If that is the way you feel about it, sir, I doubt if we shall care to do business together in the future. (*Exits left. LAWYER enters right.*)

LAWYER: Good morning, Don José. Your clerk said I would find you here.

DON JOSÉ: Ah, my lawyer. You have good news about my father's will, I trust?

LAWYER: I think so. Your brother has agreed to a settlement that is very favorable to you. He will take the house and land, and you will have everything else, about two hundred thousand pesetas, in all.

DON JOSÉ: And you think that is good? I am the oldest. I should have everything, the land as well as the money.

LAWYER: Your brother could demand much more, but he wants to settle the matter. You must admit that the land has prospered under his management.

DON JOSÉ: Management! His *mismanagement* has kept it from being worth twice as much. Think of what he has spent on the peasants' houses, on giving them gardens of their own, and that silly school for their children. I want you to sue him for wasting so much of my money.

LAWYER: In that case, you will have to get another lawyer, Don José. I will not take a case like that. (*Exits*)

DON JOSÉ (*Shouting after him*): It is impossible for an honest man to make money today! (*Exits*)

DAME FORTUNE (*To DON MONEY*): Now, there is a man who has plenty of money. You say it should bring him happiness.

DON MONEY: His good luck in business hasn't made him happy, either, Dame Fortune. He made a profit on a ship that could have been lost at sea! (MANUEL *enters left. He is well dressed, and looks happy and prosperous.*)

MANUEL: Good morning, good people. Do you remember me?

DON MONEY: Ah, Manuel! What a change! I hardly know you.

MANUEL: I well remember your kindness to me, sir. Here is the money you gave me a year ago. I have been carrying it in this little purse hoping to see you and repay you. (*Hands him purse*)

DON MONEY: Are you sure you do not need it, Manuel?

MANUEL: Truly, I have more than I need. I used some of the money to help a friend who was looking for buried treasure. He found enough to make us both rich. My family and I live in a fine house now, and I have enough to help other people who are as poor as I once was.

DAME FORTUNE: So your luck did change, Manuel?

MANUEL: Yes, madam. I remember the day you said that things would be better for me. You were right, and I have been a happy man ever since. I thank you both. (*Exits left*)

DAME FORTUNE: So you see, Don Money, all Manuel's money, without his good fortune, would be worthless to him.

DON MONEY: But I gave him the money in the first place. (*Shakes his head*) Here we are with the same old argument. Which is more powerful, money or good fortune?

DAME FORTUNE: Don Money, what is the difference between Manuel and Don José?

DON MONEY: The difference of day from night. Manuel

is a happy man with many friends, but Don José is miserable, and his misery spreads to all he meets.

DAME FORTUNE: Yet both have made money, and both seem to have good luck. Could it be that there is something more important than luck or money?

DON MONEY: Yes, there is. Don José, with all his huge fortune, will never be as happy as Manuel, who has a good and generous heart. (*Curtain*)

THE END

(*Production Notes on page 316*)

Taro the Fisherman

A Japanese folktale

by Maureen Crane Wartski

Characters

TARO, *a boy*
GORO, *his friend*
THREE CHILDREN
BIG TURTLE
SEA KING
PRINCESS SEA STAR
SIR JELLYFISH
MADAME PORPOISE
BOY
GIRL
SEA CITIZENS, *male and female extras*

SCENE 1

TIME: *Long ago.*

SETTING: *Seashore, near a fishing village in Japan. Rocks are down right. Backdrop shows the sea and sky. Baskets for fish and fishnets are scattered on stage.*

AT RISE: TARO *sits on rock, his back to audience. He holds fishing pole. A basket is at his feet.*

TARO (*Turning to face audience*): No fish at all today. (*Shows empty basket*) My master will be angry with me. (GORO *enters left.*)

GORO: Greetings, Taro! Any luck today?

TARO: No, Goro. I think all the fish are away on a holiday. My master will surely beat me for bringing home an empty basket.

GORO: If my parents treated me as badly as your master treats you, Taro, I'd run away.

TARO (*Sadly*): You're not an orphan like me, Goro. My master is harsh, but at least he gives me a place to live and food to eat.

GORO: What food! He gives you fish heads and stale barley, while he eats the best fish and rice at his inn. (TARO *suddenly tugs at pole.*)

TARO (*Excitedly*): Goro! I have a bite.

GORO: Don't let the fish get away! (TARO *pantomimes pulling in fishing line, picks up hook, and holds out imaginary fish.*)

TARO (*Disheartened*): Look at the size of this poor fish. It's so small.

GORO: A small fish is better than no fish at all. If you take it to your master, he may not beat you.

TARO (*Shaking his head*): I feel sorry for this fish, Goro. It's only a baby. (*To imaginary fish*) Here, little one, go home to the sea. (*He pantomimes throwing fish into the water. Sound of musical scale is heard offstage.*) What was that strange sound?

GORO: What sound?

TARO: Didn't you hear anything?

GORO: It was probably my mother calling me home for supper. It's getting late. Can you come to visit later, Taro?

TARO (*Shaking head; sadly*): No, I must continue fishing.

GORO: Don't stay out too long, my friend. Goodbye! (GORO *exits right. Angry voices are heard offstage.*)

1ST CHILD (*Calling from offstage*): It's mine, I tell you. Give it to me!

2ND CHILD: I want it. Let go of it. (THREE CHILDREN *enter left.* 2ND CHILD *holds small turtle, and others crowd around him.*)

TARO (*Rising from rock*): What is the matter? (*Walking to* CHILDREN *and separating them*) Here, here. Let's stop fighting. (*Sees turtle*) Why, it's a small turtle.

1ST CHILD: It's mine, Taro. I saw it first.

3RD CHILD (*Angrily*): No, it's mine. I'm going to take it home, put a string around its neck, and keep it as a pet.

TARO: I don't think the turtle would like that. Turtles don't live long when they're not in water.

3RD CHILD: I don't care.

TARO: I have an idea. I'll buy this turtle from you.

2ND CHILD: What will you buy it with? You don't have any money.

TARO: I'll give you . . . (*Digs in pocket, then shakes head*) Nothing here. I know. I'll give you my fishing pole. (*Holds out pole to* CHILDREN)

CHILDREN (*Ad lib*): A fishing pole. I've always wanted one. That's a fair trade. (*Etc.* 2ND CHILD *gives turtle to* TARO, 1ST *and* 3RD CHILDREN *take pole, and all run off, left.* TARO *pets turtle, carries it to rocks, and gently pushes it off into the "sea."*)

TARO: There you are, little turtle. Go on back to the sea. Those children didn't mean to hurt you. They were only being thoughtless. (*Shakes head sadly*) Won't my master beat me when he learns I gave them my fishing pole! (*Musical scale is heard offstage.* TARO *starts, shakes his head.*) It's that music again! Where is it coming from? (BIG TURTLE *enters right, on all fours.* TARO *looks at him, frightened.)* Why, I've never seen a sea beast as big as you. (*Hides behind rocks*)

BIG TURTLE: Come out from behind those rocks, fisherman Taro. Don't be frightened. I won't hurt you.

TARO (*Timidly*): I'm not frightened. (*Stands*) But I will feel safer when you go.

BIG TURTLE: Taro, I'm the grandfather of that little turtle you rescued from the other children. We live with many other creatures in the Kingdom under the Sea. The Sea King was touched by your kindness to the little turtle, and he wants me to take you back to our kingdom, so he can give a feast in your honor.

TARO (*Amazed*): In my honor?

BIG TURTLE: Yes, indeed. We have been watching you for some time. We see you put stranded jellyfish back into the water. We watch you as you pick up all the seashells on the beach, and return them to the sea. You care about living things, Taro.

TARO (*Coming out from behind rocks*): I can't believe this!

BIG TURTLE: If you will climb on my back, Taro, I'll bring you to my kingdom.

TARO (*Moving forward, then stopping*): This has to be a dream. How can a turtle talk? How can a turtle carry me to a kingdom under the sea? I breathe air, not water. I'd drown. (*Musical scale is heard during following dialogue.*)

BIG TURTLE: Taro, the Sea King has magical powers. He will make sure you don't drown. Aren't you curious to see my kingdom? It's more beautiful than you could ever imagine. Thousands of starfish light the way to the throne room of our great king. The King sits on a throne of coral and gold, and next to him sits Princess Sea Star, the most beautiful mermaid

in all the world. And there are so many sea creatures! Don't you want to seem them?

TARO (*Drawing closer; fascinated*): Of course, but I—

BIG TURTLE: There are sea horses and urchins, oc-
topuses, sting rays, and beautiful sea flowers. There
are great white sharks, whales, and fish that are as
bright as jewels.

TARO: I'll come! I'll come! (*He moves closer to* BIG TUR-
TLE, *then stops.*) No! I can't go.

BIG TURTLE: Why not, Taro?

TARO: If I'm not back at my master's inn, he will beat
me. It's suppertime. He needs me to carry food and
wait on customers.

BIG TURTLE: Don't worry, Taro. I promise your master
won't beat you any more. (TARO *"rides"* BIG TURTLE
off left, as curtain falls.)

* * * * *

SCENE 2

TIME: *Later that day.*

SETTING: *The Kingdom under the Sea. Backdrop shows
shells, seaweed, rocks, etc. A throne is center, and two
chairs are on either side of it. A small table, with a
box on it, is at right.*

AT RISE: SEA KING *sits on throne.* PRINCESS SEA STAR
sits next to him. SIR JELLYFISH *and* MADAME POR-
POISE *stand beside throne.* SEA CITIZENS *stand in
groups. They talk and laugh, and several dance to
lively music, which is played offstage.*

SEA KING (*To* PRINCESS SEA STAR): Where is Big Turtle, I wonder? He went to find the fisherman Taro
some time ago. (BIG TURTLE *enters, with* TARO *"riding" him. They stop before throne.*)

PRINCESS (*Excited*): Here they are, Father!

BIG TURTLE (*Bowing*): Your Majesty, here is Taro, the good fisherman.

KING: Welcome to our kingdom, Taro. (TARO *bows deeply.*)

TARO: Your Majesty, I never imagined this beautiful place was under the sea. (PRINCESS *rises.*)

PRINCESS: I am Princess Sea Star, Taro. Please come and sit down. (*She goes to* TARO, *takes his arm, and leads him to chair, left.* TARO *sits.*) I'm sure you're tired after your journey. I will send for some refreshments.

1ST SEA CITIZEN: I will bring some fruit, Princess. (*Runs off left*)

TARO (*Dazed*): Thank you, Your Highness.

PRINCESS: Please call me "Sea Star." We're so glad you could come. We're very pleased by your many acts of goodness to the creatures of the sea.

SIR JELLYFISH (*Taking out roll of parchment from pocket and unrolling it; in grand tone*): Ahem! Your Majesty, we have compiled a list of all of Taro's good deeds. (*Looks at paper, as if reading*) In the last three weeks, he threw a hundred small fish back into the sea, even though each night his master beat him for coming home empty-handed.

TARO (*Modestly*): The fish were too little to cook.

SIR JELLYFISH (*Pompously*): Don't interrupt, young sir. Ahem! Taro also tossed ten jellyfish, beached in a storm, back into the sea. He rescued twenty mussel shells, fifty clams, nineteen oysters, and two small squids.

SEA CITIZENS (*Clapping; ad lib*): Good work, Taro. You're very kind! (*Etc.*)

SIR JELLYFISH (*Sternly*): I have not finished. It gives me

great pleasure to pronounce Taro the fisherman an Honorary Citizen of the Sea. (*To* SEA CITIZENS) Now you can cheer.

SEA CITIZENS (*Ad lib*): Cheers for Taro! He's now a citizen of the Kingdom under the Sea. (*Etc.*)

KING: We are all proud of you, Taro.

TARO (*Flustered*): Sir—Your Majesty, I mean—I didn't do much at all.

MADAME PORPOISE: You did more than many other people have done, Taro. If all human beings were as kind as you are, life would be happier.

SIR JELLYFISH: Sad to say, Taro, most people are careless. They catch more fish than they need. They destroy sea creatures needlessly, and they put wastes into the sea. If we sea creatures are not treated better, many of us will be in danger of becoming extinct.

TARO (*Horrified*): That mustn't happen!

KING: It wouldn't happen if people would respect sea creatures and care for them, as you do.

SEA CITIZENS (*Together*): Three cheers for Taro! (*Lively music is heard offstage, and* SEA CITIZENS *and* TARO *form a circle and dance.* PRINCESS *dances next to* TARO, *and* SEA KING *claps hands in time to the music.* 1ST SEA CITIZEN *brings in big bowl of fruit, sets it on table, right.* TARO *sits on chair, left, and* SEA CITIZENS *bring him food. He eats, claps his hands. The music ends, and all stop dancing.*)

BIG TURTLE: Are you having a good time, Taro, my friend?

TARO: Big Turtle, I've never been to a party, much less had a party given in my honor.

KING: We want you to stay with us as long as you like.

TARO: Your Majesty, I wish I could, but I really must leave now. I have to get back to my master.

SIR JELLYFISH: Wouldn't you rather live here with us?

MADAME PORPOISE: Yes, Taro. Stay with us. We're your friends.

TARO (*Moved*): You are all my good friends. I'll never forget your kindness to me. But I have responsibilities in my village. And my friend Goro would miss me if I never came home.

PRINCESS: We understand. (*Takes box from table and gives it to* TARO) Taro, here is a gift for you to take back to your village. (TARO *begins to open it.*) No, do not open the box now! You must not open it until the time when life becomes too hard to bear.

TARO (*Repeating, as if trying to memorize* PRINCESS's *command*): I must never open this box until life becomes too hard to bear.

KING (*Going to* TARO *and shaking his hand*): That's right. And now, goodbye, good friend, Taro. (BIG TURTLE *comes forward, and* TARO *slowly "rides" him off right.*)

SEA CITIZENS (*Waving*): Goodbye, Taro. We will miss you. (*Curtain*)

* * * * *

SCENE 3

TIME: *Fifty years later.*

SETTING: *Same as Scene 1.*

AT RISE: *Stage is deserted, as* TARO, *now an old man with white hair and beard, enters left. He carries box.*

TARO: I hope it's not too late. (*Looks at the "sea"*) It all feels like a dream—a wonderful, happy dream. Was it? (*Touches box*) No. Here is Sea Star's box to remind me that I have friends. (*As he speaks,* BOY *and* GIRL *enter right.*)

BOY: Sister, who's that old man? I've never seen him in our village before.

GIRL: We'd better stay away from him. Mother doesn't like us to speak to strangers.

TARO (*Moving toward* BOY *and* GIRL): Greetings! (*As* BOY *and* GIRL *move off, right*) Wait. Uh—do you know what time it is? (BOY *and* GIRL *stop, turn around.*)

BOY: Time? It's nearly suppertime.

TARO: Thank goodness. I'm not late after all.

GIRL: Where are you going, stranger?

TARO (*Surprised*): Stranger? Hm-m-m. I've never seen either of you before. (BOY *and* GIRL *look at each other.*) What are your names?

GIRL: I'm Mari, sir.

BOY: I'm called Taro. My grandfather named me after his best friend who was lost at sea fifty years ago.

TARO: Indeed! That's a coincidence. My name is Taro, too. Who is your grandfather? (GORO *enters left. He also has white hair and beard. He leans on a cane.*)

BOY (*Pointing to* GORO): Here he is now.

GORO: Children, your mother's waiting for you for dinner. (*Sees* TARO) Who are you? Are you visiting someone in our village?

TARO (*Amazed*): It can't be. You look just like my friend Goro.

GORO: Eh? What did you say? I can't hear too well. (*Moves closer to* TARO *and peers into his face*) You look like an old friend of mine. His name was Taro. He was drowned at sea.

TARO: He drowned?

GORO: That's the only thing that could have happened to him. I left him fishing here one day fifty years ago, and when I came back, he was gone. (*Shaking head*)

Poor Taro. He didn't have a good life. He was an orphan, and his master was cruel to him.

TARO (*Dazed, to himself*): How could fifty years have passed?

GORO: Come, children, come! It's time to start for home. (GORO, BOY, *and* GIRL *start off, left.*)

TARO: Wait. Tell me what happened to Taro's master.

GORO (*Stopping and turning around; laughing*): He was furious when Taro didn't come back. He had to do all the work himself from then on, and he did badly, too. I bought his inn some thirty years ago. (*Shakes head*) You look so much like someone I once knew, stranger. What did you say your name was?

TARO (*Softly*): Never mind. (GORO, BOY, *and* GIRL *exit left, and* TARO *watches them.*) Fifty years. How could I have been away from here for fifty years? Goro is an old man now. No one in the village knows me. I don't belong here any more. (*He sits on rock and looks at box.*) Sea Star told me to open this box when life had become too hard to bear. (*Sighs*) I'm going to open it now. (*Opens box*) There's a mirror at the bottom. (*Takes out mirror, and holds it up to look at himself; horrified*) This can't be! (*Touches face*) I have a white beard. I'm old, as old as Goro. (*Musical scale is heard from offstage.* BIG TURTLE *enters right, unseen by* TARO.) This is terrible. If only I'd stayed under the sea with my friends. (*Gets slowly to his feet, then looks at ground*) Now, what's this? (*Pretends to pick up small fish*) A little fish, stranded by the tide. (*Pantomimes throwing fish back into the sea*) Back you go into the sea, little fellow. Say hello to all my dear friends in the Kingdom under the Sea.

BIG TURTLE (*Moving to* TARO): You can tell them yourself, Taro.

TARO (*Surprised*): Big Turtle! I'm so glad to see you again. What has happened to me? I'm an old man.

BIG TURTLE: Taro, time stops in the magical Kingdom under the Sea. A moment there is a year here, on the earth.

TARO (*Sadly*): I spent nearly an hour down there. So much time has passed. My life is almost over!

BIG TURTLE: Do not be sad, my friend. His Majesty and Princess Sea Star have sent me to bring you back to our kingdom. All your friends are waiting to see you. There, you'll be as young as you were on your first visit.

TARO: But, Big Turtle, I am a human being. Do I really belong in the Sea King's kingdom?

BIG TURTLE: Taro, we all belong where our hearts are happiest and good friends wait for us. Come! To the Sea King's palace.

TARO: To the Kingdom under the Sea! (*Musical scale is played offstage and swells louder and louder, as* TARO *"rides"* BIG TURTLE *right. They exit, as curtain falls.*)

THE END

(*Production Notes on page 317*)

Big Paul Bunyan

An American folktale

by Adele Thane

Characters

NARRATOR, *a lumberjack*
JIM, *a neighbor's boy*
TRAVELING LADY
PAUL BUNYAN
MR. BUNYAN } *Paul's parents*
MRS. BUNYAN }
TOWNSPEOPLE, *extras*
BABE, *the Blue Ox*
BUM } *honeybees*
BUZZ }
JOHN SHEARS, *overseer of Paul's farm*
LITTLE MEERY, *chore boy*
FARMERS }
LUMBERJACKS } *extras*

SCENE 1

BEFORE RISE: *A tree stump is down right in front of curtain.* NARRATOR, *dressed as a lumberjack and carrying an ax on his shoulder, enters and stops by the stump.*

189

NARRATOR: Big Paul Bunyan! He swung his ax (NAR-
RATOR *swings his ax and strikes the stump*)—and he
cut a road through the wilderness from Maine to
Oregon in three days. (NARRATOR *moves downstage.*)
Paul Bunyan is a real American folk hero. The stories about him came out of the Northwest in the
pioneer days of our country, when most of America
was covered with dense forests. As more and more
people settled there, these forests had to be cleared.
The men who cut down the trees were called loggers.
All day long they worked hard, but in the evenings,
they liked to sit around the camps and tell stories—
funny stories and tall tales. And the tallest tales
were told about Paul Bunyan, the mightiest man
that ever came into the woods, the greatest lumberjack of them all. (NARRATOR *sits on tree stump.*) Paul
was born in the state of Maine. As a baby, he was so
big he had to be wheeled about in a wheelbarrow.
And his mother had to use brass doorknobs instead
of buttons on his clothes. (*Curtain opens.*)

* * * * *

SETTING: *Maine. Rocky coastline in background.*

AT RISE: JIM *enters from left, with a wooden whistle.
He stops at center and tries it out.* TRAVELING LADY
enters from right, carrying a carpetbag.

LADY (*To* JIM): Excuse me, young man. Would you
direct me to the nearest hotel? I'm a stranger here.

JIM: Sure. (*Pointing off left*) Straight ahead. You can't
miss it, ma'am. It's the only hotel in town.

LADY: Thank you. (*She starts left but stops, startled, as*
MR. *and* MRS. BUNYAN *enter with a wheelbarrow
holding* PAUL. MRS. BUNYAN *pulls wheelbarrow with
a rope attached to the front, while* MR. BUNYAN
pushes on handlebars at rear. Both are panting, ex-

hausted. PAUL, *his knees drawn up against his chest and covered with blanket, wears a baby bonnet and has a thick, black beard.)*

PAUL (*In booming voice*): Hullo, Jim! Whatcha whittlin'?

JIM: Oh, just a whistle. (*He toots it at* PAUL, *who bounces with delight.)*

PAUL (*Reaching for whistle*): Let me have it. (JIM *hands him whistle, which he blasts continuously, as* MR. *and* MRS. BUNYAN *wheel him across stage and off right.)*

LADY: Good heavens! *What* was that?

JIM (*Laughing*): *That* was Paul Bunyan. His parents are taking him out for his daily airing.

LADY (*Shocked*): He should be ashamed of himself! A big heavy lummox like that making his poor parents wheel him about! *He* should be giving *them* a ride!

JIM: But he's just a baby, ma'am, only three months old.

LADY (*Incredulous*): That—that monstrous boy—with a full-grown beard—is only *three months old*? I don't believe it! Why, he *talks*!

JIM: Oh, Paul can talk like a house-a-fire. He learned his ABCs when he was two weeks old. (MR. *and* MRS. BUNYAN *return.)*

MRS. BUNYAN: There! We've put Paul in his cradle out in the bay. Jim, will you keep an eye on him?

JIM: Sure, Mrs. Bunyan. (*He exits right.)*

LADY (*In horror*): Do you mean to say you've put your baby out there in the Atlantic Ocean? He'll drown!

MR. BUNYAN: Oh, no, he won't, ma'am. I made a cradle for him out of a boat and anchored it close to shore.

MRS. BUNYAN (*Explaining*): He outgrew his cradle at home. And when we put him in a bed, he sawed off the legs and used one of them for a teething ring.

MR. BUNYAN (*Proudly*): I'll bet that boy of ours is going to be a great logger some day!

JIM (*Running in, greatly excited*): Mr. Bunyan, come quick! Paul is rocking his cradle and making waves a mile high! You have to quiet him down before the whole town is flooded! (JIM *and* MR. BUNYAN *rushes out, as several* TOWNSPEOPLE *race onstage, screaming*.)

TOWNSPEOPLE (*Ad lib*): Head for the hills! . . . Tidal wave coming! . . . Run for your lives! (*They shout at* MRS. BUNYAN.) That baby's a danger to the whole state! . . . A baby like that is against the Constitution! (*Etc.* MRS. BUNYAN *runs out right, the others, left. Curtain closes.*)

NARRATOR (*Rising and leaning ax against stump*): Well, after that, Paul's parents decided that they had better move to a place where Paul wouldn't be a public nuisance—where he could play and romp about without endangering others. So they went to Canada and, deep in the woods, they built their new home. (*Walking to center*) Paul grew up helping his father cut down trees. One winter he left his father's logging camp to do some logging on his own. That was the winter of the blue snow. Nothing like it has been seen since—bright blue snow kept falling for a week, and when it stopped, Paul heard a terrific noise outside the cave where he had taken shelter. (NARRATOR *crosses to left.*) Boom, boom! Crash! (*He sits on floor. Curtain opens.*)

* * * * *

SCENE 2

SETTING: *There is a cave left, with an opening at center. At right, several blue snowbanks stand in a field.*

Blue light floods the field. Inside the cave, but visible, a campfire burns. A large cooking kettle hangs over fire.

At Rise: Paul *is asleep inside cave.* Babe, *a baby ox, hides behind snowbank, right. A loud cracking noise is heard, and a large cut-out of a tree falls onto stage, from offstage right.* Paul *jumps up, startled, and looks out of cave.*

Paul (*In amazement*): *Blue* snow! (*Loud mooing is heard from behind snow bank.* Paul *shakes his head.*) Some poor critter is lost out there. I'd better go see what it is. (*Puts on snowshoes and walks among the snowbanks. Finally, he notices* Babe's *ears sticking out of snowbank at rear.*) There are two blue ears sticking out of the snow. (*Goes over and looks*) Why, it's a baby ox! (*He pats* Babe's *head.*) Poor little critter. He's blue with cold. (Paul *leads* Babe *inside cave, beside fire. He takes off his snowshoes and covers* Babe *with a blanket.* Babe *moos gratefully.* Paul *dips ladle into the kettle.*) Drink this hot soup, little critter. (Babe *drinks noisily from ladle, then sits up suddenly and picks up kettle and drinks down entire contents without stopping.* Paul *slaps his knee, chuckling.*) By jiminy, you feel better now, don't you? What an appetite! (*While* Paul *is bent over,* Babe *butts him from behind and knocks him flat.* Paul *laughs louder than ever.*) You young rascal! You want to play, do you? (Babe *moos loudly.* Paul *gets to his feet, pats* Babe *affectionately.*) Ah, you're a beautiful blue baby. That's what I'll call you—Babe, the blue ox. We'll be great friends, eh, Babe? (Babe *nods his head and moos.*) You'll be a giant of an ox and carry trees on your back. I'm tired of lugging logs by myself. (Babe *moos and prances about.*) Logging, Babe—that's the work for you and me! Together we'll clear the forests and make room for pioneers to build homes. Yes, sirree, Babe! We'll be the best lumberjacks in America! (*He hugs* BABE, *who moos happily. Curtain*)

NARRATOR (*Standing*): And everything that Paul said came true. He cut down the trees and Babe hauled the logs to the river to float them down to the mills, where they could be sawed into lumber. (NARRATOR *crosses slowly to the tree stump, speaking as he walks.*) Paul's fame as a logger soon spread, and men were eager to work for him. Before long, he had a crew of the best loggers in the country. (NARRATOR *picks up his ax, which is leaning against stump.*) All through the North Woods you'd hear the shout go up (*Raises his ax and brings it down on the stump*)— "T-i-m-b-e-r-r-r!" And then the echo. . . . Tim-ber!! (NARRATOR *puts down his ax.*) Paul had a farm in Smiling River Valley where the food for his loggers was raised. The overseer of Paul's farm was a man named John Shears. John and his farmhands raised so much food that it took ten thousand horse teams to carry it to the loggers. (*Strutting to center*) John Shears, well, he was *somebody,* to run a farm like that! And he began to think that if he could put an end to Paul's logging business, then all the men would have to become farmers. And if all the men were farmers, they'd make John Shears the big boss instead of that logger Paul Bunyan. (*Walking back to the stump*) One day John called some of the farmers together and told them his plan. (NARRATOR *sits. Curtain opens.*)

* * * * *

SCENE 3

SETTING: *Barnyard of Paul's farm. Babe's stable is at left. A corral-type fence runs across the back of stage and halfway down each side. Three or four wooden fruit crates are piled center. Up right, outside the fence, there is a large beehive with a sliding panel in front, now open. A gate is in fence opposite beehive.*

AT RISE: *A loud buzzing sound is heard, and* BUZZ, *a honeybee, flies out of the beehive, through gate and into barnyard, followed by* BUM, *another bee.*

BUZZ: Buzz-z-z-z! Come on, Bum!

BUM: Coming, Buzz! What'z-z-z the hurry?

BUZZ (*Pointing off right, angrily*): They're cutting down the clover! Buzz-z-z-z!

BUM: They can't do that! We haven't gathered all the honey yet!

BUZZ: Let'z-z-z go and chase-z-z-z them away!

BUM: Yez-z-z! (*They exit right.* JOHN SHEARS *and* FARMERS *enter left.* JOHN *is roughly shoving* LITTLE MEERY, *who carries two heavy pails of mash.*)

JOHN: Get a move on, Meery! Take that mash to the pigs. Then feed tho hono. (MEERY *exits through gate off left.* JOHN *laughs.*) Is he gone?

1ST FARMER (*Looking off*): Yep.

JOHN: Well, sit down, men. I've something important to tell you. (*They all sit on crates.* MEERY *comes out from behind stable and listens. Others do not see him.*) I've been trying to think of a plan to do away with logging, so you farmers can be the big shots in this country, instead of the lumberjacks. And last night I hit on a plan!

FARMERS (*Ad lib*): What is it? . . . Tell us! . . . We want to hear! (*Etc.*)

JOHN: The thing we have to do is get rid of Babe, the blue ox.

2ND FARMER: Why Babe?

JOHN: Doesn't he haul the logs to the river? Without him, Paul couldn't carry on his logging!

3RD FARMER (*Nodding*): That's true. But Babe's a powerful strong critter. How are you going to get rid of him?

JOHN: Easy. Babe's favorite food is parsnips. Right?

FARMERS: Right!

JOHN: But the crop of parsnips in the north field rotted this year. Right?

FARMERS: Right!

JOHN: So, we'll feed Babe those rotten parsnips. And *that* will put an end to Babe and the logging business!

FARMERS (*Jumping up together*): Hurrah! Three cheers for John Shears! Down with loggers! Up with farmers!

JOHN (*Pointing off left*): Go dig up the parsnips, men! (FARMERS *stand, pick up crates, and exit left.* MEERY *ducks behind stable. Off right loud buzzing of bees is heard, followed by shouts of men.*)

FARMERS (*From offstage*): Ouch! Go away! Out of here! You buzzing bumblers!

BUM *and* BUZZ (*From offstage, chanting*): We want honey! We want honey!

JOHN (*Calling*): Meery! Come here!

MEERY (*Entering left*): Yes, Mr. Shears.

JOHN: Those bees are bothering the mowers in the clover. Shut 'em up in the beehive. (*He exits left.* MEERY *runs off and returns, chasing* BUM *and* BUZZ *upstage.*)

BUM *and* BUZZ: We want honey! We want honey! (*They fly into hive and* MEERY *slams down the sliding panel. Tramping of heavy boots is heard off right, and* PAUL, *leading crew of* LUMBERJACKS, *enters with* BABE, *now a full-grown ox.*)

LUMBERJACKS (*Singing to the tune of "Oh, Sussanah!"*):
We're a crew of mighty lumberjacks,
As jolly as can be;
No matter where we have to go,
We're cheerful and we're free.

Our boss he is a powerful man,
Paul Bunyan is his name,
The hero of a hundred deeds
A lumberjack of fame.

Big Paul Bunyan!
And Babe, his ox of blue!
There's nothing that they cannot do.
Let's give them both their due!

PAUL: Relax, men! No work for a week! (LUMBERJACKS *cheer and exit left.* PAUL *scratches* BABE's *ears.*) Are you tired, Babe, old pal? (BABE *moos.*) And hungry? (*Moos and nods*) How would you like a bushel of parsnips? (*Enthusiastic nod and loud moo*)

MEERY (*Approaching timidly*): Mr. Bunyan—

PAUL: Why, hello, little Meery! Would you get some parsnips for Babe?

MEERY: I—I want to talk to you about the parsnips, Mr. Bunyan. (*He hesitates.*)

PAUL: Yes?

MEERY: The parsnips—they—

JOHN (*Entering suddenly from left*): Meery! What are you doing here? Clear out! You're needed in the kitchen. (MEERY *exits left.*) I didn't expect you, Paul. Have you broken up camp?

PAUL: We've logged off Minnesota, and I thought the

crew could use a little vacation. Put Babe in his stable, John, and let him have plenty of parsnips.

JOHN: *Yes, sir!* (PAUL *exits left.* JOHN *rubs his hands together, turns to* BABE, *grinning.*) He wants me to feed you parsnips. Well, Babe, parsnips you'll get! (*He opens stable door,* BABE *enters, and* JOHN *closes door behind him.* MEERY *peeks around corner of stable.* FARMERS *enter, stand behind fence.* 1ST FARMER *leans over fence and calls to* JOHN.)

1ST FARMER: Psst! John! The parsnips are ready.

JOHN: Good! We'll feed 'em to that ox-critter right now and he'll be a goner by nightfall. (JOHN *and* FARMERS *exit.*)

MEERY (*Anxiously, coming into barnyard*): What shall I do? I have to save Babe some way. (*Loud buzzing is heard from beehive.*) I know! I'll let the bees out. They'll sting Babe and keep him away from the parsnips. (FARMERS *and* JOHN *reenter;* MEERY *quickly hides behind beehive. They carry crates of parsnips, which they dump in center of barnyard. Then* FARMERS *line up behind fence.* JOHN *goes to stable door and opens it.* MEERY *creeps out from behind beehive, ready to open sliding panel.* BABE *moos and sniffs the air. He sees the parsnips, moos again, and gallops toward pile.* MEERY *releases* BUM *and* BUZZ, *and they fly straight for* BABE, *buzzing furiously. He starts to buck and bellow.* FARMERS *yell and run off.* JOHN *tries to climb over the fence from inside the barn, but* BABE *chases him around parsnips several times.* PAUL *enters left and shouts above the uproar.*)

PAUL: What's going on here? (JOHN *escapes, pursued by* BUM *and* BUZZ.) Slow down there, Babe! What's gotten into you? Quiet down and eat your parsnips.

MEERY (*Quickly*): Don't let Babe eat those parsnips, Mr. Bunyan! They're poison! John Shears dug up a bad crop just to kill Babe!

PAUL (*Restraining* BABE): Why would he want to kill Babe?

MEERY: He said with Babe out of the way, there would be no more logging, only farming, and then *he'd* be the big boss instead of you.

PAUL: So, John Shears is getting too big for his britches, is he? Well, we'll see about that. (*He clasps* MEERY *on shoulder.*) Little Meery, you're a real hero! What can I do to reward you for saving Babe's life?

MEERY: Oh, Mr. Bunyan, just let me go into the woods with you and be a lumberjack. I want to do that more than anything else in the world.

PAUL: You're pretty small to be a lumberjack, Little Meery.

MEERY (*Eagerly*): I'll grow, Mr. Bunyan. I'll *make* myself grow! I promise.

PAUL (*Smiling and shaking hands with* MEERY): You're hired, my boy! And while we're waiting for you to grow, you can be our chore boy in the camp, and help take care of Babe. How does that suit you?

MEERY (*Happily*): It suits me fine, Mr. Bunyan—just fine! (*Puts his arm around* BABE's *neck.* BABE *nuzzles him and moos. Curtain closes.*)

NARRATOR (*Rising*): And that's how Babe was saved. (*Walking to center*) Little Meery grew up to be a big lumberjack, just as he promised Paul he would. For years and years, Paul Bunyan and his men cleared the forests of America to make homes for the people. That's why big Paul Bunyan and Babe, his strong blue ox, will always be remembered as real folk heroes. (NARRATOR *returns to stump and picks up*

ax.) They say that when the wind is right, you can still hear Paul swinging his ax and shouting (NARRATOR *brings ax down on stump*)—*"T-i-m-b-e-r-r-r!"*
OFFSTAGE VOICES (*Echoing and fading away*): Timber-r-r-r! Timber-r-r-r! (NARRATOR *shoulders his ax and exits.*)

THE END

(*Production Notes on page 317*)

The Three Evils

A Chinese folktale

by Dorothea Smith Coryell

Characters

THREE ELDERS
COURT CLERK
CHANG
WIDOW WONG
LI
VILLAGERS, *extras*
TWO GUARDS
MANDARIN WU
JO CHOU
MRS. YEE
BOY

SCENE 1

TIME: *Morning, long ago.*
SETTING: *A courtroom of a Chinese village. Up center is a low platform with a great carved chair on top. Straw mats cover the floor around the platform. At right stands a small chair and table with pen, ink, and scroll on it.*

AT RISE: THREE ELDERS *stand on either side of plat-*
form. COURT CLERK *sits at table.* CHANG, WIDOW
WONG, LI, *and* VILLAGERS *stand at sides.* TWO
GUARDS *stand down right.*

1ST ELDER (*Stepping to front of platform and speaking*
in very official tone): We are assembled in this courtroom today for a most important occasion. Our Emperor (*All bow*) has sent us a new magistrate. His
Excellency, Mandarin Wu, is noted for his good judgment and wisdom. After we have given him greet-
ing, we will listen to the people's complaints. Now, I
beseech you, friends and neighbors, do not become a
flock of clamoring magpies. Each of you, after regis-
tering with the Court Clerk, should state your complaint simply and briefly. (*Steps back to platform*)

2ND ELDER: Quite right. Although none of us has ever
journeyed to the capital, let us give his Excellency
the impression that we are cultured and civilized
people.

VILLAGERS (*Ad lib*): Good, good. Wisely said. The Elder
is right. (*Etc.*)

1ST GUARD: His Excellency, the Mandarin Wu, approaches. (*All stand at attention.* MANDARIN WU,
dressed in richly embroidered robes and carrying
scepter, enters, and marches up onto platform. He
turns to face audience. All bow.)

1ST ELDER (*Stepping forward*): Your Excellency, the
humble members of the village greet you.

MANDARIN WU (*Graciously*): Good people, my staff and
I are most happy to be here. Only last night we
heard the great roar of a tiger in the nearby mountains. This morning we were crossing a bridge on the
outskirts of this village when the waters rose with
such speed, we were lucky we did not drown. I can
assure you I am only too happy to have arrived at

last in this peaceful village. Pray, everyone please be seated. (*He sits in chair.* ELDERS *sit on mats.*)

VILLAGERS (*Agitated; ad lib*): The tiger! The bridge! His Excellency is lucky to have escaped! (*Etc.*)

MANDARIN: Now that I am here, I hope to be a good magistrate. I wish to know more about this district. How was the harvest? Have the people enough to eat?

2ND ELDER: Your Excellency, the harvest has been abundant, rice is plentiful, and all go happily about their work.

MANDARIN: Good, good! I am glad to hear this. It is rare to find people who are completely happy. (*There is a murmur among* VILLAGERS.)

1ST ELDER: It is true, Excellency, that we have rice and clothing. Yet there is much trouble among us.

MANDARIN: I am sorry to hear these words. I wish to know more about these problems. (*All start to speak at once.*)

VILLAGERS (*Ad lib; loudly*): Yes, we are sorely afflicted! We have many complaints! (*Etc.*)

1ST ELDER (*Angrily*): Order, order! You cause His Excellency to think that we are a band of uncouth barbarians.

MANDARIN (*Holding out scepter; speaking loudly*): I cannot know what your troubles are if you all speak at once.

2ND ELDER (*Glaring*): Let each come forward as the clerk reads your name. His Excellency will hear you all, but state your complaint in one sentence only. When all the complaints are recorded, His Excellency will study each case in turn. (*To* CLERK) Clerk, you may proceed.

CLERK (*Reading*): The Widow Wong.

WIDOW WONG (*Bustling forward*): Your Lordship, my

very best laying hen was stolen, and I know who—

1ST ELDER (*Cutting her off; to* CLERK): Enough. Write down "Stolen, one hen of Widow Wong." (*To* WIDOW WONG) Please stand over there. (WIDOW WONG *stands left.*)

CLERK (*Writing, then reading next name*): The rug maker, Li.

LI: Your Highness, last night a terrible brawl was begun in my shop and the one who—

1ST ELDER (*Interrupting*): Enough. Write down "Brawl in Li's rug shop." (*Points*) Stand next to Widow Wong, please. (Li *does so.*)

CLERK (*Reading*): The fruit peddler, Chang.

CHANG: Most honorable one, last evening I had just set my baskets down and was quietly discussing with Mrs. Yee the price she would pay for peaches, when all my wares were suddenly overturned.

1ST ELDER: Enough. Please go over there. (CHANG *joins others.*)

3RD ELDER (*Stepping forward and bowing to* MANDARIN): Excellency, may I speak?

MANDARIN: Please do.

3RD ELDER: Although the people have been singularly blessed by rain and sun, three evils have caused great fear and unhappiness in recent years.

MANDARIN: Will you tell me about them?

3RD ELDER: First, there is the fiery dragon at the long bridge. Your Excellency nearly made his acquaintance this morning. The second evil is the tiger with the white forehead, who dwells in the hills. And the third evil—oh, Excellency, this is much more difficult to explain—it is a man.

MANDARIN (*Patiently*): Will someone please tell me the name of this evil one?

ALL (*Excitedly*): Jo Chou!

MANDARIN (*To* WIDOW WONG): Old woman, will you please tell us who stole your laying hen?

WIDOW WONG: It was Jo Chou, Your Lordship.

MANDARIN: Rug maker, how did the brawl in your shop start last night?

LI: Jo Chou was the instigator, Your Highness.

MANDARIN: Peddler, who upset your wares?

CHANG: Most honorable and wise one, it was—

MANDARIN (*Nodding*): Jo Chou. It would seem that if we could change Jo Chou's ways, our troubles would be over—except for the dragon and the tiger, of course. Tell me, what manner of man is Jo Chou?

1ST ELDER: Your Excellency, he is a bold and handsome man. He must be rich, for he wears a high hat adorned with two pheasant feathers. His clothes are of the finest embroidered silk and at his left hand hangs a tremendous sword. He is forever starting trouble and has been a trouble-maker in this village for many years.

MANDARIN: Why do you not keep him locked up in the village jail?

2ND ELDER: Excellency, he has extraordinary strength. Six men could not hold him, and ten men would not dare to touch him.

MANDARIN: Since he is such a strong man, perhaps it would be judicious to use other means than force to tame him. I will give the matter serious thought. The court is adjourned for the morning. However, will the three head Elders please remain? I wish to go into this situation further with them. (*All stand, bow to* MANDARIN.)

VILLAGERS (*Ad lib*): Thank you, Excellency. (*Etc. All except* ELDERS, TWO GUARDS *and* MANDARIN *exit.*)

MANDARIN (*To* ELDERS): Where does this infamous Jo Chou live?

1ST ELDER: At the end of the village, Your Lordship.

MANDARIN: Come, gentlemen. (MANDARIN *starts to lead* THREE ELDERS *off, speaking as he goes.*) I will tell you of a plan. I will dress in the clothes of a beggar . . . (*Curtain*)

* * * * *

SCENE 2

TIME: *Before dawn.*

SETTING: *In front of Jo Chou's house at edge of village. There are two huge boulders on either side of gateway.*

AT RISE: MANDARIN *enters, disguised as beggar. He looks all around, listens, then stands next to gateway, in a position of abject misery.* JO CHOU *struts in, sword at his side.*

JO CHOU (*Reciting*):

The swindler and the ruffian lead pleasant lives enough.

While judgment overtakes the good with many a sharp rebuff.

The bold Jo Chou, with sword in hand, fears neither beast nor fears he man.

If you dislike the deeds I do, then come and catch me if you can. (*Laughs uproariously to himself*)

MANDARIN (*Falling to his knees*): Please! Have mercy on me, noble sir!

JO CHOU: You want me to have mercy? (*Laughs, then prods* MANDARIN *with sword*) Get along, old man. You can't stay at my door sniffling and weeping.

MANDARIN (*Scrambling to his feet*): I weep for the distress of the poor people.

Jo CHOU: You weep for the poor people's distress, do you? (*Laughs*) What about your own distress? A more miserable looking old bag of bones I have yet to see.

MANDARIN: I weep for the people of this village who are sorely afflicted.

Jo CHOU: Old man, what are you saying? The people of this village have just harvested an abundant crop, and all have plenty to eat.

MANDARIN: True, true, and yet I say the villagers are sorely afflicted.

Jo CHOU (*Aside*): Strange that he should concern himself with the afflictions of the villagers, when it appears that no one has concern for him. (*To* MANDARIN) Speak up, old man. How are the people so afflicted?

MANDARIN: Honorable sir, the people are afflicted by three great evils. First, there is the dragon at the bridge. Second, there is the tiger who roars and has carried off men, women, and children.

Jo CHOU (*Impatiently*): I have heard of these evils, though they have not frightened me. And what is the third evil?

MANDARIN: It is hard for me to speak of the third evil, gracious sir, but the villagers say that the third and greatest evil is you.

Jo CHOU (*Stunned*): Me? Why that's impossible! It is true that I have a bold and independent nature, and (*Chuckles*) I do like a good jest, . . . but to compare me with the dragon and the tiger is ridiculous! (*Angrily*) Pray tell, who are you that you talk so boldly to Jo Chou?

MANDARIN (*Throwing off his cloak of rags, and standing*): I am the Mandarin, whom the Emperor has sent to bring the people justice. (TWO GUARDS *enter.*)

JO CHOU (*To* GUARDS): Is this really the new magistrate?

1ST GUARD: This is His Excellency . . .

2ND GUARD: The Mandarin Wu!

JO CHOU (*Incredulously*): If I am such a great evil, why did you not order forth the militia and throw me into jail?

MANDARIN: The people say that you have the strength of ten men. With that great sword you would injure many, and much blood would be shed.

JO CHOU: Still, if you call forth all the village militia, they could capture me.

MANDARIN: True. But the people are peaceable. The dragon in the river, the tiger in the mountains, and you, Jo Chou, have terrorized everyone for years, yet no one has devised a plan to eliminate these evils. I am sure that of all who live here, only you show daring and ingenuity, though you misuse these traits.

JO CHOU (*Confused*): But, Your Honor, you have humbled yourself, become a beggar, and pleaded with me.

MANDARIN: True, Jo Chou, for I had hoped that by my meekness I could show you the error of your ways— perhaps even turn your bad intentions to good.

JO CHOU (*Pleading*): Forgive me, please, noble sir. (*Contritely*) In all my life I have never concerned myself with the people's welfare. And now they say I am a greater evil than the tiger and the dragon. (*Falls to his knees*) Oh, worthy one, before you administer the punishment that I deserve, give me just a little time.

MANDARIN: Arise, Jo Chou. You may have the time, for I have not spoken of punishment. (*To* GUARDS) Come.

(*As* MANDARIN *and* GUARDS *exit,* JO CHOU *stands, his chin sunk on chest, muttering to himself.*)

JO CHOU: A greater evil than the tiger and the dragon. (JO CHOU *remains lost in thought, as* CHANG, *with pole across his shoulder, enters. He is followed by several* VILLAGERS, *including* MRS. YEE *and* BOY. *When* CHANG *sees* JO CHOU, *he stops, eyes him warily. Then he walks around him, giving* JO CHOU *a wide berth.* VILLAGERS *creep cautiously around him. Suddenly,* JO CHOU *comes out of his trance, unsheaths his sword, and brandishing it, rushes at group of* VILLAGERS *with a great cry.*) I'll show them. *Kai lu!* Make way! (*Rushes through crowd and off.* BOY *follows him.*)

CHANG: Heaven protect us! Jo Chou has become a raging madman! When we spoke to the magistrate yesterday, he should have called forth the militia and captured that monster. (WIDOW WONG, *a basket of eggs on her arm, enters, followed by* ELDERS *and* COURT CLERK)

BOY (*Returning*): Jo Chou has gone mad! He tore off his high hat and his robe, and he has plunged into the waters of the river. (*All rush to look offstage.*)

1ST VILLAGER: See how the waters swell and lash about! (*Roaring of water is heard.*)

MRS. YEE: The dragon may swallow Jo Chou alive.

2ND ELDER: The waters rise higher and higher.

BOY: Jo Chou is coming out of the water. He is breathless! (*Sound of water stops.*)

2ND VILLAGER: Look! How still the waters have become.

CHANG: He returns! Protect yourselves, everyone. (JO CHOU *rushes onstage, dripping wet, waving his sword.* VILLAGERS *scatter and cower.*)

JO CHOU (*Catching his breath*): There! I have killed the dragon!

1ST ELDER (*Calling from a safe distance*): Jo Chou, put your sword away.

JO CHOU (*Shouting*): I am not yet through. (*He dashes offstage in opposite direction.* VILLAGERS *cower.*)

WIDOW WONG: All the devils have taken possession of Jo Chou!

BOY: But it was a fine thing to have driven the dragon away.

3RD VILLAGER (*Looking off*): See, neighbors, how Jo Chou grapples with the great tiger! (*All rush to look.*)

COURT CLERK: The tiger is upon him!

4TH VILLAGER: I dare not look!

WIDOW WONG: Now he is upon the tiger.

BOY: Jo Chou raises his sword.

WIDOW WONG: He strikes the tiger, and the tiger (*Turns away*)—Oh, I cannot look!

COURT CLERK: Jo Chou strikes again.

MRS. YEE: The tiger lies still. The tiger is dead.

2ND VILLAGER: Long live Jo Chou!

BOY: He is the strongest man in the world!

COURT CLERK (*In awe*): Such bravery! Only he could have saved our village.

MANDARIN (*Entering with* GUARDS): What is all this? Is there another disturbance in the village?

ALL (*Together*): It was Jo Chou!

MANDARIN: I must say I'm surprised. I rather thought I had reformed the man. (JO CHOU *enters.*)

VILLAGERS (*Ad lib*): Long live Jo Chou! The bravest man in the village! (*Etc.*)

JO CHOU (*Kneeling before* MANDARIN): Your Excellency, I shall go to a far country and never return. Watch over my village and tell the Elders I will trouble them no more.

COURT CLERK (*Excitedly*): He killed the tiger.

2ND ELDER: He drove the dragon away!

MANDARIN: Jo Chou, your fellow villagers no longer seem so anxious to have you leave. (*Gesturing for* JO CHOU *to stand*) Arise. The people will judge you. (*To* VILLAGERS) Do you now wish to banish this villain, Jo Chou?

BOY: No, he is a hero!

COURT CLERK: He has such prowess!

MANDARIN (*To* JO CHOU): How fickle the public is. Only yesterday they would gladly have seen you banished. Today they call you a hero (*To* VILLAGERS) I hereby appoint Jo Chou Honorable Protector of the village. (*All cheer.*)

WIDOW WONG (*To* JO CHOU): Most valiant one, may I offer you this basket of eggs as a small token of my esteem? (*Hands basket to* JO CHOU)

CHANG: Most brave of the brave, may I also present this basket of fruit? (*Hands basket to* JO CHOU)

MANDARIN: To celebrate the end of the three great evils, and my appointment as magistrate, I wish to announce that there will be a feast in the courtyard tonight. Everyone is invited. (*All cheer as curtains close.*)

THE END

(*Production Notes on page 318*)

The Clever Dog of Hawaii

A Polynesian folktale

by Barbara Winther

Characters

STORYTELLER
HOMOKU
DOG, *"Puapualenalena"*
NANI, *the Queen's stepsister*
TWO WORKERS
QUEEN LUKIA
AKUA ⎤
PAPUA ⎬ *evil spirits*
TURI ⎦

SCENE 1

BEFORE RISE: STORYTELLER *enters in front of curtain.*
STORYTELLER (*To audience*): Here on the Kona Coast of
the big island of Hawaii there once lived a blind old
man named Homoku and his little dog, Puapualenalena. Their story began one afternoon as Homoku went to look for his dog. (STORYTELLER *exits.*

212

HOMOKU *enters left, slowly, as if blind.* DOG *enters center through curtains, carrying fish in mouth. He drops fish at* HOMOKU's *feet and barks.*)

HOMOKU: Why, that must be my little dog, Puapualenalena. (*Bends over and picks up fish*) What's this? My clever dog has caught a fish! (*Patting* DOG) Thank you, my faithful friend. Without you I would surely starve. (DOG *barks happily.*) If only I had some delicious poi to eat with my fish! (*Wistfully*) What is fish without creamy poi? When I was young and could see, I used to grow taro plants and make my own poi from them. However, I have no taro plants now. (DOG *whines sadly.*) Come, come, little dog, don't be unhappy. I shall forget all about poi and enjoy this fine fish. We cannot all be rich and grow taro plants, as Queen Lukia does. (*Turns and starts off.* DOG *yips and begins to sniff ground, then exits through center of curtains.* HOMOKU *calls.*) Dog! Dog! Where have you gone? (*Sadly*) I'm afraid he thought I didn't like the fish he brought me. I should never have mentioned poi. (*Exits, shaking head*)

* * * * *

SETTING: *Queen Lukia's royal taro field in the Waipio Valley, on the Island of Hawaii. Backdrop of mountains and a fiery volcano center, palm and banana trees at sides. The palace, a large, thatched hut, is at right, potted taro plants stand at left.*

AT RISE: TWO WORKERS *with hoes are cultivating the taro patch.* NANI *at center, plays with a coconut. Slow drumbeat is heard under following chant.*

NANI (*Chanting*):
Every day I come to play.

WORKERS (*Chanting as they work*): Hoe the royal taro field.

NANI:

I wish someone would play with me!

WORKERS (*Chanting*):

We must hoe the taro field

In the Valley Waipio.

1ST WORKER (WORKERS *stop working and lean on hoes*):

All is not well in the Valley Waipio.

2ND WORKER: Queen Lukia is angry. (*Loud sound of horn is heard from offstage.*)

NANI (*Putting her hands over her ears*): What was that?

1ST WORKER: The Queen's conch-shell horn!

2ND WORKER: The evil spirits who live on the cliff have stolen it.

1ST WORKER: All night and all day they blast away on it.

2ND WORKER: Our Queen has not had a night's sleep since the horn was stolen. (QUEEN LUKIA *enters.*)

QUEEN (*Gazing out over audience angrily*): Bring back my horn, you thieves! I, Queen Lukia, should be treated with respect. (*Blast on horn is repeated.*) Stop mocking me! (*All put hands over ears. Aside*) Someone must go up to that cliff and bring back my horn! (*To* WORKERS) Attention!

1ST WORKER (*Bowing*): How can we help you, oh Queen?

2ND WORKER (*Bowing*): What can we do for you?

QUEEN: Call a meeting of the villagers. (WORKERS *bow again, then put down hoes and start to exit.*)

WORKERS (*Ad lib*): Everyone, gather! Gather for a meeting! The Queen calls a meeting of the village! (*Etc. Exit*)

QUEEN (*Turning to* NANI): As for you, little Nani, make yourself useful, instead of playing with that silly coconut.

NANI (*Eagerly*): What shall I do, stepsister?

QUEEN (*Haughtily*): Guard the royal taro field, while I conduct the meeting. See that no one steals any of my taro plants, or I will make you find the thief— even if you have to climb the volcano!

NANI (*Fearfully*): But, stepsister, the goddess Pele will surely kill me if I go up there! No one has ever done it.

QUEEN: Then make sure that no one goes near my taro plants.

NANI (*Trying to smile*): Very well, stepsister.

QUEEN: I must go now. (*Exits*)

NANI (*To herself*): I'd better watch the taro plants. (*Looks all around at taro plants*) I don't see anyone. I hope my stepsister won't mind if I play with my coconut ball, just for a few minutes. (*Tosses coconut and catches it*) I wish I had someone to play with. Just because I am the Queen's stepsister, none of the other children will play with me! (DOG *enters, circles stage and sniffs.* NANI *does not notice.* DOG *crosses to taro plants, sniffs them, then yips excitedly.*) What was that? (NANI *turns and sees* DOG.) Why, it's only a dog. (*To* DOG) Hello, there! This is Queen Lukia's royal taro patch. You'd better not disturb it. (DOG *sits.*) Why don't you play ball with me? I'll roll the ball and you bring it back. (*Rolls coconut and* DOG *chases it, retrieves it, and then rolls it offstage right.*) Why did you roll it way out there? Oh, well, I'll go get it. (NANI *exits right.* DOG *quickly crosses to taro plants and digs one up, then exits, left, carrying plant in mouth.* NANI *reenters right with coconut again.*) Here it is! Now we can play catch again. (*Looks around*) Where did the dog go? (WORKERS *enter right.*)

1ST WORKER: No one in the village is brave enough to get the Queen's horn.

2ND WORKER: The Queen is even angrier than before.

1ST WORKER: I would go myself except that I'm frightened of the evil spirits.

2ND WORKER (*Shaking his head*): They can play terrible tricks on a person. (WORKERS *pick up hoes.*)

1ST WORKER (*Alarmed*): Look! (*Points to empty pot*) One of the royal taro plants is missing!

2ND WORKER: The Queen will be furious!

QUEEN (*Entering*): What is all the commotion?

WORKERS (*Ad lib*): More thievery! A taro plant is missing. Someone has stolen it! (*Etc.*)

QUEEN: So! Nani, you were supposed to watch my taro plants. If you had guarded them as I asked, this would not have happened.

NANI: But, I did. I've been watching the whole time. No one came to the field. No one except a little dog.

QUEEN (*Angrily*): Excuses, excuses! Little stepsister, I warned you about what would happen if you were careless. You must stand guard until you catch the thief.

NANI (*Fearfully*): But what if I cannot catch him?

QUEEN (*In threatening voice*): I will give you three days to find the thief. If you don't, you will have to climb to the top of the fiery volcano where Pele the goddess lives! (*Blast on horn is heard offstage.*) There's the sound of my horn again! (*Puts hands over ears*) I can't stand it! Something must be done about those evil spirits. (*Quick curtain*)

* * * * *

SCENE 2

TIME: *Several days later.*
SETTING: *Same as Scene 1.*

AT RISE: NANI *is walking back and forth in front of taro plants.*

NANI (*Wearily*): For the last two days I have watched over the royal taro field. All night long I guard it. (*Yawns*) I am so tired! (DOG *enters left.*) Why, it's the little dog that I played with a few days ago. (*To* DOG) Hello, little dog. Do you want to play ball again? (DOG *barks.*) I wish you were my dog. We could have such fun together! (DOG *cocks head one way, then the other.*) Here, catch the ball. (NANI *rolls coconut, and* DOG, *as before, rolls it off right. Exasperated*) Not again! (*Starts right after coconut.* DOG *at once crosses to taro plant and begins to dig it up.* NANI *pauses.*) There's something strange about this dog. (*She turns and sees* DOG *digging up plant.*) So, the dog is the thief! I'll keep out of sight and follow him to see where he takes the taro plant. (*Hides at right.* DOG *exits left with plant in mouth.* NANI *runs after him. Blackout to indicate passage of time. When lights come on again,* QUEEN *enters right, and* NANI *enters left followed by* DOG *and* HOMOKU. WORKERS *enter behind* QUEEN. QUEEN *has large sponges in her ears, and cloth wrapped around her head, like a turban.*)

QUEEN: Nani, your time is almost up. Have you found the thief who stole my royal taro plant?

NANI: Yes, Your Majesty. (*To* HOMOKU) I am sorry, old man, but the Queen said that I had to bring you back or face Pele, the goddess of the volcano.

HOMOKU: We understand, Nani. (*To* QUEEN) Here I am, Your Majesty.

QUEEN: What? I can't hear you.

1ST WORKER: Let me help you, Your Majesty. (*Takes sponges out of* QUEEN'*s ears*)

2ND WORKER: Now you will be able to hear.

QUEEN: I put sponges into my ears so I will not be able to hear the horn. Tell me, what did you say, old man?

HOMOKU: My dog, Puapualenalena, stole your taro plants, Your Majesty, to make me some poi. It was the most delicious poi I have ever eaten! I am too poor to buy poi, and I have no taro plants of my own. But I know I am as guilty as my dog.

QUEEN: I am touched by your story, old Homoku.

NANI: Stepsister, this man meant you no harm. Do not punish him!

HOMOKU (*Proudly*): We are willing to face whatever punishment we deserve. There is no excuse for theft. (DOG *whines*.)

QUEEN: If you can repay your dog's theft, you will be forgiven.

HOMOKU: I am too poor, Your Majesty. I have nothing with which to repay you.

QUEEN: Then you must be punished (DOG *howls*.) I decree that you and your dog shall go to the fiery volcano. (*Suddenly loud horn blast is heard from offstage. All cover ears.*) That terrible sound again! (*Horn is heard again.*) Oh-h-h! Can nothing be done about those evil spirits?

NANI: I have an idea, stepsister.

QUEEN (*Impatiently*): Well, what is it?

NANI: If this dog played ball with the evil spirits, perhaps he could bring back your conch-shell horn. (DOG *yips excitedly*.)

HOMOKU: An excellent idea.

QUEEN: Hm-m-m. If the dog can do this, he and his master will go free. (DOG *barks excitedly.* NANI *gives coconut to* DOG, *who takes it in his mouth and exits left. Curtain*)

* * * * *

SCENE 3

TIME: *A short time later.*

SETTING: *Before curtain. The cliffs where the evil spirits live.*

AT RISE: *The three evil spirits,* AKUA, PAPUA, *and* TURI, *enter from the back of audience, jumping and frolicking. They move down aisle and onto stage, squealing in high-pitched tones.* PAPUA *carries conch-shell horn.*

AKUA (*Pointing to audience*): Look! Look! There in the Waipio Valley! Queen Lukia has wrapped her head in a cloth!

PAPUA: She doesn't want to hear us play her horn. (*Blows loud blast on horn*)

TURI: Soon she will be so distracted that we will be able to swoop into the valley and take over everything! (DOG *enters, left, with coconut. He puts it down and barks.*)

AKUA (*In surprise*): What is this animal doing here?

PAPUA (*To* DOG): How dare you come to our cliff?

TURI: Let's use our magical powers to turn him into a banana! (DOG *plays with coconut, knocking it back and forth between his front paws, then rolls it toward them.*)

AKUA: The dog has come to play with us.

PAPUA: Let's play a game of catch!

TURI: What fun! What fun!

AKUA (*To* DOG): Here—roll the ball to me. (DOG *rolls coconut to* AKUA.) Here—catch! (*Rolls coconut to* TURI)

PAPUA: Roll it to me! Roll it to me! (TURI *rolls coconut to* PAPUA, *who puts conch-shell horn on ground and catches coconut.* DOG *barks.*)

TURI: Roll it to the dog. (PAPUA *rolls ball to* DOG.)

AKUA: This is fun! (DOG *gets coconut and rolls it into aisle.* AKUA, PAPUA, *and* TURI *scramble after it into aisle.* DOG *creeps across stage, picks up horn, and exits quickly.* AKUA *gets coconut and runs onto stage, with* PAPUA *and* TURI *following.*) Catch! (*Rolls coconut to* TURI)

TURI: This is more fun than the conch-shell horn. (*Rolls coconut to* PAPUA)

AKUA (*Suddenly*): Where is the conch shell? (*Looks around*)

PAPUA: It has disappeared!

TURI: The creature must have stolen it. Shall we go after it?

PAPUA: No, it is more fun to play catch. I was tired of blowing the horn, anyway. (*They toss coconut to each other, as curtain falls.*)

* * * * *

SCENE 4

TIME: *Immediately following.*

SETTING: *Same as Scene 1.*

AT RISE: NANI, QUEEN, WORKERS, *and* HOMOKU *are onstage. Slow drum beat is heard from offstage.* DOG *enters, with conch-shell horn in his mouth.*

1ST WORKER: Look! Look!

2ND WORKER: The dog is bringing back the Queen's horn! (DOG *crosses to* QUEEN *and drops horn at her feet.*)

QUEEN (*Patting* DOG): You have returned my royal conch-shell horn, little dog. You and your master are free. (DOG *barks and crosses to sit by* HOMOKU.) You have done me such a great service that I hereby give you part of my royal taro patch, to use whenever you want poi.

NANI: Please, stepsister, may I go with the dog and his master, to help them? I can make poi for old Homoku, and the rest of the time, I can play coconut ball with the little dog, Puapualenalena!

HOMOKU: This would please me greatly, Your Majesty. (DOG *barks*.)

QUEEN: It is a good plan. I agree!

WORKERS: Long live the Queen! Hooray for Nani! Hooray for Homoku! Hooray for the little dog, Puapualenalena! (HOMOKU *and* NANI *wave, then exit with* DOG *following them. Hawaiian music is heard.* QUEEN *and* WORKERS *begin to do hula dance. Sound of thunder is heard from offstage.*)

1ST WORKER: What was that noise?

QUEEN: It is the evil spirits on the cliff. They are playing a game with the coconut ball that the little dog gave them! (*Curtain*)

THE END

(*Production Notes on page 318*)

The Green Glass Ball

An Irish folktale

by Hazel W. Corson

Characters

TINKER
DONKEY
TERRY
TWO WOMEN
BOY
GIRL
TWO MEN
MIKE
BOY'S MOTHER
OLD WOMAN
TIM

SCENE 1

TIME: *Long ago.*
SETTING: *A small village in Ireland.*
AT RISE: TINKER *and* DONKEY *enter right and walk slowly to center.*

TINKER: 'Tis a beautiful day. The sun is shining! The birds are singing!

DONKEY: That's all right for you to say! All you have to do is stroll around without a care in the world while I have to carry a heavy pack.

TINKER: Oh, I work, too. And we both have a chance to move about, meeting people and hearing the news. Isn't that better than staying on a farm, plowing the same field and talking to the same three people day after day?

DONKEY: I suppose so. (*Looks around*) Here we come to a village.

TINKER: I can see that you are in a bad mood this morning, donkey. Cheer up! Things aren't that bad. Who knows what the day will bring? (TINKER *and* DONKEY *stop at center.* TINKER *shouts in a loud, sing-song voice.*) Any rags, any bottles, any bones today? Scissors sharpened! Knives ground! Pots and pans mended! I buy old rags, old bottles, old bones! (*He takes pack off* DONKEY's *back and sets it on ground. He takes small grindstone and iron kettle out of pack.* TERRY *enters carrying hoe, goes up to* TINKER.)

TERRY: Good morning, tinker.

TINKER: Good morning, lad.

TERRY: Can you use a boy to travel with you and help you, and learn to be a tinker?

TINKER (*Doubtfully*): Well, I don't know. What is your name, lad?

TERRY: My name is Terry, sir.

TINKER: You are a likely-looking lad, Terry, and could make a good tinker, if you tried.

TERRY: Then you'll take me?

TINKER (*Shaking head*): No, my lad, I'm sorry. I have a young nephew, Tim, who is lame. There are many things that Tim cannot do, but he could be a tinker, and I plan to teach him.

TERRY: But how can Tim walk about the country?

TINKER: I must find a way for him to ride. Someday in my travels, I'll find someone with a cart to sell or trade. But you must keep trying to learn a trade, Terry. Be your own man. (1ST WOMAN *enters, carrying a pot and sack.* TERRY *stands back, and watches* TINKER.)

1ST WOMAN: Good morning, tinker. Here is a pot I've been saving for you to mend. (*Hands* TINKER *pot*)

TINKER: A good morning to you. (*Looks the pot over*) There's many a good soup been cooked in that pot, I'll be bound.

1ST WOMAN: Yes. And there'll be many a good soup to come, if you can fix it.

TINKER: It can be fixed, and it will still be a better pot than you can buy today. I've heard there's a new ironmonger in the next village who makes good wares, but I've not seen his work.

2ND WOMAN: That would be young Jock. He's an honest lad, and will do a good job of work at anything he tries. (TINKER *finishes mending pot, looks it over, and gives it to* 1ST WOMAN.)

TINKER: There you are, ma'am. That should serve you for a good long time.

1ST WOMAN: Thank you, tinker. What do I owe you?

TINKER: Fourpence would be about right.

1ST WOMAN: And cheap enough, too. I don't have fourpence, but here is a sack of potatoes. They should be worth fourpence. (DONKEY *stamps feet impatiently as* TINKER *takes sack.* 2ND WOMAN *enters, carrying basket.*)

TINKER: Thank you. One can always eat potatoes.

2ND WOMAN (*Stepping forward*): Here are some knives to sharpen, tinker.

TINKER: I'll gladly sharpen them. (*He takes knives and pretends to sharpen them on his grindstone. As he works,* BOY, *carrying kettle and sack, and* GIRL *with wooden doll enter right.* TWO MEN *enter left. All gather around* TINKER.) A dull knife can be as dangerous as a sharp one, you know. (MIKE *rushes in right.* TERRY *ducks down behind others, and exits quickly.*)

MIKE: Has anyone seen that good-for-nothing lad, Terry?

1ST MAN: And where should Terry be, Mike?

MIKE (*Angrily*): Hoeing beans in my field—that's where he *should* be!

2ND MAN: Maybe that's where he is.

MIKE: I doubt it!

TINKER: And what is this Terry to you, sir?

MIKE: He is a boy I keep out of the kindness of my heart, because he belongs to no one. And a great worry he is, with his hungry mouth and his shiftless ways.

TINKER: Then why not take him to young Jock, the ironmonger, in the next village? He may need a boy.

2ND MAN: Aye. Jock *is* looking for a likely boy.

MIKE: I may do that. The boy will never make a farmer! (*Stomps off*)

TINKER (*To* 2ND WOMAN): Now, here are your knives, ma'am. Be careful. Very sharp they are. (*Hands them to* 2ND WOMAN)

2ND WOMAN: Thank you, tinker. How much do I owe you?

TINKER: Sixpence, all told.

2ND WOMAN: I have no money, but here are some cabbages that should be worth sixpence. (*Hands him cabbages from basket*)

TINKER: Thank you, ma'am. (DONKEY *stamps.*)

BOY: My mother wants to know if you can mend her kettle. All she has to pay is this bag of apples. (TINKER *takes kettle and examines it.*)

TINKER: I guess I can do it. It isn't a very big hole. (*Starts to work on kettle*)

1ST MAN: How is the haying around the country coming on, tinker?

TINKER: It looks like a good crop this year, but with all the rain, hard to dry. It doesn't do to put green hay in a barn, or even in a haycock. The hay heats up and may catch on fire. Why, only last week such a thing happened to Jim Kelly. His barn was filled with green hay and it caused a fire.

2ND MAN: What a terrible thing!

TINKER (*Handing kettle to* BOY): Here you are, my lad.

BOY: Thank you, tinker. (*Takes kettle, but stays to watch*)

GIRL: My doll has a broken leg, tinker. Can you fix her? (TINKER *looks at doll, hunts through his pockets.*)

TINKER: Now, I have no wood like that at all. Do you have the broken leg, by any chance?

GIRL: Here it is. (*Hands it to him*)

TINKER: Well, that's not bad. (*He works on doll.*) I'll make a little hole here, and one here. Now a bit of wire to fasten it together, and here she is. She can bend her knee now. (*Hands doll back*)

GIRL: Oh, thank you, tinker. Here is a pretty pebble for you. It is my good luck pebble.

TINKER (*Taking pebble*): Thank you. It is a very pretty pebble. (DONKEY *stamps.*)

BOY'S MOTHER (*Rushing in*): So here you are! I've been

waiting for that kettle! (*Takes* BOY *by ear and leads him offstage.* TINKER *starts to pack up his things.*)

1ST MAN: I'd better go, or my wife will be after me by the ear. (*As he exits*) Come again soon, tinker. You always bring us news.

2ND MAN: 'Twas a good thing you did for young Terry. I'll put in a good word with Jock for the boy myself. Now I must be off, too. Goodbye, tinker. (*He exits, followed by* GIRL *and* WOMEN.)

TINKER (*Waving*): Goodbye. (OLD WOMAN *hobbles on, carrying kettle.*)

OLD WOMAN (*In a quavering voice*): Can you fix my kettle, tinker?

TINKER (*Examining kettle*): Now, that is as old a kettle as I have ever seen, but still, a good kettle. Yes, I can fix it.

OLD WOMAN: Many a year has that kettle hung in the fireplace, and strange stories it could tell. (TINKER *works on kettle and soon finishes.*)

TINKER: Here is your kettle, Mother.

OLD WOMAN: Bless you, tinker. It has been many a year since anyone called me "Mother." "Old Witch Blakewell," but never "Mother."

TINKER: The more shame to them for their bad manners, Mother.

OLD WOMAN (*Taking kettle and looking it over*): Now that is a fine job of mending. I can see that you are no ordinary tinker.

TINKER: Thank you. That will be fourpence.

OLD WOMAN: I have no money to pay you, tinker, but you have been so kind to a poor old woman that I will give you a special gift. (*She takes green glass ball from her pocket and hands it to* TINKER. DONKEY *stamps and sniffs loudly.*)

TINKER (*Holding up ball*): This is very pretty, Mother, but neither my donkey nor I can eat it.

OLD WOMAN: Ah, but this is a magic ball, and better than food.

TINKER (*Sighing*): I know of nothing better than food.

OLD WOMAN: Hold this magic ball in your hand and make a wish—and one wish only—for the thing you want most in the world, and that wish will come true.

TINKER: Oh, I don't believe it.

OLD WOMAN: It is true. The fairies made this ball many years ago and gave it to a mortal. Since then, it has passed from person to person, each one making one wish. I was the last to have it, and now it will be yours.

TINKER: Why didn't you wish for gold when you had the chance, Mother? Then you could be paying me now.

OLD WOMAN: Alas, I wished my one wish when I was young, and it was not a kind wish or a generous wish and little good it did me. Think well before you wish and perhaps you will fare better than I. And remember, wishes can be dangerous. No good comes from them, unless you make the wish for someone else. (*She exits.*)

TINKER (*Watching her exit*): Well, donkey, now we have a green glass ball, and one wish.

DONKEY (*Crossly*): And much good may it do us. (*Curtain*)

* * * * *

SCENE 2

TIME: *A short while later.*

SETTING: *A country road. Scene is played before curtain.*

AT RISE: TINKER *and* DONKEY *enter right and walk to center.*

TINKER: It's been a good day, donkey. Jock the ironmonger will take young Terry, we will be getting home early, and a fine lot of business we did today!

DONKEY: If you call it business—listening to a lot of chatterboxes.

TINKER: Everyone brought me something to mend or sharpen.

DONKEY: Yes, and not so much as one tuppence in the lot of them.

TINKER: They all gave me something—potatoes, apples, cabbages—

DONKEY (*In disgust*): And the green glass ball! That was the most useless thing of all!

TINKER: I am not so sure of that.

DONKEY: Well, I am. Pray, what am I to eat tonight?

TINKER: There is plenty of grass to eat, and I know you always like a fine red apple.

DONKEY: You should have kept the old woman's kettle, and exchanged it for oats for me.

TINKER: Donkey, you have been complaining all day. Look—here comes Tim to meet us. Be done with your complaints. (TIM *enters. He pats* DONKEY *on head and smiles at* TINKER.)

TIM: Donkey, I suppose you and Uncle have been quarreling. What is it this time?

DONKEY: The usual thing. I can't teach him anything. He works for nothing. Today we did not take in even one coin.

TINKER: But we did a good day's work, and are better off than we were this morning. Besides, we have a magic ball.

TIM: A magic ball?

TINKER: See how beautiful it is, and how the light

shines through it. (*Holds up ball*)

DONKEY: Humph! You said yourself that we can't eat it.

TINKER: True enough! But something beautiful is worth any price.

TIM: How did you get it?

TINKER: An old woman gave it to me for mending her kettle. She said I must hold it in my hand and make a wish—only one wish—for the thing I want most in the world, and it will come true.

TIM: Are you going to try it?

TINKER: I am, indeed! I have been waiting for you to help me. Now, what shall I wish for?

TIM: Don't you think you should put the ball down until you are ready to wish, Uncle? It would be too bad to wish by accident.

TINKER: True enough. (*They all sit, with* DONKEY *in front of curtain opening.* TINKER *places ball in front of him.*)

TIM: What do you want most?

DONKEY: Why don't you wish for a lot of money? Then you could buy me oats every day.

TINKER: Money isn't everything. Why don't I wish for a fine cart?

DONKEY: So I can pull it around the country, I suppose. No, thank you.

TINKER: If you are so smart, what would you have me wish for?

DONKEY: Why don't you wish to be a king? Then I could be the king's donkey. I would have a fine stable to live in, and grooms to care for me. What a life!

TINKER: What a life indeed! A king has many worries. He may live in a fine palace, with many servants, and fine food, but a king can never be sure who his friends are. That is a stupid wish, donkey. (TINKER *picks up ball and watches light shine on it.*)

DONKEY (*Angrily*): So now you say I am stupid! I don't know what you would do without me to help you. If it were not for me, you would starve. Stupid, indeed!

TINKER (*Angrily, to* DONKEY): I have listened to your scolding all this day. I wish you were at the ends of the earth! (*There is a crash, then a bang.* DONKEY *disappears through opening of curtain.*)

TIM (*Standing*): Oh, Uncle! What have you done?

TINKER (*Jumping up*): I didn't mean it! I forgot that the ball was in my hands. How could I know that the wish would really come true? 'Twas only a little old woman who said so! What can I do?

TIM (*Slowly*): Do you think I could have a wish?

TINKER: I don't know why not.

TIM: Then I will wish for donkey to be back.

TINKER: Oh, Tim! 'Twould please me greatly to have the donkey back, cross as he is, sometimes. But what about you? Would you not like to be cured of your lameness?

TIM: I would rather have the donkey back, and see you happy again, Uncle. Let me give my wish to you and the donkey. (TINKER *gives ball to* TIM, *who places it carefully on ground.*)

TINKER: Wish carefully then, Tim. (*Puts ball into* TIM'S *hands, and leans forward, anxiously*)

TIM (*Slowly*): I wish the tinker's little donkey back alive and well. (*There is a crash, then a bang, and* DONKEY *bursts in through curtains.*)

DONKEY (*Angrily*): What a trick to play on your faithful donkey! How could you be so thoughtless? Now you have wasted your wish!

TIM: But, donkey, we used *my* wish to bring you back. If you are going to be so bad-tempered, we shall be sorry that we didn't leave you at the ends of the earth. (DONKEY *hangs his head.*)

TINKER: Oh, my poor little donkey. How glad I am to have you back! Are you all right?

DONKEY (*Thoughtfully*): Yes, I guess I'm all right. It's too bad we lost the wishes. It was my fault. I complained too much.

TINKER: It was as much my fault. I lost my temper. (TINKER *hugs* DONKEY.)

TIM: What are you going to do with the ball now, Uncle?

TINKER: It isn't any good to us any more, and somehow it doesn't seem beautiful to me now. I'll toss it away. (*Starts to throw ball away*)

TIM: Wait, Uncle! Suppose someone finds it and makes a terrible wish?

DONKEY: Or a careless wish, not knowing it would come true?

TINKER: I didn't think of that. This magic ball could cause a lot of trouble. I'll smash it.

TIM: But what if each piece is magic? There might be millions of terrible wishes made.

DONKEY: That would be worse than ever! What can we do with it? (*They all think.*)

OLD WOMAN (*Calling from behind curtain*): Tinker! Tinker! (OLD WOMAN *enters.*) Oh, tinker! Such a time as I've had! Are you all right?

TINKER: Yes, Mother. I'm all right. But how did you find me? How did you get here?

OLD WOMAN: Never mind that. I've come to stop you from making a bad wish. I've been worried ever since I gave you that ball.

TINKER (*Sadly*): It's too late, Mother. I wished foolishly. If I had only wished for the cart, Tim could go with us when we travel.

OLD WOMAN: But no one was hurt by your foolish wish?

TINKER: No. Tim made a wish that fixed everything.

OLD WOMAN: What's done is done! Give me the ball. (TINKER *hands ball to* OLD WOMAN.)

TINKER: And what will you do with it?

OLD WOMAN: It is a dangerous thing. I know a place, far from here, where there is a deep bog, filled with quicksand. I will drop it in the middle of that bog.

DONKEY: When you drop the ball into the quicksand, it will drop out of sight forever.

OLD WOMAN: Yes, but it will not soon be forgotten. This green glass ball has taught us all a good lesson: Never make a mean wish. When you wish for something, make it a kind wish, a generous wish. (*She exits, as curtain falls.*)

THE END

(*Production Notes on page 319*)

The Pie and the Tart

A medieval French folktale

by Margaret Hall

Characters

PIERRE ⎫ *beggars*
LOUIS ⎭
GAUTIER, *pastry cook*
MARIANNE, *his wife*

TIME: *Long ago; winter.*
SETTING: *A village in France. The backdrop shows several houses facing street. At left is shop, with sign above door reading,* GAUTIER, PASTRY COOK. *A low wall is at right. A bench stands center.*
AT RISE: PIERRE *and* LOUIS, *two ragged beggars, enter from opposite sides of stage and meet at center.*
PIERRE: Good day, Louis. (*Shivering*) Br-r-r! (*Walks rapidly, clutching arms to chest*)
LOUIS: Good day, Pierre. What is the matter?
PIERRE: I am so cold, I can't stand still. And the wind blows through these rags!

LOUIS (*Sighing*): Mine are no better. My coat has more holes than a sieve.

PIERRE: If that isn't bad enough, I have not eaten all day and don't have a penny to buy bread.

LOUIS: Alas, I am starving, too.

PIERRE: There must be something for us to do.

LOUIS: I have an idea. Let's hunt for a house where we could get food and lodging for nothing. I am going to rap at all the doors and ask for charity. (LOUIS *exits right.*)

PIERRE (*To himself*): I may as well do the same. (*Crosses to door of shop and knocks.* GAUTIER *opens door.*)

GAUTIER (*Gruffly*): Yes, what is it?

PIERRE: My good sir, will you take pity on a poor, unhappy fellow who has eaten nothing for two days?

GAUTIER: I'm sorry, but my wife holds the purse, and she is not at home. (*He closes door.*)

PIERRE (*Sighing*): I should have known I would not meet with success. (*Exits left.* LOUIS *reenters, looks about, then knocks at pastry shop door.* MARIANNE *puts her head out.*)

LOUIS: Please, my good woman, have pity on a poor beggar who has not eaten for a week.

MARIANNE: My husband is not here. It is he who has the money. Come back later when he has returned. (MARIANNE *closes door.* LOUIS *shrugs and trudges toward bench. He sits, shivering, as* GAUTIER *opens shop door and steps out.*)

GAUTIER (*Calling*): Wife! (MARIANNE *comes to doorway.*) I forgot to tell you that I am going to have dinner tonight with the doctor. I promised him the large eel pie in the window. (LOUIS *watches with interest.*)

MARIANNE: I hardly like to see my beautiful pie disappear so soon. Are you taking it with you?

GAUTIER: No, I have a stop to make first. I shall send a messenger for it. (*Pauses*) I shall pay the first beggar I meet to come for the pie and deliver it. To identify himself, he must kiss your hand and say, "I've come to fetch the pie on behalf of Master Gautier." Do you understand?

MARIANNE: Of course, I understand.

GAUTIER: I must hurry, or I shall be late. Goodbye. (*Exits left.* MARIANNE *closes door.* LOUIS *jumps up and rubs his hands together eagerly.* PIERRE *enters, discouraged.*)

LOUIS: Pierre! Come quickly.

PIERRE: I will try, but hunger has left me weak. (*Walks slowly to bench*)

LOUIS (*Rubbing his hands together*): You want a good dinner, don't you?

PIERRE: I would do anything for a morsel of food.

LOUIS: If you follow my directions, you'll have more than a morsel. (PIERRE *nods.*) Knock on that door (*Points at shop*) and ask the woman to give you the pie of eels.

PIERRE: Oh, no! She will just give me blows and send me away. (*Turns away*)

LOUIS: Wait. I know it sounds like a joke, but it is true. Say, "Fair lady, I come on behalf of Master Gautier, who sends me to fetch the large eel pie." Can you remember all that?

PIERRE: Let's see. I come on behalf of Master . . . Master who?

LOUIS: Gautier. Master Gautier. Don't forget the name.

PIERRE: Master Gautier sends me to fetch the big eel pie.

LOUIS: Right, and it's very important that as soon as you ask the woman for the pie, you kiss her hand.

PIERRE (*Surprised*): Kiss her hand? What will her husband say?

LOUIS: He's left. You need not be afraid. Think of it, Pierre—a fat pie, succulent, crusty, and delicious. Hurry. I'll wait for you out here. (LOUIS *exits right.* PIERRE *crosses to door and knocks.*)

MARIANNE (*Appearing at door*): What do you want?

PIERRE: Madame, I come on behalf of Master Gautier, who sends me to fetch the great eel pie.

MARIANNE: How do I know you are the man he sent?

PIERRE: Please, Madame, allow me to kiss your hand. (*He takes her hand. She pulls it away swiftly.*)

MARIANNE: It is not worth the trouble. I am going to give you the pie. (*She exits briefly, then returns with pie and hands it to* PIERRE.)

PIERRE (*Politely*): Be assured, lady, I'll take good care of it. (MARIANNE *closes door.* PIERRE *carries pie to center stage.*) I have it! I am holding it! I see it! I feel it! (*Inhaling deeply*) What a delicious smell! What a beautiful pie, what a magnificent pie! This monarch of pies is all mine! (*He puts pie on bench, and* LOUIS *enters.*) Have you ever seen such an eel pie? *Magnifique, non?*

LOUIS: I never guessed it was so large. You have done well. Let's see how it tastes.

PIERRE: Let's go behind this wall where we can have privacy. (*They take pie and exit right.* GAUTIER *reenters left, crosses to door, knocks impatiently.*)

GAUTIER: Open the door! Marianne, where are you?

MARIANNE (*Opening door; surprised*): Why did you come back so soon? Didn't you stay at the doctor's?

GAUTIER: Nobody was there. I called, knocked, I rang

the bell, but nothing happened. (*Shrugs*) We shall
eat at home. We may as well enjoy the eel pie.

MARIANNE (*Surprised*): But you sent a man to fetch it.
He came just as you said, and I gave it to him.

GAUTIER (*Astonished*): What are you telling me? I did
not send anyone. Whom did you give it to?

MARIANNE: A beggar. He followed your instructions
exactly. He even wanted to kiss my hand.

GAUTIER: What? I don't believe you. I'll wager you have
sold it and were afraid to tell me.

MARIANNE: That is ridiculous. Calm down and go inside. (*She enters shop.*)

GAUTIER: You just wanted to play a trick on me.
(*Laughs*) I know the pie is really here. I'll get it and
put it on the table. (GAUTIER *enters shop, closing
door.* PIERRE *and* LOUIS *enter slowly, smiling happily.*)

PIERRE: What a pie! In all my life I never tasted anything so good. Tell me, what do you say to some
sweets?

LOUIS (*Interested*): I shouldn't refuse. But where can
we get any?

PIERRE: In Gautier's shop I saw a delicious apple tart.
It would be a shame to let such a tart go to common
folk, who would not appreciate it.

LOUIS: Agreed. Master Gautier is a great artist, and we
two are the only ones who can appreciate his master-
pieces. But will the trick work a second time?

PIERRE: Why not? The husband is not home yet.

LOUIS: Very well. I'll try. (PIERRE *exits right.* LOUIS *goes
to door and knocks.* MARIANNE *opens it.*) Madame,
Master Gautier has sent me to fetch the apple tart.
He says the eel pie was not enough. To let you recog-
nize me, he asks me to kiss your hand. (LOUIS *takes
 MARIANNE's hand. She pulls it away.*)

MARIANNE (*Suspiciously*): Very well, I shall give you the tart. But didn't he also tell you to bring a bottle?

LOUIS: You are right; I forgot. He wants two bottles of that fine grape juice that came from his own vines.

MARIANNE: I'll fetch them from the cellar. (MARIANNE *enters shop, closes door.* LOUIS *walks back and forth.*)

LOUIS: This woman is really easy to fool. (GAUTIER *opens door, a stick in his hand.*)

GAUTIER (*Collaring* LOUIS): Rascal! Bandit! Where is my pie? You are the one who stole it!

LOUIS (*Terrified*): Monsieur, someone has lied to you! I never took your pie. I swear it!

GAUTIER (*Raising his stick*): Rascal! Villain! Thief!

LOUIS (*Cowering*): Sir, I beg you, don't strike me, and I'll tell you where your pie is.

GAUTIER (*Shaking him*): Well, speak up.

LOUIS: Here is what happened. My friend Pierre heard you tell your wife, as you were leaving, that you would send someone to fetch the pie. He presented himself and took it. If you release me, I'll get him for you. He is not far off. I promise he will come.

GAUTIER (*Releasing* LOUIS): Then have him hurry. I'll wait for you in the shop. (GAUTIER *enters shop, closing door.* LOUIS *starts to exit right, as* PIERRE *enters.*)

PIERRE: Where is the tart?

LOUIS: She didn't want to give it to me. She said she would only give the tart to the same person who took the pie.

PIERRE: Well, that is simple enough. I shall get it myself. (LOUIS *exits right.* PIERRE *knocks at door.* MARIANNE *opens it.*) Your husband sent me to fetch the tart. He told me to hurry.

MARIANNE (*Feigning surprise*): Is it you again? Well, wait a moment. I'll go get it. (*She reenters shop, closes door.*)

GAUTIER (*Flinging open door*): You stole my pie. I am going to have you arrested. (*Seizes* PIERRE *by the collar.* PIERRE *struggles to escape.*)

PIERRE: Stop, stop—don't hit me! Let me explain.

GAUTIER: What have you to say?

PIERRE: I heard you say that you needed someone to take the pie to the doctor. I wanted to spare you the trouble of waiting, and so I carried your message to your wife. She gave the pie to me, and I ran to the doctor's, hoping for a little reward.

GAUTIER: You are lying. The doctor was not at home.

PIERRE: Sir, I beg pardon. The doctor asked me to tell you that he had to go out to see a patient, and he would return in an hour.

GAUTIER (*Reflecting*): Ah, I understand now. That explains why I found nobody there.

PIERRE: And the doctor asked me also to fetch the apple tart, which he wanted for dessert. I was tired of running, so I asked my friend to do the second errand in my place.

GAUTIER: Why didn't he explain this to me? I regret having treated him roughly. Well, you run off, and tell the doctor I shall arrive in five minutes. He must surely have returned by now.

PIERRE: May I take the tart?

GAUTIER: Yes, I have confidence in you. (*He exits briefly, returns with tart and hands it to* PIERRE.)

PIERRE: Thank you, sir. (GAUTIER *closes door.* PIERRE *crosses right, meeting* LOUIS, *as he enters.*)

LOUIS (*Astonished*): You have the tart! (*Shop door opens.* PIERRE *and* LOUIS *rush off right.* GAUTIER *is speaking to wife, as he walks out door.*)

GAUTIER: Now, Marianne, I am going for good this time. By the way, if the doctor wants grape juice, I shall send the same person to fetch a bottle or two.

You will recognize him now. Goodbye. (GAUTIER *closes door and exits left*. PIERRE *and* LOUIS *reenter right, carrying tart, and cross to bench stealthily. They sit and greedily eat tart.*)

PIERRE: Now, this is what I call living! A free meal, to be topped off by fresh juice of the grape, from the finest vineyards in France!

LOUIS: With two such clever minds combined, we should be able to eat this royally for many days to come. Tomorrow we shall try another pastry shop! (*Curtain*)

THE END

(Production Notes on page 319)

Night of the Trolls

A Norwegian folktale

by Suzanne Rahn

Characters

ERIC ERICSSON, *a boy*
BEAR
LARS LARSSEN
LOTTE LARSSEN, *his wife*
TROLL KING
THREE TROLLS

SCENE 1

SETTING: *Mountain country of Norway. Backdrop shows snowy mountains and pine trees.*

AT RISE: ERIC *enters, playing a tune on his whistle. He is followed by* BEAR, *walking on all fours.*

ERIC: Come on, old bear! Can't you walk a little faster? It's a long way to the next village. And it's getting dark. We don't want to be caught out of doors when night falls. (BEAR *grunts loudly and sits up.*) Yes, I know you're hungry. You're not the only one! But there isn't a scrap of food. You'll just have to wait. (BEAR *groans and drops to all fours again. He and*

ERIC *continue across stage, but after only a few steps,* LARS *and* LOTTE *enter right, carrying bundles.)*

LARS: Good heavens! It's a bear!

LOTTE (*To* ERIC): Run, boy, run!

LARS (*To* LOTTE): Get behind a tree! (LOTTE *runs behind tree.*) I'll kill him with my ax! (ERIC *quickly steps between* BEAR *and* LARS.)

ERIC: Stop! Don't hurt him! He's my bear, and he's perfectly tame.

LARS (*Doubtfully*): Are you sure?

ERIC: Just watch! (*He turns to* BEAR.) Roll over! (BEAR *lies down and rolls over.*) Sit up! (BEAR *sits up.*) Play dead! (BEAR *falls over and lies motionless.*)

LARS: Amazing! (LOTTE *comes out of hiding.*)

ERIC (*To* BEAR): All right, you're alive again. (BEAR *gets up, and* ERIC *pats him. To* LARS *and* LOTTE) I don't know what I'd do without my bear. I have no parents, so he's all the family I have.

LOTTE: You poor boy! What is your name?

ERIC: Eric Ericsson, ma'am.

LARS: I'm Lars Larssen.

LOTTE: And I'm Lotte Larssen, his wife. How do you manage, Eric, with no one to look after you?

ERIC: Well, my bear and I travel from village to village, all over Norway. I play my whistle, and Bear does tricks and dances.

LARS: Can you make a good living that way?

ERIC (*Reluctantly*): Not too good. The trouble is, most people don't stay long enough to watch. They see Bear coming, and zoom—they're gone! I hope we'll have better luck on the other side of the mountains.

LOTTE: I wish we could offer you a place to sleep! But you see how it is. We've had to leave home ourselves.

ERIC: Why?

LARS (*In a low voice*): Trolls!

ERIC: Trolls?

LARS: Once a year on this night they come creeping out of their mountain caves, down through the trees, to our little house. They break in and eat all of our food. Then they sing and dance and romp through the house, smashing the furniture.

ERIC: What can you do about it?

LOTTE: Nothing! If we stayed home, the trolls would eat us for dessert.

LARS: We'll spend the night at our neighbor's house. (*He sighs.*) Tomorrow morning we'll go home and pick up the pieces.

LOTTE (*Sadly*): All my good dishes!

ERIC (*Suddenly struck by an idea*): Perhaps I can save your dishes!

LOTTE: What do you mean?

ERIC: Let me stay in your house tonight.

LOTTE: Oh, no!

LARS: Thanks for the offer, Eric. But we couldn't let you do that.

ERIC: Why not? I'll have my bear to protect me. Besides, I have a plan.

LARS (*Hopefully*): Really?

ERIC: If it works, I don't think those trolls will ever bother you again. There's just one thing you'll have to do. First, you'll have to hide somewhere near the house. Can you do that?

LARS: Yes. We can hide in the cowshed.

ERIC: Then, when you hear me blow my whistle, you must both come running and pound on the door of the house as hard as you can.

LARS (*Doubtfully*): All right, but I don't see what good it'll do.

ERIC: You'll see! But we'll have to hurry—the sun is setting.

LOTTE (*Still hesitating*): You will be careful, won't you, Eric?

ERIC: I'll be careful. Come on, Bear! (*All exit right, as curtain falls.*)

* * * * *

SCENE 2

SETTING: *The Larssens' cottage. A large table with cloth that hangs nearly to floor is at center. On wall is shelf with bowl and pitcher. A large wooden door is on one side. A fireplace, cupboards, benches complete setting.*

AT RISE: ERIC *and* BEAR *enter through door and look around.*

ERIC: Nice place, isn't it, old Bear? (*He sighs.*) Makes me feel homesick. (BEAR *grunts and sits up, waving his paws.*) All you can think about is food! Well, maybe I can find you a little milk. Lotte told me to help myself. (*He takes pitcher and bowl off shelf and pours some milk into bowl. He sets bowl in corner, and* BEAR *crouches to drink milk.* ERIC *yawns.*) I'm too tired to eat. I'd like to take a nap. But the trolls may come. Do you know something, Bear? I'm not looking forward to meeting those trolls. In fact, I'm scared. (BEAR *comes over to him and nuzzles him affectionately.* ERIC *pats him.*) That's my good old Bear! (*Notices table and peers under it*) Say, Bear, this table looks like a safe place to hide. Let's crawl under here and get some sleep. (*He crawls under table and* BEAR *follows him.*) Wake me up when the trolls get here. (*After a brief silence, wild whoops are heard outside door. Door is flung open, and* TROLLS *rush in, running and leaping around room, shoving furniture around. Suddenly* TROLL KING *holds up his hand.*)

TROLL KING: Stop! Do you smell something funny? (TROLLS *stop and sniff loudly.*)

1ST TROLL: Yes! Something very funny!

2ND TROLL: I smell it, too!

3RD TROLL: What could it be, Your Majesty?

TROLL KING: It smells to me like (*Sniffs again*)— human being!

1ST TROLL: Boy or girl?

TROLL KING (*Sniffing*): Boy. Right here in this room! (TROLLS *begin searching room, sniffing as they go.* TROLL KING *moves toward table.*) Warmer . . . warmer . . . aha! He's under that table! Drag him out! (TROLLS *pull* ERIC *out.*)

TROLLS: Mm-m-m, yum-yum!

TROLL KING: What a fine surprise. (*Laughs evilly*) I hope you will stay for supper, my boy.

ERIC (*Boldly*): Of course—as long as my little dog can stay, too.

TROLL KING: A little dog? (*He turns to others.*) Well, why not?

1ST TROLL: Yes, why not?

3RD TROLL: Dogs are quite tasty!

TROLL KING: So they are! (*Looks around*) Where is this little dog of yours?

ERIC: Oh, he's right here. (*Bends down to look under table.*) Come on—that's a good little fellow! Come on out! (BEAR *crawls out from under table, facing* TROLLS. *They all leap backward at once.*)

1ST TROLL: Help!

3RD TROLL: A monster!

TROLL KING (*Laughing nervously*): Ho-ho! That's a fine dog, a very fine dog. Does he bite? (TROLL KING *edges closer to* BEAR *and reaches out to pat him.* BEAR *rears up on his hind legs and growls loudly.* TROLLS *all cower against wall.*)

ERIC (*Smiling*): I should have told you—he's not friendly to trolls.

TROLL KING: Just tell me one thing. Why do you call him your "little" dog?

2ND TROLL: Yes, why? He's the biggest dog I ever saw!

ERIC: If you think this dog is big, you should see his brother!

TROLL KING: His brother?

ERIC: Yes, his brother! His brother's five times as big, and ten times as heavy. If he sat down on this house, he'd smash it flat. He's still just a puppy. You should see his mother!

TROLLS (*Together*): His mother?

ERIC: Yes, his mother! His mother could swallow this house in one gulp. She's got a nasty temper, too. (*Suddenly*) Listen!

TROLL KING: What is it?

ERIC: She must be somewhere near. I can hear the mountains shaking. Shall I call her? Then you can see her for yourselves.

TROLLS (*Together*): No! No! (ERIC *blows loudly on his whistle.*)

ERIC: Here she comes! She's getting closer—closer. She's at the door! (*A thunderous knocking is heard.* TROLLS, *howling with terror, run madly in all directions, falling over each other. Still howling, they leap off front of stage into aisle or run off right and left.* LARS *and* LOTTE *burst in through door.*)

LARS: That noise! What's happening?

ERIC: Come in! It's all right. You scared off the trolls, that's all.

LOTTE: Just by knocking on the door?

ERIC: They were nervous.

LARS: I don't know how you did it, but I'm very grateful. I wish we had a son like you.

LOTTE: We've never had any children of our own. And we like you, Eric.

LARS: We'd like you to stay with us and live as our own son. Someday, this farm will be yours.

ERIC: Why—that would be wonderful! But what about Bear? Can he stay too?

LARS: We need a watchdog. And (*Laughing*) something tells me he'd make a good one.

LOTTE: Of course, he can stay! (*She pats* BEAR's *head.*)

ERIC: Then I can promise you one thing—you've seen the last of the trolls! (*Curtain*)

THE END

(*Production Notes on page 319*)

Big Cat, Little Cat, Old Man Monkey

A Japanese folktale

by Gillian L. Plescia

Characters

NARRATOR
BIG CAT
LITTLE CAT
MASTER OWL
OLD MAN MONKEY

TIME: *Long ago.*
SETTING: *A bare stage. A stool stands at one side of stage.*
AT RISE: NARRATOR *enters, bows to audience.*
NARRATOR: Honorable ladies and gentlemen, welcome. Today we bring you a play from Japan. It is about two cats, Big Cat and Little Cat. Now, these two cats were the very best of friends, until, one day—well, watch and see what happened one day. It was a day that started out like any other. The two friends were playing together as usual. (NARRATOR *bows and sits on stool. Large ball of yarn rolls onstage.* BIG CAT

249

enters and pounces on it, then picks it up. LITTLE CAT
runs in.)

BIG CAT: Here, Little Cat, catch this! (*Throws ball of
yarn.*)

LITTLE CAT (*Catching it*): Meow! Got it! Now it's your
turn. (*Rolls ball along ground.* BIG CAT *chases it and
pounces on it again.*)

BIG CAT: Meow! Ha! This is fun!

LITTLE CAT: Yes, it is. But tiring too. Pouf! Let's rest for
a while. (*They sit on ground.*) We certainly do have
fun playing together, don't we?

BIG CAT: Yes. No one has a better time than we do. It's
good to have a friend.

LITTLE CAT (*Grinning*): And we'll always be friends,
won't we, Big Cat?

BIG CAT: Of course! Nothing can change that. (*They sit
contentedly, cleaning faces and whiskers with their
paws. Then* BIG CAT *sighs.*) My, my! All that exercise
has made me hungry. Do you have anything to eat?

LITTLE CAT: Not a thing. I wish I had. My stomach's
quite empty.

BIG CAT: Meow! So's mine.

LITTLE CAT: Meow! (*They sit meowing mournfully.*
MASTER OWL *enters.*)

MASTER OWL: My, my, young cats. What a noise you are
making. What is the matter? Are you lost?

BIG CAT: No.

OWL: Then are your stomachs hurting?

LITTLE CAT: Our stomachs are empty!

BIG CAT: And we have no food with us.

OWL: Ah, well, then that is a problem easily solved. I
have food here in my pack, left over from my own
dinner. You are welcome to it. (*Opens pack and takes
out two cakes*) Here—two rice cakes. One for you
(*Gives larger cake to* LITTLE CAT)—and one for you.

(*Gives smaller cake to* BIG CAT) There now. That should fill your stomachs for a while.

LITTLE CAT: Oh, thank you, Master Owl.

BIG CAT: We are very grateful.

OWL: You are most welcome. And now, I must be on my way, as I have a long way to go. Farewell, and enjoy your meal.

LITTLE CAT: Goodbye.

BIG CAT: And thanks again. (OWL *exits.*)

LITTLE CAT: That was a lucky chance. A whole rice cake each. Oh, it looks delicious!

BIG CAT: Mine, too. Look—plump and delicious. (*Shows cake*)

LITTLE CAT: But look at mine. Even plumper.

BIG CAT (*Looking back and forth at cakes*): Why, so it is. Master Owl must have made a mistake. It is clear that I should have the larger cake. After all, I am the larger cat. Here, let's exchange.

LITTLE CAT: Now, just a moment. I don't think there was a mistake. You are larger, it is true, but that was why he gave me the larger cake. I need to grow.

BIG CAT: That's nonsense. Just give me the cake and let's say no more about it. (*Stretches out paw for cake.* LITTLE CAT *hisses and moves cake out of reach.*) You *hissed* at me!

LITTLE CAT (*Loudly*): Just keep your paws off my cake!

BIG CAT: I thought you were my friend. Friends don't hiss at each other.

LITTLE CAT: And I thought you were *my* friend. Friends don't try to snatch each other's cakes.

BIG CAT: I wasn't snatching. I was exchanging. I'm bigger and I should have the bigger cake.

LITTLE CAT: No!

BIG CAT: Yes!

LITTLE CAT: No! Meow! Hiss-s-s-s!

BIG CAT: Meow! Hiss-s-s-s! (*They eye each other angrily, clutching cakes in their paws. Then* BIG CAT *moves back.*) This is ridiculous. We're quarreling—over two rice cakes.

LITTLE CAT: Yes, it's really very silly.

BIG CAT: And we could solve it so easily. If you'd just hand over the big cake, everything would be settled.

LITTLE CAT: No! (*Moves away. They glare at each other again.* LITTLE CAT *looks at rice cake and shakes his head.*) We'll have to solve this quarrel soon, or the rice cakes will be all dried up. What shall we do?

BIG CAT: We could ask Old Man Monkey. I hear he's very good at settling quarrels.

LITTLE CAT: Good! Let's go see him now. The sooner we settle this, the sooner we can enjoy the rice cakes. (*They exit.* NARRATOR *comes forward.*)

NARRATOR: And so Big Cat and Little Cat went into the forest to see Old Man Monkey. Now, Old Man Monkey was very wise, but spent a good deal of time sleeping. And that is exactly what he was doing when Big Cat and Little Cat came to see him. (NARRATOR *returns to stool.* CATS *enter, carrying rice cakes.*)

BIG CAT: This is where Old Man Monkey lives.

LITTLE CAT (*Calling*): Oh, Mr. Monkey. Old Man Monkey!

BIG CAT: We have a favor to ask you.

LITTLE CAT: We need your wisdom to settle a quarrel.

BIG CAT (*Loudly*): Meow!

LITTLE CAT (*Even more loudly*): Meow! (*They continue to meow until* OLD MAN MONKEY *enters, yawning, stretching, and looking cross.*)

OLD MAN MONKEY: My, my! And what can be the matter with you two young cats? I've never heard such a commotion in my whole life.

BIG CAT: We want you to settle our quarrel.

LITTLE CAT: So we can be friends again.

MONKEY: Oh? And what is the quarrel about?

BIG CAT: It's about these two rice cakes Master Owl gave us. He made a mistake and gave Little Cat the larger cake, when I clearly should have it, since I am the larger cat.

LITTLE CAT: It wasn't a mistake. I need to eat more so I can grow, and that's why he gave me the larger cake.

MONKEY: Ah, is that all? That is a quarrel I can easily settle. Wait here a minute while I fetch my scales. (*He exits.*)

BIG CAT: Good. Soon we shall be able to eat our cakes. My mouth is watering at the thought.

LITTLE CAT: I certainly hope he hurries. I'm getting hungrier every minute. (MONKEY *returns with balance scales.*)

MONKEY: Now, give me the cakes. (CATS *do so, and he places them on scales.*) Aha! This one is larger. That is very easy to fix. I will make them the same size. (*He takes large bite of bigger cake.*)

LITTLE CAT (*Taken aback*): Oh! (MONKEY *puts cake back on scales.*)

MONKEY: Hm-m-m-m. They are still not of equal size. Well, that can soon be fixed. (*He takes large bite from second cake.*)

BIG CAT: Oh! (MONKEY *replaces cake on scales again.*)

MONKEY: Hm-m-m. Still not quite equal. Ah, well. (*He get ready to bite larger cake.*)

LITTLE CAT: Oh, Mr. Monkey, do you really think this is right?

MONKEY: Hush! Do not interrupt me while I am working. You asked me to settle your quarrel. Well, I am settling it. But I can't do it if you interrupt me.

LITTLE CAT: Oh, but—(MONKEY *glares.* CATS *watch*

glumly as MONKEY *continues to take bites from each cake in turn, muttering to himself. Finally, nothing is left but one small piece.*)

MONKEY (*Slyly*): Still not quite equal. Oh, well—(*He pops last morsel into his mouth.*)

LITTLE CAT: But our cakes! Meow! You ate them all.

MONKEY: Why are you complaining? I settled your quarrel, didn't I? You were quarreling about the cakes and now the cakes are gone, so you have nothing left to quarrel about, do you?

BIG CAT: Well . . .

LITTLE CAT: I—I suppose you're right.

MONKEY: Of course, I'm right.

BIG CAT: But we're still hungry.

MONKEY: That may be, but it was not the problem you asked me to solve. Perhaps, another time, you'll settle your quarrels yourselves. (*He smacks his lips, pats his stomach and yawns.*) Incidentally, the cakes were delicious! (*He exits.* CATS *look sadly after him.*)

BIG CAT (*Sighing*): We were awfully silly.

LITTLE CAT: He's right! We could have worked it out ourselves.

BIG CAT: Let's go home now.

LITTLE CAT: Yes, let's. (*Brightening*) You know, I have a fish at home that I was saving for my supper. We can share it, if you like.

BIG CAT: And I have a bowl of milk. You can have half. Let's hurry. (*They exit.* NARRATOR *comes forward.*)

NARRATOR: So Big Cat and Little Cat shared everything equally from then on, and in that way they avoided quarrels. Honorable audience (*Bows*), with that thought, I leave you. Goodbye. (*Bows again and exits. Curtain*)

THE END

(*Production Notes on page 320*)

Barnaby the Brave

An English folktale

by Lenore Blumenfeld

Characters

BARNABY, *a baker*
MARGARET, *his wife*
MR. STRUDELMEISTER
GRANNY
TRUMPETER
BANNER BEARER $\Big\}$ *Royal Procession*
TWO FOOTMEN
KING
THIEF
MAN IN TORN SHIRT
REDHEADED MAN
REDHEADED WOMAN

SCENE 1

TIME: *Once upon a time.*
SETTING: *A village. Sign on backdrop reads,* VILLAGE OF NORTHCHESTER. *Also painted on backdrop, at right, is a bake shop, with sign above it reading* BAKE

SHOP, *and at left, a cottage. Bake shop and cottage have working doors.*

AT RISE: BARNABY, *wearing baker's hat and apron, steps out of cottage.* MARGARET *stands at doorway.*

BARNABY: Goodbye, Margaret. I'm off to set the bread to rise.

MARGARET: Goodbye, Barnaby, my dear. I'll see you this evening. (*She goes inside cottage.* BARNABY *strides toward bake shop.*)

BARNABY: Ah, the sun is smiling, and so am I—for I've a wonderful family and work I love. Yes indeed, I'm always happy when I've got my arms elbow-deep in flour and the air is thick with the fragrance of (*Inhaling*) fresh bread baking. (*Arrives at bake shop, tries to open door, but finds it locked*) What's this? The door is locked? (*Calling out*) Mr. Strudelmeister! It's Barnaby. Open up! (MR. STRUDELMEISTER *opens bake shop door slightly and comes part way out.*)

MR. STRUDELMEISTER (*Rapidly*): Barnaby, after fifty years in business, I'm finally closing the shop. Here are your wages. (*Hands him money*)

BARNABY: But you can't . . .

STRUDELMEISTER: There's nothing more to say, Barnaby. Goodbye. (*Closes door*)

BARNABY (*Stunned*): Wait, Mr. Strudelmeister! (*To himself*) It can't be! I have no job. (*Downcast, he trudges back toward cottage.*) How will I support my family? (*Arrives at cottage;* MARGARET *opens door.*)

MARGARET (*Concerned*): Barnaby, why are you home so early?

BARNABY: Margaret, prepare yourself for terrible news.

MARGARET (*Upset*): What is it, Barnaby?

BARNABY: I've lost my job.

MARGARET (*Relieved*): Oh, that's not such a catastrophe. At least you're all right.

BARNABY: Margaret, it *is* a catastrophe. How am I to earn a living? (*Holds up money*) As soon as these last wages are spent, I'll be out in the street begging for bread, instead of baking it.

MARGARET (*Cheerfully*): What a gloomy fellow you are. Surely you can find some other job.

BARNABY (*Shaking head*): Like my father and his father, I have only one skill—baking. And now that the only bake shop in Northchester is closed, I am doomed to life as a beggar.

MARGARET: Cheer up, Barnaby. Northchester is not the only village in the world. You've two sturdy feet—go take a good long walk to the next village. You'll find another bake shop to work in.

BARNABY (*Shocked*): What a ridiculous idea! Why, neither my father nor my father's father ever journeyed past the edge of that village green.

MARGARET: Then you shall be the family's first explorer.

BARNABY: Margaret, are you trying to make me into some kind of Marco Polo?

MARGARET: Indeed I am! Oh, think, Barnaby—when our baby grows up she can say to her friends, "No man in my family ever dared venture past the village green—'til my famous father, Barnaby the Brave, came along!"

BARNABY (*Musing*): Barnaby the Brave—I like the sound of that name!

MARGARET: Then go forth and earn it.

BARNABY (*With determination*): All right, I shall! Farewell, my dear. Like the great Marco Polo, I'm off to explore uncharted lands. (*He strides toward exit.*)

MARGARET (*Waving*): Farewell, Barnaby the Brave. Watch out for monsters. (BARNABY *looks alarmed, stops in his tracks, then walks back toward* MARGARET.)

BARNABY: Margaret—

MARGARET: What is it now?

BARNABY: Margaret, there may be danger lurking beyond the edge of this green.

MARGARET: There may also be golden opportunities waiting, Barnaby. You're a master baker. This is your chance to show the world your skill. (*Closes door*)

BARNABY (*Proudly*): She's right. I am a master baker. I can bake the crustiest breads, the lightest cakes— and my pastries just melt in the mouth. Wherever I go I'm sure to find a job. As for danger, why, these sturdy feet of mine can outrun any monster. (*Strides out, as curtain falls*)

* * * * *

SCENE 2

TIME: *Later.*

SETTING: *Village of Southchester. Setting is the same, except that sign over bake shop reads,* GRANNY'S PIE SHOP, *and sign on backdrop reads,* WELCOME TO SOUTHCHESTER.

AT RISE: BARNABY *enters.*

BARNABY (*Looking around*): Well, after hiking all morning, I've finally reached Southchester. It reminds me of my own village. (*Spots sign over bake shop*) "Granny's Pie Shop." I wonder if Granny needs a baker? (*Knocks on door.* GRANNY *opens it.*)

GRANNY: Yes?

BARNABY: Good day, madam. I'm Barnaby the baker, looking for work.

GRANNY: What kind of pies can you bake?

BARNABY: Why, I can bake—(*Chants rapidly*)
Fruit pies, cream pies, chocolate and cheese pies—
Custard, squash, pumpkin, and mince—
Pies stuffed with partridge and peacock and pheasant—
And I even have a recipe for one made with twenty-four blackbirds!

GRANNY: Barnaby, you're just the baker I need, for the King himself wants 101 assorted pies for a breakfast banquet tomorrow. Can you bake that many before dawn?

BARNABY (*Confidently*): Of course, I can.

GRANNY: Then, come right in and get to work.

BARNABY (*Hesitantly*): Ma'am, what will my wages be for the job? I have a family to support.

GRANNY: If you get those pies baked on time, I'll pay you three times the wages you earned at your last job.

BARNABY: Triple wages! (*Happily*) Granny, lead me to your kitchen. (*They enter shop, close door. Curtain*)

* * * * *

SCENE 3

TIME: *The next morning.*

SETTING: *The same as Scene 2.*

AT RISE: *Cock crowing is heard, then trumpet fanfare. Royal Procession—TRUMPETER, BANNER BEARER, TWO FOOTMEN, and KING—march in, cross to bake shop. TRUMPETER blows trumpet. GRANNY and BARNABY come out of bake shop and stand on either side of doorway, as Royal Procession files into bake shop, then files out, each footman carrying a stack of pies.* KING *brings up the rear, carrying pie filled with blackbirds.* TRUMPETER *trumpets.* GRANNY *curtsies, and* BARNABY *bows, and Royal Procession exits.*

BARNABY: Well, Granny, now that my job's done, I'll be on my way.

GRANNY: How can I thank you, Barnaby, for staying up all night to get those pies baked for the King?

BARNABY: By giving me my wages this minute.

GRANNY: Your wages—oh, yes. Now, where's my purse? *(Pats pockets of skirt and apron)*

BARNABY: I hope you can find it, Granny, for I've a family to support.

GRANNY *(Taking purse from pocket)*: Oh, here it is. I've forgotten how much I promised to pay you.

BARNABY *(Impatiently)*: Triple wages, Granny.

GRANNY: Oh, yes—triple. *(Counts money in purse)* Thirty, forty-five, sixty—I have exactly triple wages here in my purse, so you may as well take the whole thing. *(Holds it out)*

BARNABY *(Reaching out)*: Thank you. *(Before he can take it,* GRANNY *pulls hand back.)* Hey!

GRANNY: Before I pay you, Barnaby, I must warn you— the road ahead is long, danger lurks at every turn, and money won't buy safe passage home.

BARNABY *(Suspiciously)*: Are you trying to talk me out of my hard-earned money?

GRANNY: No, I merely wish to offer you a choice. You can have your wages *(Holds out purse;* BARNABY *reaches for it, but* GRANNY *snatches it back again.)*, or you can have three pieces of good advice, guaranteed to get you home safely.

BARNABY *(Shaking his head)*: I can't support a family on good advice, Granny, so I'll take *(Snatches purse out of her grasp)*—the purse.

GRANNY: Very well. I just hope you don't run into any thieves, vandals, or bandits along the way. Goodbye. (*Goes into pie shop, closes door*)

BARNABY (*Shaking fist at door*): Sly old woman, trying to trick me out of my wages. Well, I'm Barnaby the Brave. She can't scare me with her talk of (*With each word his tone changes from defiance to anxiety to fright.*) thieves, vandals, and bandits! (*Terrified, he beats fist on pie shop door and cries out.*) Granny, open up!

GRANNY (*Opening door*): What is it, Barnaby?

BARNABY: Granny, I don't want to be robbed, beaten, or murdered, so (*Thrusting purse at her*) I'm returning your money. Now, quickly, give me your three pieces of good advice.

GRANNY: Very well. First piece of advice—don't take any shortcuts.

BARNABY (*Nodding*): No shortcuts.

GRANNY: Second piece of advice, don't accept anything from a redhead.

BARNABY (*Nodding*): No redheads.

GRANNY: Third piece of advice—just a moment, I'll be right back. (*She goes into pie shop, returns with very long loaf of bread, hands it to* BARNABY.) Take this loaf on your trip, but don't break it until you get home, when you must have your wife spread her apron to catch the crumbs.

BARNABY (*Taking loaf*): I'll remember. Thank you, Granny. Now I can start my journey with a carefree heart. Farewell, Granny.

GRANNY: Go safely, Barnaby. (*Goes into pie shop*)

BARNABY: Off I go, home to Margaret. (*Exits as curtain falls*)

* * * * *

Scene 4

Time: *Several hours later.*

Setting: *Same, except that sign over bake shop reads* jail, *and sign on backdrop reads* crimechester. *Sign also has small print that cannot be seen by audience.*

At Rise: Barnaby *staggers in, falls down.*

Barnaby: Oh, my poor feet. As soon as I get home I'll give them a good, hot soak. (*Notices jail*) Jail! I don't remember passing that. (*Peeks inside*) Nobody there. (*Gleefully*) A village with no criminals! (*Nervously*) Or maybe their criminals are too smart to get caught! (*Reads sign*) Crimechester! (*Frightened*) I'm leaving! But, which way? (*Peers at small print on sign*) "Go right to Northchester." Aha! That's the road for me! (*Reads further*) "Go left for *shortcut* to Northchester." (*Happily*) Better still! (*Starts left, then halts*) Uh-oh. Granny said no shortcuts. Then again, she's the one who tried to talk me out of my rightful wages—so I'll show her! I'll take the shortcut, anyway! (*Starts left, but stops when* Man In Torn Shirt, *holding coil of rope, runs in, followed by* Thief, *who chases after him. They run back and forth on stage.* Barnaby *takes loaf of bread and hits* Thief *on head.* Thief *falls, and* Man In Torn Shirt *ties rope around* Thief's *hands.*)

Man In Torn Shirt (*To* Barnaby): Thanks, my good man. I'd give you a reward, but I've no money. (*Points off left*) That shortcut road is lined with thieves, vandals, and bandits. Why, I was attacked three times this morning. One chap took my overcoat, another snatched my wallet, and this bloke wanted the very shirt off my back! I'm taking him right to jail. (*Pulls* Thief *to his feet*) Step lively, you! (*To*

BARNABY) Thanks again. (*Drags* THIEF *into jail*)

BARNABY (*To himself*): No wonder Granny advised me not to take the shortcut. From now on I'll follow all her advice. (*Wearily, he starts trudging right.*) Oh, I'm so weak. I haven't eaten a crumb since yesterday. (*Holds up loaf of bread*) Granny told me to keep this loaf until I get home—but if I don't eat some of it now, I'll collapse and will never get there. (*He is about to break bread when* REDHEADED MAN *comes out of cottage.*)

REDHEADED MAN: Good morning, stranger.

BARNABY (*To himself*): Hm-m-m. Granny told me to watch out for redheads. (*He turns his back on* RED-HEADED MAN. REDHEADED WOMAN *comes out of cottage, holding dish.*)

REDHEADED WOMAN: Good morning, friend. (BARNABY *looks over his shoulder.*)

BARNABY (*To himself*): Dear me. Another redhead. (*Turns away again*)

REDHEADED WOMAN: Won't you come in? (BARNABY *shakes head.*)

REDHEADED MAN· We'll give you some lunch.

BARNABY (*To himself*): Food!

REDHEADED WOMAN: We're having sausages. (*Holds out dish*)

BARNABY (*To himself*): My favorite! My mouth is watering! But I must follow Granny's advice. (*To* RED-HEADED MAN) I'm not hungry. (REDHEADED WOMAN *steps in front of* BARNABY.)

REDHEADED WOMAN: Just take one bite.

BARNABY (*Looking at dish*): I really shouldn't.

REDHEADED MAN (*Winking*): No one will ever know.

BARNABY (*Eagerly*): All right! (REDHEADED WOMAN *uncovers dish and thrusts it under* BARNABY's *nose. He recoils, holds his nose.*) That sausage smells terrible!

REDHEADED WOMAN (*Suddenly unpleasant*): What did you expect?

REDHEADED MAN (*Also unpleasantly*): If you're so hungry, you can't be fussy.

BARNABY: I don't eat smelly sausages. (REDHEADED MAN *and* REDHEADED WOMAN *advance on him.*)

REDHEADED WOMAN: Well, you're going to eat this one.

BARNABY: How do I know it's not poisoned?

REDHEADED WOMAN: You don't. (*She and* REDHEADED MAN *laugh.*)

BARNABY: I know. You're going to poison me and steal my valuables.

REDHEADED MAN *and* REDHEADED WOMAN: Right!

BARNABY: But I have no valuables.

REDHEADED MAN: I don't believe you.

BARNABY: Well, at least grant me one last wish.

REDHEADED WOMAN: Fair enough.

BARNABY: I wish to break off a piece of my bread to eat with the poisoned sausage so it won't taste so bad.

REDHEADED MAN: All right. But be quick about it. (BARNABY *whacks* REDHEADED MAN *and* REDHEADED WOMAN *over the head with loaf.*)

REDHEADED MAN *and* REDHEADED WOMAN (*Ad lib*): Oh! Ow! Stop! (*Etc. They run into cottage.*)

BARNABY (*Jubilantly flourishing loaf*): Barnaby the Brave strikes again. (*Strides off; curtain*)

* * * * *

SCENE 5

TIME: *Some time later.*

SETTING: *Same as Scene 1.*

AT RISE: BARNABY *staggers on.*

BARNABY: I just can't walk another step. (*Looks up at sign; elated*) Praise   be! Northchester! I'm home!

(*Suddenly revived, he runs to cottage*) Margaret! Gentle patient, soft-spoken Margaret! Your Barnaby the Brave is home at last! (MARGARET *opens door.*)

MARGARET (*Screeching*): Where have you been all night? (*Speaking very rapidly*) And why are you so tattered and dirty, and did you find a job, and how much money did you earn, and where is it, for I need to buy food and a warm blanket for the baby—not to mention new shoes for myself—and why aren't you answering any of my questions—why, why, why?

BARNABY: Gentle, patient, soft-spoken Margaret—why do you treat me as if I were a mongrel dog, when I worked all night just to earn triple wages for you?

MARGARET: Triple wages! (*Suddenly sweet*) Barnaby, dear—how I've missed you. (*Hugs him*)

BARNABY (*Tenderly*): And I've missed you. (*They hold hands and gaze at each other.*)

MARGARET (*Matter-of-factly*): Now, give me your triple wages, so I can buy all the things we need.

BARNABY (*Hesitantly*): Margaret, the only way I could get home safely was to exchange my wages for some good advice.

MARGARET (*Angrily*): Good advice? What are you telling me? Will good advice keep a baby warm or mend the holes in an old shoe? Because of your precious good advice, we'll all starve. There's not a morsel of food in the house.

BARNABY: I do have a loaf of bread.

MARGARET: I must say it's a good-sized loaf. Come inside and we'll slice it.

BARNABY: No, I have to break it, and you must hold out your apron to catch the crumbs.

MARGARET (*Haughtily*): Barnaby, only low-class people break their bread. Proper folk cut it into neat slices. Let me have it now.

BARNABY: I'll let you have it, all right. (*Whacks her on the head*)

MARGARET: Oh, Barnaby! (*Holds head, howls in pain*)

BARNABY: Oh, Margaret, what have I done?

MARGARET: You brute! You've hit your own wife on the head. (*Tragically*) I fear I'm fading fast. Farewell, dear world. (*Sits*)

BARNABY (*Distraught*): Dear me! I'd better take Granny's advice. (*He breaks bread over* MARGARET's *apron. Money flutters out.*) Money! The loaf was filled with money! (MARGARET *springs up, scrambles about stage, picking up bills.*)

MARGARET (*Counting*): Ten, twenty, fifty—(*Excited*) Barnaby, we're rich! The baby shall have a blanket of lamb's wool, I'll wear shiny shoes with no holes, and you—Barnaby, what is it that you want most?

BARNABY: Why, I already have a lovely family and a nice little house. I've traveled, I've battled scoundrels and seen the King, so there's nothing I really want—except a chance to work at my trade. But alas, Mr. Strudelmeister has closed the bake shop forever.

MARGARET (*Brightly*): I have the answer. You can use this money to buy the shop from Mr. Strudelmeister!

BARNABY (*Delighted*): Of course! Now I can spend the rest of my life elbow-deep in flour, breathing the sweet perfume of fresh bread baking. (MARGARET *picks up a piece of bread and flourishes it.* BARNABY *takes her arm and gallantly escorts her into cottage. Curtain*)

THE END

(*Production Notes on page 320*)

Puppet Plays

Why the Sea Is Salt

A Norwegian folktale

by Lewis Mahlmann and David Cadwalader Jones

Characters

SHARKIE
FLIPPER
CHARLIE
GILLIE
GRANNY, *Gillie's grandmother*
OLIVER, *a poor man*
MARTHA, *his wife*
MERVIN, *his rich, greedy brother*
DWARF

SCENE 1

TIME: *The present.*

SETTING: *The ocean floor. This scene is played behind a sea scrim.*

AT RISE: SHARKIE, FLIPPER, CHARLIE, *and* GILLIE *swim in, in front of scrim.*

GILLIE: 'Bye, Sharkie. 'Bye, Flipper. 'Bye, Charlie. See you tomorrow. (SHARKIE, FLIPPER, *and* CHARLIE *swim off.* GILLIE *calls.*) Granny—I'm home! (GRANNY *swims in.*)

GRANNY: My, you're home early, Gillie. You weren't naughty at fish school today, were you?

GILLIE: Oh, no, Granny. Miss Trout let us out early on porpoise.

GRANNY: That's nice. Just so you weren't playing hookie. You know what a nasty word that is! Now, tell me what you learned in school today.

GILLIE: Well, Mr. Bass taught us how to catch a fly. And Miss Trout taught us something very silly.

GRANNY: What was that, Gillie?

GILLIE: She said that the sea was salt! She *was* fooling us, wasn't she?

GRANNY: Oh, no! What she said is very true.

GILLIE: But how can that be, Granny?

GRANNY: Well, it's a very long story, child. Swim over here closer to Granny, and I'll tell you how it all happened. (GILLIE *swims over to* GRANNY.) A long time ago there lived on the dry part of the Earth a poor tailor and his wife. They were good people—not like the ones who hunt us in these waters now. They were very, very poor and ate only once or twice a week. One day the wife went to the cupboard . . . (*Curtain*)

* * * * *

SCENE 2

TIME: *Long ago.*

SETTING: *The interior of a poor cottage in Norway. There is an empty table center, an open window in backdrop, and a shelf painted on backdrop, with only an empty breadbox on it.*

AT RISE: MARTHA *and* OLIVER *are onstage.*

MARTHA: Oh, my poor, dear husband. What are we to do? The cupboard is bare and Christmas is only two days off.

OLIVER: Don't worry that pretty head of yours, Martha. We'll manage somehow. We always have. Remember last year? We had nothing in the cupboard, and brother Mervin gave us a box of crackers.

MARTHA: Yes, we are so fortunate that you have such a rich and generous brother.

OLIVER: Perhaps I could ask him for another box of crackers, and we can pay him before the year is over.

MARTHA: That sounds reasonable. With all the food he keeps stored in his larder, he could feed the entire army of the kingdom.

OLIVER: A clever businessman like my brother deserves to have lots of food and belongings.

MARTHA: Oh, I wasn't criticizing him, Oliver. What would we do with all that food, anyway? It would just spoil on our shelf.

OLIVER: Or make us fat and lazy.

MARTHA: Or give us gout and indigestion.

OLIVER *and* MARTHA (*Sighing wistfully*): Ah-h-h!

OLIVER: I shall go right now to see my brother, and ask him to lend us those crackers.

MARTHA: Dress warmly. Be sure to button up your coat.

OLIVER: But, Martha—I have no coat! I sold it to the peddler last month to buy you a broom.

MARTHA: Oh, dear. And I sold the broom to buy you tobacco for your pipe.

OLIVER: But, Martha, I sold the pipe . . .

MARTHA: You'd better go now, dear.

OLIVER: 'Bye, Martha.

MARTHA: 'Bye, Oliver. (*He exits. Curtain*)

* * * * *

SCENE 3

SETTING: *Outside Mervin's mansion. A corner of the mansion, with a working door, is at one side of stage. A tree stands at opposite side of stage. This scene may be played before curtain.*

AT RISE: OLIVER *is talking to* MERVIN *outside the door.* OLIVER *holds box.*

OLIVER: Thank you, Mervin. You are most generous. After all, half a box of crackers—even soggy crackers—is better than none at all. And I shall repay you as soon as possible.

MERVIN: Yes, yes. Now be off. You're letting in cold air. I may have to throw another log on my fire.

OLIVER: Oh! I didn't mean to keep you standing at your door. And I don't blame you for not letting me in. After all, my feet are soaking wet, and I would have tracked water all over your beautiful marble floors. Good day, and thank you.

MERVIN: *Humph! (He goes inside mansion and slams door.)*

OLIVER: How lucky I am to have such a kind and wealthy brother! I wish I could visit with him more often, but I know he has many things to do. He counts his money daily—and keeps a daily account of his possessions. It must be terrible to have such wealth and responsibility. I am glad I am not so rich. Why, what would I do with all that gold and all that food? These crackers do look good. Maybe if I had just one. . . . (*Strongly*) No! Martha must have the first one. How selfish of me to think of myself. (DWARF *steps out from behind tree.*)

DWARF: Crackers? Did I hear someone say crackers? I must have them. Please let me have them! I love soggy crackers!

OLIVER: Who are you, sir?

DWARF: I might ask you the same—but I won't. I'm too hungry. What will you trade for those crackers?

OLIVER: Why, if you are hungry, I will *give* them to you—all but one. I must save that for Martha.

DWARF (*Shaking his head*): Dwarfs never take something for nothing. Won't you trade them for this magic mill? (*He takes small mill out from behind tree.*)

OLIVER: Well, I know nothing of magic. But if it will please you and ease your hunger . . . (*He holds out box of crackers.*)

DWARF: Good! (*Taking box*) I'll take these crackers—all but one. (*He eats hungrily.*) Yum, yum! (*He presents mill and cracker box to* OLIVER, *and recites.*)

> Here's a magic mill for you.
> 'Twill make your wishes all come true.
> Whatever you want it grinds with ease.
> All you have to say is "please."
> When the mill has ground enough,
> Just say "thank you" for the stuff.
> And should it fall in greedy hands,
> It will return unto the lands.

Those are the magic words to operate the mill. Remember to say, "please" and "thank you." No other words will do. (DWARF *exits.*)

OLIVER: I must hurry home and show Martha. She will like this little mill. It will go nicely with the empty breadbox on the shelf. And she'll have her cracker for Christmas, too! (*Curtain*)

* * * * *

Scene 4

SETTING: *The same as Scene 2.*

AT RISE: MARTHA *and* OLIVER *are talking.*

MARTHA: Oh, Oliver. Did you see the smiles on those poor little orphans' faces when we took them all that food and clothing this afternoon?

OLIVER: Yes—thanks to our little mill. (OLIVER *places mill on stage.*) And now we shall have more than enough crackers to pay back Mervin. I hope he received the invitation we sent for dinner tonight. It was the least we could do to pay him back.

MARTHA: Oh, I won't blame him if he doesn't come. Our cottage is so small and cold compared to his home.

OLIVER: Why don't we ask the mill to churn us out a delicious turkey dinner? If Mervin doesn't come, we can give it to our kind neighbors. (MERVIN *appears at window, unnoticed by* MARTHA *and* OLIVER.)

MARTHA: Good idea. And how about a nice, clean table-cloth, too?

OLIVER: Very well. (*Addresses mill*) Magic mill, please turn out a turkey dinner on a nice, clean tablecloth. (*Table top flips over to reveal turkey dinner on white tablecloth.*) Thank you, mill. (*There is a knock on door.*) Perhaps that's Mervin, now. (*He opens the door.*) Oh, dear brother. You did come! (MERVIN *enters.*)

MERVIN: What is this I see? You ask me for crackers one day, and the next you have a table laden with goodies.

OLIVER: Brother, you wouldn't believe our good fortune! I have here a magic mill that can grind out our every wish.

MERVIN: I don't believe it. You probably stole that turkey and are making up that story about the mill.

MARTHA: No, no! It's really true, as you will see. Just name something you like very much, and we shall ask the mill to grind it out for you.

MERVIN: Something I like, eh? Let me think! Well . . . how about some hard-boiled eggs? I do like them.

OLIVER: Oh, that should be easy enough. (*To mill*) Magic mill—please grind out some hard-boiled eggs for brother Mervin. (*Mill begins to grind out eggs.* NOTE: *There is a disc inside mill with eggs painted on it, which is slowly turned from backstage, to give illusion that mill is grinding out eggs.*)

MERVIN: Well—you weren't lying, after all. It *is* a magic mill. (*There is a knock on door.*)

OLIVER: Now, who could that be? (*He goes to door, opens it.*) Why, it's little Tiny Tim, Bob Cratchit's boy from down the street. Here. . . . (OLIVER *goes back to table, picks up turkey and carries it to door.*) Take this turkey, Tim. I can always get another one. (*He hands turkey out door, closes door, and returns to center.*)

MERVIN: What? Are you out of your mind? Giving up a perfectly good turkey? (MERVIN *races out door.*)

OLIVER: We can always get another where that came from. (*Sees mill still grinding eggs*) Oh, my goodness! The magic mill! (*He runs to mill.*) What were the magic words? Oh, yes. (*To mill*) Thank you for the hard-boiled eggs. (*Mill stops.* MERVIN *reenters, carrying turkey.*)

MERVIN: You obviously haven't priced turkey lately. I made that ragamuffin give it back. Oh! You stopped the mill.

MARTHA: Let's have dinner now.

MERVIN (*Craftily*): I don't see any cranberries on the table.

OLIVER: Oh, I'll ask the magic mill.

MERVIN: No, no. You can't waste the mill's magic on such a trifle. (*Holds out hand*) Here's a nickel. Run down to the store and buy some cranberries.

OLIVER: But, it's a five-mile walk!

MERVIN: And Martha, you go with him to make sure he picks out the right kind.

MARTHA: But, the turkey will get cold.

MERVIN: Never mind, I'll put it back in the oven. Now, run along.

OLIVER: Come along, Martha. Mervin's right. Turkey dinner wouldn't be right without cranberry sauce.

MARTHA: You're right, Oliver. Goodbye, Mervin. We will see you in about three or four hours. (*Exit*)

MERVIN: Ha! Ha! They are gone at last. (*Picks up mill*) Now I shall have everything my greedy heart desires. (*He laughs and exits. Curtain*)

* * * * *

SCENE 5

TIME: *A few days later.*

SETTING: *On the sea. This scene may be played on top of the puppet stage. A cutout of Mervin's ship is at center, with a cutout of the magic mill on the deck.*

AT RISE: MERVIN *is on board ship with* DWARF, *disguised as a sailor.*

MERVIN: Ah—at last! On board my merchant ship. And now I'll make a fortune with this stupid mill.

DWARF: How will you make money from the mill?

MERVIN: Sailor, I've found out that the people at the next port are badly in need of salt. I'll sell it to them.

DWARF: But those townspeople are poor.

MERVIN: They need salt, and I'll make them pay heavily for it. Now, how do you make this mill work? (*To mill*) Mill! Grind salt! (*Nothing happens.*) Grind salt, I tell you! (*Still nothing happens.*) It's not working!

DWARF: Maybe it needs the magic words.

MERVIN: Stay out of this, if you please. (*To mill*) Grind salt! (*It begins grinding salt in great quantities.* NOTE: *A triangle of shiny white fabric is attached behind ship cutout. Point of the triangle is slowly pulled up by a thread to look as if it is salt filling the ship.*) Look! It's working! Look at all the beautiful salt! Wonderful!

DWARF (*To audience*): It's best I go now. I think he will learn his lesson. (DWARF *disappears.*)

MERVIN: Why, where did that sailor go? Oh, well—never mind. I'll be extra rich when I get into port with all this salt. Grind away, mill! Ha, ha! A whole ship full of money-making salt. (*Salt continues to rise in the ship.*) Oh-oh! The boat is beginning to list. Guess that's enough salt. Magic mill—stop grinding salt. (*Salt continues to rise.*) Stop, I say! Stop! (*It continues.*) Oh—the ship is beginning to sink! Help! (*He tries to throw salt over side of ship, to no avail.*) Help! (*The ship sinks out of view of the audience. Curtain*)

* * * * *

SCENE 6

SETTING: *Same as Scene 1.*

AT RISE: MERVIN'S *ship is seen slowly sinking into sea. It settles on the bottom.* GRANNY *and* GILLIE *swim in, in front of the scrim.*

GRANNY: And so, Gillie, the ship sank and the magic mill continued grinding out salt, and as far as anyone knows, it still grinds out salt to this day.

GILLIE: Wouldn't it be exciting if someone could find that ship and stop the mill?

GRANNY: That's very unlikely, Gillie. There must be a million ships at the bottom of the sea. Come. Let's swim to dinner now. (*They swim off, then reenter behind scrim, and swim across stage, passing ship. A puff of salt emerges from ship as curtain closes.*)

THE END

(*Production Notes on page 320*)

Monkey Business

An Indian folktale

by Claire Boiko

Characters

FOUR STORYTELLERS, *actors*
RAJAH
SCHOLAR
GARDENER
JIBBA
SHIMPU } *three foolish monkeys*
MUJ

TIME: *Ancient India.*
SETTING: *Rajah's garden.*
AT RISE: FOUR STORYTELLERS *dressed in turbans and robes sit cross-legged in front of puppet stage at center. Puppet stage curtains are closed. Offstage sound of cymbal is heard. Each* STORYTELLER *presses hands together and bows. Puppet stage curtains open, revealing garden, with three trees in pots, left and right.*
1ST STORYTELLER (*Rising*):
In the olden days, in the golden days,
In the days before we came to be,

There bloomed a garden, a Rajah's garden,
Most beautiful to see.
2ND STORYTELLER (*Rising*):
In this garden, this Rajah's garden,
Grew three fine trees, most strange and rare,
And tending these, most precious trees,
A gardener beyond compare.
(GARDENER *enters, carrying watering can. He waters
trees.*)
GARDENER:
I am a gardener beyond compare.
I can coax the stones to grow,
For me, the lilies bloom in snow.
Come with me now. Come with
   me please,
And meet my most celestial trees.
(*Pointing to first tree*)
A tree of golden apples.
(*Pointing to second tree*)
A tree of silver pears.
(*Pointing to third tree*)
A tree of rainbow blossoms.
(*Bowing to audience*)
3RD STORYTELLER (*Rising*): You cannot imagine how
the Rajah loved his garden. (RAJAH *enters, walks
back and forth, as* GARDENER *sprinkles trees.*) Every
day the Rajah would admire his precious trees. And
he would ask the Gardener the same questions.
RAJAH:
Gardener, gardener, tell me please,
How are all my lovely trees?
3RD STORYTELLER: And every day, the Gardener would
make the same reply.
GARDENER (*Bowing to* RAJAH):
Most royal Rajah, come right this way.

All goes well with your trees today.
(RAJAH *and* GARDENER *exit.* SCHOLAR *enters, reading from a scroll.*)

4TH STORYTELLER (*Rising*): Now, besides the Rajah and the Gardener, there was another person who loved the garden—the Scholar. . . .
Beneath each splendid, royal tree
Walked a Scholar of high degree.
(MONKEYS *enter, in line, imitating* SCHOLAR'S *actions.*)
And following him were Monkeys three,
Who copied the Scholar with mirth and glee.
(SCHOLAR *nods.* MONKEYS *nod.*)

1ST STORYTELLER: One day, the Scholar caught the monkeys mocking him. He spoke angrily. (SCHOLAR *turns around quickly, and monkeys collide.*)

SCHOLAR: Rogues! Rascals! (*Shakes his finger at them. Monkeys shake their fingers back at him.*) Stop that. Do you think you can become wise by copying me? (*Monkeys nod their heads.*) Indeed? What books have you read? What thoughts have you thought? What dreams have you dreamed? (*Monkeys put their hands over their ears.*) I thought so. There is nothing in your heads but bananas! (*Nose in air, he exits haughtily.*)

1ST STORYTELLER: But that scolding did not stop the Monkeys. They were so puffed up with pride that they said to each other:

MONKEYS (*Together*): Ho, ho, ho. We walk like Scholars. (*They walk proudly.*) We scratch our heads like Scholars. (*They scratch their heads.*) We shake our fingers like Scholars. (*They shake fingers.*)

JIBBA: Therefore . . .

SHIMPU: Wherefore . . .

MUJ: Thenceforth . . .

MONKEYS (*Together*): We *are* Scholars. (*With their heads in their hands, they stare at audience.* GARDENER *enters.*)

2ND STORYTELLER: Now, who should come upon the Monkeys as they tried to look so wise, so very wise, but the Gardener.

GARDENER: How I would like to go to the Festival and buy some honey cake. But who would water the trees? Who is wise enough to tend the Rajah's garden? (*He turns slowly and looks at monkeys; amazed*) Lo and behold! A miracle has come to pass. The foolish monkeys have grown wise. Ah-h-h!

MONKEYS (*Together, mimicking* GARDENER): Ah-h-h!

GARDENER: Good monkeys, you have grown wise before my eyes. I must ask you a favor.

JIBBA: Ask . . .

SHIMPU: Ask . . .

MUJ: Ask away.

GARDENER: Would you please water the trees of the Rajah while I go to the Festival?

MONKEYS (*Nodding together*): We will. We will. We will.

GARDENER: But remember. Do not waste any water, and do not harm the trees.

MONKEYS (*Shaking their heads; in unison*): We won't. We won't. We won't.

GARDENER: Farewell. (*He exits.*)

MONKEYS (*Together*): Farewell. (*Monkeys form circle and dance.*) We're going to water the trees—tra la.

JIBBA: Not the flowers,

SHIMPU: Not the birds,

MUJ: Not the bees, tra la.

JIBBA:
    In a trice and a twinkle
    We'll splash and we'll sprinkle,

Those thirsty old, dusty old trees.

Tra la!

JIBBA (*Breaking off, scratching his head*): The Gardener said to remember something. What was it?

SHIMPU: He said not to forget something. But I don't remember what he said not to forget.

MUJ: I know, I know. He said, "Do not harm the water, and don't waste any trees." That's what he said.

JIBBA: You have it all wrong, as usual. He said not to harm the *trees* and not to waste any *water.*

SHIMPU: That's it. But how much water is too much water?

MUJ: And how much water is too little water?

JIBBA: And how much water is just enough water?

MONKEYS (*Holding their heads, pondering*): Hm-m! Hm-m! Hm-m!

MUJ: I have a thought. (*Pause*) It flew away like a moth.

SHIMPU: Ah! I have a thought. (*Pause*) It slid out my ears.

JIBBA: A thought! I have a thought. A real, live thought.

MUJ: Tell us. Tell us the thought.

JIBBA (*Slowly*): We will pull up the trees. We will see how long the roots grow. If the roots grow long, the tree will need much water. If the roots grow short, the tree will need a little water.

SHIMPU *and* MUJ (*Clapping*): Clever! Very clever!

JIBBA: I know. Now, you two take the trees out of the pots. I will water them. (SHIMPU *and* MUJ *pull up first tree.* JIBBA *takes watering can and sprinkles it. They pull up second tree, which has short roots.* JIBBA *gives it a quick sprinkle. As they uproot the third tree,* RAJAH *enters. Sound of clashing cymbals is heard.*)

RAJAH (*Angrily, and greatly agitated*): Monkeys, what are you doing? (*Monkeys try to hide behind pots, quivering with fear.*) Come out, you three villains! Come out before I shake you out of your silly skins! (*Monkeys come forward, heads hanging.*)

JIBBA: We were only watering the trees, Most Royal Rajah.

SHIMPU: We meant well. We meant the very best, Most Royal Rajah. The Gardener told us to water the trees.

MUJ: Perhaps you can cut them up for firewood.

RAJAH (*Roaring*): Silence! I'll cut up your tails for firewood. Blundering Monkeys, begone! Never let me see your Monkey faces in my garden again. Out, I tell you! (*Monkeys scamper off.* GARDENER *enters.* SCHOLAR *follows him, but stays at distance, listening.*)

GARDENER (*Raising his hands in dismay*): Oh, the trees! Who has done this to the trees?

RAJAH: The Monkeys. Did you tell the Monkeys to water the trees?

GARDENER: Yes, Most Royal Rajah. But the Monkeys seemed so wise.

RAJAH: They seemed wise to you? Then you seem foolish to me. You shall no longer tend my garden! Begone! (*He waves* GARDENER *away, then exits.*)

GARDENER (*Upset*): I will catch those Monkeys. I will catch them by their monkey tails. I will tie their monkey tails in one great knot and hang them from the Rajah's tower. (*He exits.*)

SCHOLAR (*To audience, shaking his head*): Did I not tell you so? Monkeys can only pretend to be wise. (*Pointing finger at audience.*) There are persons in this world who appear very clever on the outside. But inside, they are only foolish Monkeys. And before *you* try to do a good deed, be sure that *you* are wise inside and outside. (*He bows and exits.*)

1ST STORYTELLER: All was not lost in the garden, the garden of the Rajah. For behold! A seed dropped from each tree.

2ND STORYTELLER:
A golden seed,
A silver seed,
A seed of rainbow hue.

3RD STORYTELLER:
From every seed, a sapling rose,
And a tall tree grew.

4TH STORYTELLER:
With apples bright as noonshine,
And pears as light as moonshine,
And a thousand blossoms shimmering,
With every color glimmering.

1ST STORYTELLER: And the Rajah was content. But he built a strong gate around that garden. (RAJAH *enters, carrying gate, which he puts at front of puppet stage. He exits.*) And on that gate he placed a large, bold sign. (RAJAH *reenters, carrying sign, which he hangs on gate. Sign reads:* NO MONKEYS ALLOWED.)

STORYTELLERS (*Together*): No monkeys allowed! (*Puppet stage curtains close.* STORYTELLERS *bow. Curtain*)

THE END

(*Production Notes on page 321*)

The Strongest Being

A Japanese folktale

by Helen L. Howard

Characters

OTOSAN, *Father*
OKASAN, *Mother*
MUSUME, *daughter*
DEDMU, *young man*
SUN
CLOUD
WIND
WALL

TIME: *Long ago.*
SETTING: *Japanese garden. Tree large enough to hide behind stands right. Corner of house is painted on backdrop, right. Stone wall divides stage in half.*
AT RISE: CLOUD *is in sky, left.* MUSUME *is crouching on right side of* WALL. *She is talking through a chink in the* WALL *to* DEDMU, *who stands on other side.*
MUSUME (*Sadly*): Oh, Dedmu, what are we going to do? I am afraid that my father will not let us marry.

NOTE: For definitions of Japanese words, see glossary at end of play.

DEDMU (*Speaking through hole in* WALL): Don't despair, Musume. Our love will find a way.

OTOSAN (*Calling from off left*): Okasan!

MUSUME: That's Father calling Mother. He must not find me here talking to you. *Sayonara*, Dedmu.

DEDMU: *Sayonara, Musume.* (MUSUME *hides behind tree.* DEDMU *exits, and* WALL *turns to stand across the back of stage.*)

OTOSAN (*Entering left*): Okasan!

OKASAN (*Entering right*): Did you call me, Otosan?

OTOSAN: Yes, I did. I have decided who shall marry our lovely daughter, Musume. She is so fair, so intelligent, so graceful that anyone would be honored to have her for his bride. I have decided that the strongest being in the world shall marry her. I shall tell her. Where is she?

OKASAN: She was just here in the garden. (*Calling*) Musume, come! Your father wishes to speak with you.

MUSUME (*Coming from behind tree*): Here I am, Noble Father.

OTOSAN: Musume, it is time for you to marry. You are to be betrothed to the strongest being in the world—the Sun.

MUSUME (*Protesting*): No! No! I love Dedmu! I cannot marry the Sun—or anyone but Dedmu!

OTOSAN: No, Musume. Dedmu is only a common young man. The Sun is the strongest being in the world. His rays keep us warm and make the rice grow. You must marry him. I'll go to him at once, to tell him of the great honor we will bestow upon him. (OKASAN *and* MUSUME, *weeping, exit right.* SUN *enters right, and* OTOSAN *approaches it.*)

OTOSAN: *Ohayo goziamus*, Sun.

SUN: *Ohayo goziamus.*

OTOSAN: Sun, since you are stronger than anyone else in the world, I will give you my daughter's hand in marriage.

SUN: Ah, my good friend, I am honored, but I am not the strongest being in the world. There is one stronger than I.

OTOSAN: Who can that be?

SUN (*Pointing*): Do you see that Cloud? Soon he will scurry across the sky and cover me. I am powerless when the Cloud comes between me and the earth.

OTOSAN (*Bowing*): *Arigato goziamus,* Sun. *Sayonara.*

SUN: *Sayonara.* (SUN *exits right.* OTOSAN *turns and crosses left to* CLOUD.)

OTOSAN (*To* CLOUD): *Ohayo goziamus,* Cloud. Sun says you are stronger than he, because you can hide him so that he cannot shine on the earth. I want my daughter to marry the strongest being in the world; therefore, I offer you Musume, my daughter, for your bride.

CLOUD: It is true that I can hide the Sun, and the moon, as well. But I am not the strongest being on the earth. The Wind can blow me wherever it likes.

OTOSAN (*Bowing*): Then I must seek the Wind. *Arigato goziamus,* Cloud. *Sayonara.*

CLOUD: *Sayonara.* (WIND *enters blowing. He blows* CLOUD *off right, then turns and blows across the sky again.* OTOSAN *addresses him.*)

OTOSAN: *Ohayo goziamus,* Wind. (WIND *slows and stops.*)

WIND: *Ohayo goziamus.*

OTOSAN: Cloud can hide the Sun and the moon, but he says you are stronger because you can blow him about. Since you are the strongest being in the world, Cloud, I would like you to marry my daughter, Musume.

WIND: *Arigato goziamus,* my friend. I am honored by your praise, but I am not the strongest being in the world. When I blow against the stone wall in your garden, I cannot move it at all.

OTOSAN: Then the stone wall must be the strongest being in the world. *Arigato goziamus* for the advice. *Sayonara,* Wind.

WIND: *Sayonara.* (WIND *blows off.* OTOSAN *crosses to* WALL.)

OTOSAN: *Ohayo goziamus,* Wall. I have heard that you are stronger than the Wind who can scatter the Clouds that can cover the Sun. You must be the strongest being in the world. I have come to offer you my daughter, Musume, as your bride.

WALL: I have no trouble stopping the Wind, that is true. But there is someone stronger than I—someone I cannot stop.

OTOSAN: Someone you cannot stop? Who can that be?

WALL: When Dedmu, the young man next door, wanted to talk with your daughter, he removed one of my stones. He can take me apart, stone by stone, and I cannot stop him. Dedmu's love is stronger than I am.

OTOSAN (*Bowing*): *Arigato goziamus. Sayonara,* Wall.

WALL: *Sayonara.*

OTOSAN (*Calling*): Okasan! Musume! Come here! (OKASAN *and* MUSUME *enter.*) I have wonderful news for you. I set out to find the strongest being in the world, so that I could offer him Musume's hand. Who do you think is the strongest one in the whole world?

OKASAN: I thought you said it was the Sun.

OTOSAN: Yes, but the Sun told me that the Cloud is stronger than he. When I asked the Cloud, he told me that the Wind is the strongest one.

MUSUME (*Protesting*): But I don't want to marry the Wind. I love Dedmu. (*Pleading*) *Dozo,* Honorable Father. (DEDMU *stands up behind* WALL, *then walks around it and enters garden. He crosses and stands beside* MUSUME.)

OTOSAN: Let me finish. The Wind said the Wall was the strongest, but when I spoke to the Wall, he told me that Dedmu's love was stronger than he, because Dedmu made a hole in the Wall, so that he could speak to Musume. (*To* DEDMU) Dedmu, I offer Musume to you as a bride, because your love is stronger than anything else on the earth.

DEDMU (*Bowing to* OTOSAN): *Arigato goziamus.* I shall cherish her forever.

MUSUME (*Joyfully*): *Arigato goziamus,* dear Father. (*To* OKASAN) *Arigato goziamus,* dear Mother. (MUSUME *takes* DEDMU's *hand.*) Dedmu, I am so happy! Love *is* the strongest thing on earth. (*Curtain*)

THE END

(*Production Notes on page 321*)

GLOSSARY

Otosan (*oh toh san*): Father

Okasan (*oh kay san*): Mother

Musume (*moo soo me*)

Dedmu (*ded moo*)

Ohayo goziamus (*aw high oh gaw zeye mus*): Good morning.

Sayonara (*say aw nah rah*): Goodbye.

Arigato goziamus (*ah lee gah toh gaw zeye mus*): Thank you very much.

Dozo (*daw zaw*): Please.

The Perfect Gift for a Princess

by Phyllis J. Perry

Characters

PRINCESS CLARE
QUEEN WINIFRED
KING HENRY
MESSENGER
COOK
GARDENER
JACK
ANNIE
TROLL

SCENE 1

SETTING: *Princess Clare's bedroom.*

AT RISE: PRINCESS CLARE *is in her bed, crying softly.* QUEEN WINIFRED *enters.*

QUEEN WINIFRED: Princess Clare, why are you crying? Are you ill?

PRINCESS CLARE (*Drying her eyes with lace handkerchief*): No, Mother. I'm not ill. I'm just lonely.

QUEEN (*Surprised*): How can you be lonely, dear?

(QUEEN *goes to comfort* PRINCESS.) Your father and I are with you every day. The cook lets you bake in her kitchen and play with her daughter. The gardener lets you play with his son and help in the garden. Your teacher reads with you and shows you how to draw and paint. Your days are busy.

PRINCESS: My days are busy, Mother, but I'm lonely here in my bedroom at night. I need a pet to keep me company.

QUEEN: Perhaps that can be arranged. You have a birthday soon, and your father and I thought you might like a pony.

PRINCESS: Thank you, Mother, but I don't really want a pony. A pony would have to sleep in the stables. I want a pet that I can keep in my room.

QUEEN: What about a dog or a cat?

PRINCESS: Everyone has dogs and cats. I want something unusual, a warm, furry animal that will snuggle up and sleep at the foot of my bed at night.

QUEEN: What do you have in mind?

PRINCESS: I want a snugabed.

QUEEN (*Surprised*): A snugabed! I'm afraid that's one pet you can't have, dear. Snugabeds live in the Enchanted Forest, guarded by an awful Troll. Only a few people have gone into the Enchanted Forest and come back safely. The Troll captures people and makes them his servants. Isn't there some other pet that will do?

PRINCESS: No, Mother. (*Sighs*) If I can't have a snugabed, I'll just have to be lonely. (*Curtain*)

* * * * *

SCENE 2

TIME: *The next day.*

SETTING: *The throne room.*

AT RISE: KING HENRY *and* QUEEN WINIFRED *are on thrones, talking.* MESSENGER *stands nearby.*

QUEEN: Dear King, our daughter's very lonely. I found her crying in her room last night. I wish we could make her happy.

KING: Surely we can think of some special birthday present that would make her happy. Perhaps a ruby ring? Or a necklace?

QUEEN (*Shaking head*): She wants a pet. I suggested a pony or a dog or cat, but Princess Clare says there is only one pet that will do. A snugabed!

KING (*Surprised*): A snugabed? Impossible! We'll have to think of some other gift. (*Waves his hand to summon* MESSENGER)

MESSENGER: Yes, Your Majesty.

KING: Good Messenger, bring the cook and the gardener here at once.

MESSENGER: Yes, Your Royal Highness. (*Bows, exits*)

KING: Princess Clare loves to play in the kitchen and in the garden. Perhaps her friends there can help us think of something that will keep her from being so lonely. (MESSENGER *reenters with* COOK *and* GARDENER.)

MESSENGER: Your Royal Highnesses, I have brought the cook and gardener as you commanded. (*All bow.*)

KING: Good cook and kind gardener, we are very worried about the Princess. She gets lonely and sad at night. Could you help us think of a birthday present that would make her happy again?

COOK: I'd be glad to bake her a very special cake. And

my daughter would be happy to come and play with her.

GARDENER: I'll pick a big bouquet of flowers for her, and my son will come and keep her company.

KING: Thank you both. I knew you would do all you could. But I'm afraid that will not be enough. The Princess wants a snugabed.

COOK (*Shocked*): Oh, dear, no!

GARDENER: (*Shaking head*): But that's impossible.

QUEEN: Yes, it is. For as you know, the only place to find a snugabed is in the Enchanted Forest, which is so dangerous that no one who goes there comes back safely.

GARDENER: Your Majesty, my son Jack has gone into the Enchanted Forest several times. (*All gasp.*)

COOK: Can that be?

GARDENER: It's true, and Cook's daughter, Annie, has gone with him.

COOK (*Upset*): Oh, no! This is the first I've heard of this.

KING: Why did Jack go? He must have known how dangerous it was.

GARDENER: Jack and Annie were playing in the woods and wandered further than they intended. They came upon a circle of stones, and saw a Troll sitting there, eating breakfast. The children hid and watched. When the Troll finished eating, he left, and Jack and Annie slipped away.

COOK: Annie never mentioned this to me. How did Jack happen to tell you about these visits to the Enchanted Forest?

GARDENER: Just two days ago, when they were walking home through the Enchanted Forest, they saw a family of strange-looking animals sleeping in a tree. Jack didn't know what they were, and he asked me what animal looks like a tiny brown bear but has a long, bushy tail. I remembered from my childhood that it was a snugabed. I asked Jack where he's seen such an animal, and that's when he confessed. I made him promise never to return to the Enchanted Forest.

QUEEN: What an incredible story! I should like to talk to the children about it. Messenger, would you please call Jack and Annie?

MESSENGER: At once, Your Majesty. (*Bows, exits*)

KING: I wonder if the children could lead us to the forest so that we might bring back a baby snugabed?

QUEEN: It may be too dangerous! What if the Troll sees you? You could be held captive forever. (MESSENGER *reenters with* JACK *and* ANNIE. *All bow.*)

KING: Jack, your father has told us that you and Annie have entered the Enchanted Forest. Is that true?

JACK (*Embarrassed*): Yes, Your Majesty, but I have promised Father that I would never go again.

QUEEN: Is it true that you saw a family of snugabeds?

ANNIE: Yes, Your Majesty.

KING: If some soldiers and I went with you, would you be willing to lead us to the spot where the snugabeds live? We want to bring one back for Princess Clare's birthday.

JACK: I'd be happy to try, Your Majesty, but I don't think it would be safe for you to go with your soldiers. Soldiers would make too much noise tramping through the woods. Annie and I are small and quiet. The Troll has never noticed us.

ANNIE (*Bravely*): Jack and I will bring back a snugabed for Princess Clare.

COOK (*Protesting*): No, Annie, you must never go there again.

QUEEN: You're quite right, Cook. It's far too dangerous for the children or for the King, even with his soldiers. We must think of something else to give Princess Clare for her birthday.

KING: Our thanks to you all. You may go now. (*All bow and exit. Curtain*)

* * * * *

Scene 3

TIME: *Early the next morning.*

SETTING: *The Enchanted Forest. There are bushes scattered about and circle of stones center, in the middle of which is a fire. Pot sits over fire. Basket, bowl, and spoon are nearby.*

AT RISE: JACK *and* ANNIE *enter, each carrying knapsack.*

ANNIE: If my mother finds out that I've come to the Enchanted Forest again, she'll be very angry.

JACK: But you know we're the only ones who can catch a snugabed for Princess Clare. (*Looks around*) I wonder where the Troll is this morning? He should be here eating his breakfast. (TROLL *suddenly appears behind them. He has long white beard and wears pointed green hat.*) You're right, young man. It's *past* my breakfast time. You two will stay here and work for me. You can pick berries and make bark tea, while I sit back and relax. (ANNIE *and* JACK *try to run away, but* TROLL *grabs them.*)

TROLL: You two aren't going anywhere. First you will gather berries. (TROLL *gives* JACK *a basket and points him toward bushes.*) And you, young lady, will stir my bark tea. (TROLL *pushes* ANNIE *toward fire. She begins stirring pot while* JACK *picks berries and put them into basket.*)

ANNIE: Forgive me, Sir Troll, but bark tea isn't very tasty. I can make you something much better.

TROLL (*Scornfully*): What could that be?

ANNIE: I'll show you. (*She opens knapsack, takes out small bottle of milk.*) Jack, bring me some berries, please. (JACK *brings over berries and puts them into bowl.* ANNIE *pours milk over them and hands bowl to* TROLL, *who picks up spoon and begins to eat.*)

TROLL: Mm-m! What is this delicious white liquid?

JACK: It's called milk.

TROLL: Where do you get it?

ANNIE (*Giggling*): Why, it comes from an animal called a cow.

TROLL (*Thinking*): A cow? I don't believe there are any cows in the Enchanted Forest.

ANNIE: Would you like to make a trade with us?

TROLL (*Suspiciously*): What kind of a trade?

ANNIE: We'll give you a cow for a baby snugabed.

TROLL (*Suspiciously*): This sounds like a trick. You'll just pretend to go for a cow, but you'll run away and never come back. I won't get any milk and I'll lose two servants.

ANNIE: Don't worry. I'll stay with you until Jack comes back with a cow.

TROLL: All right. After I finish my breakfast, I'll catch a snugabed for you. (TROLL *resumes eating.* ANNIE *sits on rock.* JACK *exits. Curtain*)

* * * * *

SCENE 4

TIME: *Princess Clare's birthday.*

SETTING: *Same as Scene 2.*

AT RISE: COOK *holds cake and* GARDENER *holds bouquet of flowers.* KING, QUEEN, *and* PRINCESS CLARE *enter.*

PRINCESS (*Admiring cake*): Thank you, Cook. What a beautiful cake you've made.

COOK: You're very welcome, Princess Clare.

PRINCESS: And Gardener, what lovely flowers. Thank you very much.

GARDENER: You're very welcome, Princess Clare.

QUEEN: Before we cut the cake, be sure to make a wish. (PRINCESS CLARE *puts her hands over her eyes.* JACK *and* ANNIE *tiptoe in, carrying box. They stand behind* PRINCESS, *where she cannot see them.* PRINCESS *removes hands from her eyes.*)

KING: What did you wish for?

PRINCESS: If I tell you, Father, it won't come true.

KING: Perhaps this is what you wished for. (*Hands her a ring*)

PRINCESS: Thank you, Father. What a beautiful ring!

QUEEN: And here's a birthday present from me, dear Princess Clare. (*She hands* PRINCESS *a necklace.*)

PRINCESS: Thank you, Mother. It's a lovely necklace.

JACK *and* ANNIE (*Together*): Surprise! We have a present for you, too. (PRINCESS *turns, surprised.* JACK *and* ANNIE *hand her the box.*)

PRINCESS (*Peeking into box; delighted*): Oh, my goodness! It's a baby snugabed! (*Takes small stuffed bear gently from box*) This is what I wished for! How happy I am! I'll never be lonely at night again! (*Cradles snugabed in her arms*) How did you find him?

KING: Come, everyone. While we have our cake, Jack and Annie can tell how they went into the Enchanted Forest, and convinced the Troll to trade them a snugabed for a cow. (*All gather excitedly around cake, as curtain falls.*)

THE END

(*Production Notes on page 322*)

How the Little Dipper Came to Be

by Lewis Mahlmann

Characters

NARRATOR
CLARA, *a good little girl*
MOTHER
OWL
OLD MAN
DOG
NIGHT, *a shadowy lady*

SCENE 1

SETTING: *Bedroom in a cottage in the woods. Window right overlooks garden and woods.*

AT RISE: MOTHER *is in bed.*

NARRATOR: Once upon a time there was a little girl named Clara. She lived with her sick mother in a little cottage deep in the woods. Although she was a brave child, the one thing she was afraid of was the night, when it was dark.

CLARA (*Entering with tray of food*): How do you feel, Mother?

297

MOTHER: Not very well, Clara. But I am so lucky to have a dear daughter like you.

CLARA: Do you think you can eat something? I've made pudding, tea, and cinnamon toast for you.

MOTHER: Not now, Clara. Maybe later.

CLARA (*Feeling* MOTHER's *forehead*): You are so warm. I fear you have a fever.

MOTHER: If I could only have a cold drink of water. . . . Is there any left in the rain barrel?

CLARA (*Shaking her head*): I used the last of it for the tea.

MOTHER: I'm so thirsty. I just know I'd feel better if I had a cool drink.

CLARA: I'll go to the well, Mother.

MOTHER: But that's so far away, deep in the woods, and it's so late. It's much too dangerous for you.

CLARA: Do not worry, Mama. I'll be careful. And I will be back as soon as I can. (*She kisses her.*) Now, try to rest.

MOTHER: I'll try, dear. Come back soon. (CLARA *exits. Curtain*)

* * * * *

Scene 2

SETTING: *The deep dark woods. Backdrop is black. There are a few trees.*

AT RISE: CLARA *enters, with tin water dipper in her hand.*

NARRATOR: And so Clara entered the deep dark woods, with her simple tin water dipper. She walked on and on, and it became darker and darker.

CLARA: Oh, dear. I hope I don't get lost. It is so dark and mysterious here!

OWL (*Flying by*): Whoo-o-o-o! Whoo-o-o-o!

CLARA: What was that?

OWL (*Swooping by her*): Whoo-o-o-o! Whoo-o-o-o! Whoo-o-o-o! (*Exits*)

CLARA: It's only an old hoot owl. I shouldn't be afraid.

NIGHT (*Entering and crossing stage*): Clara! (*Exits*)

CLARA (*Frightened*): Who is that? I'd like to go home, but I promised Mother I'd get her some cool water from the well. I must try not to be afraid. (*Exits; curtain*)

* * * * *

SCENE 3

SETTING: *Another part of the woods. A well is center.*

AT RISE: CLARA *enters, humming to herself.*

NARRATOR: Clara did her best to lift her spirits and not be frightened. Finally, she found her way to the well.

CLARA (*Happily*): Here it is at last. Now, to dip my tin dipper into the sweet, cool water. How good it will taste to Mama.

OLD MAN (*Entering*): Dear little girl, please help me!

CLARA: How can I help you, old man?

OLD MAN: I am so thirsty. Can you give me a drink from your tin dipper?

CLARA: Of course. But please don't drink it all. It is for my sick mother.

OLD MAN: Just a sip will do. (*He drinks.*) Thank you, little girl. You are so kind. You will not be forgotten. Goodbye. (*He exits. The dipper has turned to silver; see Production Notes.*)

CLARA: I must hurry home now. I'll just take my dipper and . . . (*Surprised*) Oh, my! What has happened? My dipper has turned to pure silver! What magic could have changed it? Mama will be so pleased!

NIGHT (*Entering and crossing stage*): Clara! (NIGHT *exits.*)

CLARA (*Frightened*): There's that mysterious voice again. Why does she call me? I . . . I will *not* be afraid. (*She exits. Curtain*)

* * * * *

SCENE 4

SETTING: *Still another part of the forest.*

AT RISE: CLARA *enters.*

NARRATOR: Clara walked as fast as she could, being careful not to spill the water in her dipper.

CLARA (*Nervously*): I hope I'm not lost. No—here's the path again.

DOG (*Howling offstage*): Oo-oo-ooo!

CLARA (*Terrified*): What was that?

DOG (*Limping on*): Ooowww. (*Whines*)

CLARA: You poor old thing. Are you lost? You are panting so. Poor doggie. You look so thirsty. Here! Drink a bit of water from my hand. It will make you feel better. (*She pours a bit of the water from dipper into her hand, and* DOG *laps it up.*) Ha, ha! You are licking my hand. (*Laughs again*) Now, be off with you. I hope you find your way home. (*Dipper has changed to gold; see Production Notes.*) I do hope there is enough water left for Mother. (*Suddenly*) Oh, my! (*Happily*) The dipper has turned to pure gold!

NIGHT (*Entering*): Clara! Clara! (*Exits*)

CLARA (*Frightened*): Oh, no! (*She runs off. Curtain*)

* * * * *

Scene 5

SETTING: *Same as Scene 1.*

AT RISE: MOTHER *is in bed.* CLARA *enters, holding golden dipper.*

CLARA (*Softly*): Mother! Mother! I have some nice cool water for you.

MOTHER (*Stirring*): Oh, I'm so glad to have you back, Clara. (*Sits up*)

CLARA (*Handing her the dipper*): Here—drink! (MOTHER *does.*)

MOTHER: My, that tasted good! I was so thirsty! I feel much better now. Thank you, dear. (*Suddenly*) Clara! How did this dipper turn to gold?

CLARA: First I gave a drink to a poor old man, and it turned to silver. A little dog came along, and when I gave him a drink, it turned to gold. Perhaps now we can sell this golden . . . (*Dipper flies from her hand and disappears out window.*)

MOTHER: What happened? Your beautiful golden dipper jumped out of your hands and flew through the open window. (CLARA *runs to window and looks out.*)

CLARA: I can't believe what I see! Mother, you must come see for yourself. (CLARA *goes to bed and helps* MOTHER *to window.*)

MOTHER: Why, your dipper has turned into many stars, and is flying through the night sky. Let's go outside to get a better view. (*As they exit, the house moves to one side, revealing night sky. Dipper in star form sparkles in the sky.*)

CLARA: How beautiful! (NIGHT *enters, and* CLARA *hides behind* MOTHER.)

MOTHER: Don't be afraid, Clara. It is only Lady Night.

NIGHT: My dear child, don't be afraid of me. I am the time when you sleep and replenish your spirit. I bring you peace and quiet. To reward you for your kindness, I will make sure that you will never be in need again. Look at your Little Dipper in the sky. Do you see where the handle points?

CLARA: It points right here to our garden. (*Chest of sparkling diamonds appears.*) Look, Mother! Night has given us a wonderful present. A chest of beautiful diamonds that sparkle like the stars.

MOTHER: Oh, how wonderful!

NIGHT: Now, Clara, everyone will remember your kindness when they look up in the heavens and know "How the Little Dipper Came to Be." (*She flies off, as curtain falls.*)

THE END

(*Production Notes on page 322*)

Spinning a Spider's Tale

An African folktale

by Sari Ross

Characters

STORYTELLER, *actor*
ANANSI, *spider man*
ASO, *his wife*
INTIKUMA } *their sons*
KWEKU TSIN }
OSEBO, *leopard-of-the-terrible-teeth*
ONINI, *the great python*
TWO MMBORO, *hornets-who-sting-like-fire*
TWO VILLAGERS

SCENE 1

TIME: *Long ago.*
SETTING: *Forest in Ghana, Africa. Backdrop may be painted with lush green trees and bushes. Cutout of tall tree, big enough for puppets to hide behind, with low, hanging branches is on right side of stage. A low stool for* STORYTELLER *is in front of stage, left.*

AT RISE: STORYTELLER *enters, beating drum, goes down aisle and stops in front of stage, turns to face audience, then walks back and forth, drumming loudly.*

STORYTELLER (*Beating drum and pacing before stage*): In the beginning, O my friends, my friends. . . . Kwaku Anansi, the spider man, lived in Ghana, Africa. Many tales are told about the spider man, and one is that Anansi's thin belly came from greed. The spider carries with him forever the mark of that greed. It is said that one year there was a wedding feast in the town of Kibbes, in the country of Ghana, and another wedding feast in the town of Diabee, and they were both on the same day. (STORYTELLER *crosses to stool and sits on it.* ANANSI, *followed by his wife,* ASO, *enters, wearing black costume. Foam padding is tied to* ANANSI's *stomach under costume.*)

ANANSI: Which of the two wedding feasts shall I go to? I am very hungry! (*Pauses, thinking*) Ah, I shall go to both! First I will eat at the wedding where the food is served first, and then I will go to the other feast to eat again.

ASO (*Angrily*): Anansi, you have just eaten a big meal. How will you be able to eat two more? And how will you know which town will have its wedding feast first?

ANANSI (*Firmly*): There is a way to find out, wife; you shall see. Send for our sons and tell them to bring a long stout rope.

ASO (*Irritated*): I will do as you say, Anansi. (*Calling off left*) Intikuma! Kweku Tsin! Come quickly and bring a rope for your father. Hurry! (INTIKUMA *and* KWEKU TSIN *enter left, carrying long rope between them.*)

INTIKUMA *and* KWEKU (*Ad lib*): Here we are, Father, and here is the rope. We came as quickly as we could.

What is it for? Do you want us to tie something up? (*Etc.*)

ANANSI: Tie me up. I'm hungry!

ASO: For what purpose?

INTIKUMA *and* KWEKU (*In puzzled voices*): Why, Father?

ANANSI: Intikuma, take this end of the rope with you (*Hands it to him*) and go to the village of Diabee. I will then tie the rope around my middle, like this. See? (*As he does so,* INTIKUMA *and* KWEKU *try to help, become tangled, and all three try to get untangled.*) And then I will give the other end to Kweku Tsin to take to the village of Kibbes. Intikuma, when they start to give out food at the wedding feast, pull hard on the rope, and I will come. Kweku Tsin, when the feast begins in your town, you pull, too. In that way I will know where the food is given out first, and I will be able to eat twice! (INTIKUMA *and* KWEKU *scratch heads, look at one another, puzzled, holding end of rope.*)

INTIKUMA *and* KWEKU (*Ad lib*): Yes, Father. We will do as you say (ASO *makes impatient gesture and rushes off right. Sons run in place at opposite ends of stage, holding rope panting, simulating running to villages.* ANANSI *stands center, swaying slightly.*)

STORYTELLER (*Beating drum*): Yiridi, yiridi, yiridi, along the jungle paths, yiridi, yiridi, yiridi.

INTIKUMA: I am here now in Diabee.

KWEKU: I am here now in Kibbes.

INTIKUMA: I can see the feast is ready to begin, and I must signal Father.

KWEKU: This feast is about to begin and I will pull hard on the rope so Father can come in time. (INTIKUMA *and* KWEKU, *with backs to* ANANSI, *pull hard on rope.* ANANSI *is pulled first in one direction, then the other.*)

ANANSI (*Crying out*): Oh, eeeee, pui, pui, poor me, eeeeeeee, which way shall I go? They both pull at once, and I cannot tell which feast begins first. They are pulling me too hard . . . pui, pui! (*Both sons continue to pull,* ANANSI *moans as invisible string tied around costume and foam is pulled until waist is made small.*) Oh, dear me, the food will be gone by the time I get out of this rope. The feast will be over. Eeeeeee!

KWEKU: What can be keeping Father? I have signaled and signaled. Where can he be?

INTIKUMA: The feast is almost over. I must go look for Anansi and find out why he did not come when I pulled. (KWEKU *and* INTIKUMA *drop rope ends.* AN-ANSI *falls to ground. Sons run in place, panting, as if returning to village.*)

STORYTELLER (*Beating drum*): Yiridi, yiridi, yiridi . . . (KWEKU *and* INTIKUMA *continue running motion and move closer, stopping in front of* ANANSI, *who still lies on ground, holding stomach and groaning.*)

KWEKU *and* INTIKUMA: Father! What is wrong? (ASO *reenters.*)

ASO (*Shocked*): Anansi, what has happened to you? Where the rope has squeezed you around the middle, you have become very small.

KWEKU (*Laughing*): Oh, Father, you are small in the middle. You now have a thin belly!

INTIKUMA: The rope has squeezed you in the middle. (*Laughing*)

ASO: You will never be the same! (ASO, KWEKU *and* INTIKUMA *untie* ANANSI, *who lies gasping. Sons take rope and run off, pointing, and laughing at* ANANSI, *who covers head with hands.*)

ANANSI (*Crying*): Pui, pui, pui . . .

STORYTELLER (*Rising and going around circle*): And so Anansi carries with him forever the mark of his greed, a thin belly. And every spider after him has a thin belly, too. (*Blackout*)

* * * * *

SCENE 2

TIME: *Another day long ago.*

SETTING: *Same as Scene 1.*

AT RISE: ANANSI *lies on ground asleep.* STORYTELLER, *seated on stool, drums for few moments, then rises.*

STORYTELLER: O my friends, my friends, if you look closely, you will see that every spider has a bald head. In the old days, Kwaku Anansi had hair, but he lost it through his vanity, vanity, vanity! (ASO *enters and stands over* ANANSI, *who stands slowly as* ASO *speaks.*)

ASO (*Scolding*): Get up, Anansi, get up! I have news for you, sad news, and I must leave immediately. My mother has died in our own village, and I must go there at once. The funeral is tomorrow. I will go now, and you can follow.

ANANSI: That is sad news indeed, wife! Mother-in-law has died! Yes, you must go ahead. I will follow you later. Goodbye, Aso.

ASO: Goodbye, Anansi. Come soon. (*Exits*)

ANANSI (*Standing*): Hmm-m-m-m. When I go to my dead mother-in-law's house, I will have to show great grief over her death. I will have to refuse to eat. Therefore, I will eat now! (*Ducks behind tree, reappears shoving hands into mouth as though eating. He mumbles.*) I will eat a huge meal to prepare myself. Now, I must put on my mourning clothes and hat and follow Aso to our village. (*Hides behind tree and reappears with dashiki and hat on over spider costume.*) Now I will run to the funeral. (*Dances across stage to drum beat. Exits*)

STORYTELLER (*Drumming*): Yiridi, yiridi, yiridi . . . (OSEBO, ONINI, *and* 1ST *and* 2ND MMBORO *enter, carrying table, bowls, pot, ladle, and tripod.*)

1ST MMBORO: Come, we must lay the funeral feast here in the forest for Aso's dead mother. (*They pull out tripod with pot and table set with bowls from behind tree.*)

OSEBO: Yes, Onini and I will help; but I see that rascal, Anansi, coming. I suppose we must invite him to join us as he is Aso's husband.

ONINI (*Sighing*): Yes, I'm afraid so. (ANANSI *approaches, breathing heavily.*) Welcome, Anansi. We are ready for the funeral feast. Come and eat.

ANANSI (*Indignant*): What kind of man would I be to eat when I am mourning for my mother-in-law? I will eat only after the eighth day has passed.

OSEBO: This is not required of you, Anansi; you need not starve because your mother-in-law has died.

ANANSI (*Protesting*): No, I will not eat. . . . I am the greatest mourner of all, especially at my mother-in-law's funeral. (*Sniffs food in pot, but turns away quickly, pretending not to be interested; wrings hands and moans loudly.*)

ONINI: Anansi is the kind of person who, when he eats, eats twice as much as others, and when he dances, dances more vigorously than others. And when he mourns, he has to mourn more loudly than anyone else.

ANANSI (*With louder and louder moans*): I am so hungry now, oh, eeeeeeee! Eat, my friends, but as for me, I shall do without.

2ND MMBORO: We shall eat without you, but as each

day passes, you will get more and more hungry. (*All but* ANANSI *gather around table and eat.* ANANSI *sniffs food longingly.*)

OSEBO: Will you watch the beans for us, Anansi, while we call the other funeral guests?

ANANSI (*Eagerly*): Yes, I will watch them, but I will not eat. (*All rise.*)

ONINI: We will return in a short time. Don't let the beans burn!

ANANSI: I will be careful of them. Oh, poor mother-in-law! (*All but* ANANSI *exit. He rushes to pot, sniffs deeply, looks around stage, then takes hat off and bends over to hoist pot up to his mouth. Suddenly voices of* OSEBO *and* ONINI *are heard from offstage, and in panic* ANANSI *pours "beans" over his head, replaces pot, and puts his hat back on, just as* ASO, INTIKUMA, KWEKU, OSEBO, ONINI, TWO MMBORO, TWO VILLAGERS *enter.*)

1ST VILLAGER: Come, Anansi, you *must* eat with us. (*Others ad lib agreement.*)

ANANSI: Never! What kind of man would I be to eat at this time? (*Beans start to burn his head.* ANANSI *begins a jiggling dance, slowly, holding hat. Aside*) Oh! Oh! The beans are too hot. I am burning! I am on fire! (*To others, hastily*) Just at this very moment, in my village, the hat-shaking festival is taking place. (*All turn to look at him. He moans in pain, dancing faster and faster.*)

ASO: Anansi, what are you saying? What are you doing? Stop!

ANANSI (*Shouting*): They are shaking and jiggling the hats in our village like this. It is a great festival! I must go!

INTIKUMA: Father, before you go, eat something with us. There is plenty. (*He ladles out food for guests.*)

ANANSI (*Jumping and writhing with pain*): Oh, no, they are shaking hats, they are wriggling hats and jumping like this! I must go to my village. They need me!

KWEKU: Eat before your journey, Father. (*Eating*) The beans are delicious.

ANANSI (*Running down aisle, screaming*): I could not, with my mother-in-law just buried!

ASO: We will all come with you to the festival. (*Follows him*)

OSEBO: We should like to see this dance in your village. We will learn to do it, too. (*Runs after* ANANSI)

ANANSI (*With a howl*): I cannot stand this pain! (*Tears off hat, and with it wig, leaving "skin head." Holds wig and hat in one hand, and covers face with other, crying*) Oh, poor me. Tall grass hide me, hide me, hide me. I am overcome with shame. The beans have burned off all my hair. I am bald! (*Wails*)

ASO, SONS, ANIMALS, VILLAGERS (*Pointing, laughing, ad lib*): Look at that! His hair is gone! He's bald! (*Etc.* ANANSI *runs around stage twice, in attempt to hide, then exits, followed by others, all laughing.*)

STORYTELLER: That is why Anansi is often found in the tall grass. The spider was driven there by shame. And you will see that his head is bald, for the hot beans burned off all his hair. All this happened because Anasi tried to impress people, but his vanity and greed cost him his dignity. (*Rises, drumming softly*) And now, children, our spider tales are finished. (*Begins to drum more loudly as he exits*)

THE END

(*Production notes on page 322*)

Production Notes

Production Notes

THE BELL OF ATRI

Characters: 3 male; 16 or more male and female for all other parts.

Playing Time: 15 minutes.

Costumes: Medieval. King, Herald, and Attendants, belted tunics of rich materials, tights and slippers. King can wear short mantle over costume. King wears gold crown, Herald and Attendants, caps with feathers. Magistrate, long velvet robe, chain of office, and turban or round hat. Sir Rolfo, sleeveless tunic over coat of mail, belt with sword in scabbard, silver helmet with plume. He changes into shabby brown smock, tights, sandals, and shapeless brown cloth hat later in play. Peter, Townspeople and Children, peasant costumes (Howard Pyle's illustrations for Robin Hood and Maxfield Parrish's illustrations for fairy tales are excellent sources of reference for medieval costumes.) Horse costume (for two actors) for Trojan: In Scene 1, bridle is decorated with tassels, and ornamental cloth covers the body. Later, horse has no bridle or covering, and actors should limp.

Properties: Lance; shield.

Setting: Marketplace in Atri, Italy. Up center is archway with an open bell tower. A large golden bell hangs in tower. Fastened to the bell is a long rope that reaches to the ground. (In Scene 2, the rope is much shorter.) A platform is on left side of archway; on right side are a bench and trellis overgrown with leafy vines. Behind archway is a painted drop of distant hills. Market booths and carts are left and right (in Scene 2, vegetables and fruits are in booths, flowers and pastries in carts). Stepladder is also in one of booths.

Lighting: No special effects.

Sound: Deep-toned bell, fanfare, horse's whinny, barking, as indicated in text.

THE SLEEPING MOUNTAINS

Characters: 7 male; 4 female.

Playing Time: 25 minutes.

Costumes: All wear simple costumes with an Aztec influence. Old Woman wears black. Prince and guards wear swords.

Properties: Pouch containing white powder, swords, large fan on the end of long stick, rope and handkerchief to bind and gag Terana, flute or recorder.

Setting: The courtyard in the palace of King Papantco in Mexico. A well is at center, and a bench is at right, both painted to look like stone. Throne is at left, painted gold, and draped with bright cloth. The backdrop is a

311

painting of a dull red-colored plastered wall, with potted tropical plants hanging from it. Actual potted plants may be set upstage to give dimension to the backdrop.

Lighting: Scene 2 is a moonlit evening; Scene 3 is at dawn.

Sound: Horn blast (like a conch shell) and drum roll (played on a tom-tom); snarling wild cat, and howling coyote; flute or recorder music, played live, recorded, or whistled offstage by crew, if desired.

THE BOY WHO WENT TO THE NORTH WIND

Characters: 2 male; 2 female; 3 male or female for North Wind, Goat, and Stick.

Playing Time: 20 minutes.

Costumes: Ned, Mother, Innkeeper, and Wife wear appropriate peasant costumes. North Wind wears a cape. Stick is dressed in brown, and Goat wears horns or appropriate mask and tail.

Properties: Bowl, shredded white paper for flour; tablecloth; silver coins; gold coin; stick (hobby-horse) goat.

Setting: A sign down left reads NORTH WIND'S DEN. A screen up center represents the front of inn. It may have sign on it reading INN. Table and two chairs down right represent Ned's home. Exits are down right, up center, and down left.

Lighting: No special effects.

A TRIUMPH OF WITS

Characters: 1 male; 4 female.

Playing Time: 12 minutes.

Properties: Two serving trays with covered dishes and two pairs of chopsticks; two clothing bundles; small flashlight "candle"; candlestick; papers; four colored papers pleated into fans; paper lantern.

Setting: Scenes 1 and 3: A Chinese garden near a doorway to a house. A large, majestic chair is at center, and a low tea table is in front of it. A low stool or chair is at right, a rug at left. Scene 2: A country road. This scene may be played before curtain.

Lighting: No special effects.

THE MICE THAT ATE MONEY

Characters: 4 male.

Playing Time: 10 minutes.

Costumes: Banker, colorful robe and jewelry; Son, shorts; Servant and Young Man, simple tunics.

Properties: Ball, umbrella, piece of brown paper, jug.

Setting: Garden, with several potted plants. Couch with colorful coverlet is center.

Lighting: No special effects.

BARON BARNABY'S BOX

Characters: 5 male; 4 female.

Playing Time: 15 minutes.

Costumes: Old-fashioned dress. The women wear long, brightly colored skirts and peasant blouses. Bess Goodwin wears cape with hood over her skirt and blouse. The men wear dark-colored knee breeches and white shirts. Will Goodwin also wears cape. Baron Barnaby is dressed in elaborate knee breeches and wears vest over his shirt. He also wears a hat.

Properties: Two pennies; a wooden box filled with gold-paper coins (the box is tied shut); knife.

Setting: A village green. If a backdrop is used, it could show a few small houses and some distant hills. A row of small bushes stands in front of backdrop. At right and left are cardboard trees. A log lies at an angle up left.

Lighting: No special effects.

THE KING AND THE BEE

Characters: 4 male; 2 female.

Playing Time: 10 minutes.

Costumes: The men wear long robes with wide belts, heavy necklaces, and turbans. The King has a crown. The Keeper may have a slightly humorous touch, such as a long, curved feather. The Queen may wear full Turkish trousers and a filmy veil or scarf held in place by a small crown or circlet. The Bee may wear a black and yellow tunic, dark stockings, a glittering cap with antennae, and cellophane wings.

Properties: Cardboard dagger, several jars or boxes, a large magnifying glass, a roll of bandage, a scarf, two bouquets of artificial flowers.

Setting: The garden of King Solomon. A long, low wall with many brightly colored flowers is in the back. In front of it is a long bench draped with a rich, colorful fabric. There may be trees, shrubs, etc.

Sound Effects: During the Bee's scenes there should be a continuous low buzzing sound, or the very soft playing of "Flight of the Bumblebee." A trumpet or gong may announce the Queen.

Lighting: No special effects.

THE HODJA SPEAKS

Characters: 4 male, 1 female; 1 male or female for Narrator.

Playing Time: 20 minutes.

Costumes: Turkish. Baggy pants for everyone, with sandals or slippers. Men wear sashes, full-sleeved shirts, and loose vests. Jamal and Mustafa each wear a red fez with a black tassel. The Hodja has a beard and a large turban attached to felt cap. Wife wears a head scarf, pulled across face so only eyes show. Knee-length dress extends over pants.

Properties: Scene 1: large sack; dish of pilaf. Scene 2: two small glasses of tea; brass teapot; blanket.

Setting: Inside a simple house in Turkish village. There is a low table with vase on it, two large pillows, and an old trunk containing household items. Exit right leads to kitchen; exit left to outside.

Lighting: Blackout and dimming of lights, as indicated.

Sound: Recorded Turkish music. Narrator uses backstage microphone or a megaphone for amplification.

THE BREMEN TOWN MUSICIANS

Characters: 8 male or female.

Playing Time: 15 minutes.

Costumes: Donkey, Hound and Cat wear one-piece suits with tails, hoods, and appropriately sized ears held up by wires or sewn on. Cock may wear a feathery, brightly colored costume and cardboard wings covered with feathers. The robbers wear long, black beards and dark clothes with bright red handkerchiefs around their necks.

Properties: Lute; kettledrum on a cord; two drumsticks; four money bags; carrot; ear of corn; one large and one small bone.

Setting: Scene 1, a country road. May be played before curtain. Scene 2, a forest. Downstage left is a large tree with overhanging branches. Upstage left is the front of a house, with a door and a window. The backdrop may be a forest. If desired, the house front may be a part of the backdrop.

Lighting: No special effects.

THE SNOW WITCH

Character: 5 female, 1 male; 1 male or female for Driver; male and female dancers.

Playing Time: 15 minutes.

Costumes: Peasant dresses for Marina and Katya. Flowing white gown for Snow Witch. Royal robes and fur for Princess. Uniforms for Ivan and Driver. Peasant costumes for Dancers.

Properties: Whip for Driver; gold ring for Snow Witch.

Setting: Simple peasant kitchen: fireplace down right with large tea kettle on hearth; be-

hind table and two stools up right is wall shelf with three or four cups and plates. Window in rear wall; outside door left; rocking chair between window and door.

Sound: Wind; sleigh bells; suitable folk music for dance; wolf howl.

THE WHITE SPIDER'S GIFT

Characters: 6 female; 7 male; 2 male or female; male and female extras.

Playing Time: 20 minutes.

Costumes: Girls wear simple "sack-style" dresses with wooden beads or colorful sashes and flower wreaths or headbands. All characters are barefoot or wear simple leather sandals. Boys wear loose shorts of solid color. Some also wear capes, headbands, and beaded ankle bands. Piki and Kuma wear some distinguishing item, such as colorful armband or headpiece.

Properties: Walking stick; burlap sack; two large water jars; spider made of large cotton ball sprinkled with glitter, with eight small pipe cleaner legs; basket; bows and arrows; drum; large feather made of construction paper, cut partway down the middle as if split by arrow; sturdy stick or dowel; blowtube; comb; flowers; feathered headdress; gold necklace; lace mantle. (Note: lace mantle should already be hidden somewhere around the bush at beginning of Scene 3.)

Setting: Before Rise, forest of Paraguay. Murals on walls flanking stage depict trees and undergrowth. One large bush, displayed on right wall outside curtain, represents spider's home, and must be visible throughout the play. Large spider's web of white yarn covers most of the bush. At Rise, Chieftain's home. Cloth-covered wooden frame center has leafy branches laid across the top. Large earthen jars, weaving frame, and wood for fire are on either side. Background mural shows forest.

Lighting and Sound: In Scene 3, lights dim, then come up, and soft music is played, to indicate passage of time.

THE KING'S DREAMS

Characters: 5 male; 1 female; 1 male or female for Serpent.

Playing Time: 20 minutes.

Costumes: King and Queen wear crowns. In Scene 1 he wears nightshirt and she wears nightgown with old bathrobe. In later scenes they wear royal robes. In Scene 2, they wear boots. Advisers wear appropriate court costumes. Ivan wears plain, dark clothes, and Serpent wears leotard and appropriate mask.

Properties: Pillow; blanket; items for Queen's pockets: comb, stocking, apple, ribbon, scissors, harmonica, red rose, medals, trumpet (or whistle); three handkerchiefs and daggers for advisers; chunk of black bread, hoe for Ivan.

Setting: Scene 1: A palace in Old Russia. Background may show view of colorful Russian towers. Other scenes take place in a field. If desired, tall grain may be seen growing.

Lighting: No special effects.

THE STRANGE AND WONDERFUL OBJECT

Characters: 3 male; 2 female; 4 male or female for Narrator, trees, and servant. As many male and female neighbors and musicians as desired.

Playing Time: 15 minutes.

Costumes: Chinese costumes. Narrator and Musicians wear black. Priest wears colorful headdress. Trees carry branches.

Properties: Mirror; instruments (triangle, Chinese block, gong, jingle bells, xylophone, wind chimes).

Setting: Ancient China. On raised platform up center is a reversible, free-standing archway representing on one side the entrance to Chang's house, on the other the entrance to the Temple. At front of platform is a large Chinese vase. A bench is at front of stage or to one side.

Lighting and Sound: No special effects.

THE MILLER'S GUEST

Characters: 5 male; 3 female.

Playing Time: 15 minutes.

Costumes: Hunter wears trousers, shirt with vest, high boots, and hat with plume, and carries bow and quiver of arrows. Miller and Richard wear peasant shirt, trousers, and heavy boots. Miller's

Wife, Margery, and Dora wear long skirts, peasant blouses, kerchiefs in their hair; Miller's Wife wears apron.
Properties: Large heavy sack; hunting horn; coin purse; two swords.
Setting: Scene 1: A footpath near the King's forest, may be played before curtain. Scene 2: Inside Miller's cottage. Doors are left and right. On stove, rear, are large pot and ladle; over stove is window. Table with five chairs is center; extra chair is at rear. Plates, mugs, bowls, and eating utensils are on stove.
Lighting: No special effects.
Sound: Hunting horn, as indicated in text.

CAP O' RUSHES

Characters: 5 male; 10 female.
Playing Time: 20 minutes.
Costumes: Medieval dress. Alicia, Louisa, and Catherine wear rich, silk dresses; Catherine wears an old cloak over her dress when she is disguised as Cap o' Rushes, and a cap that covers her hair. Alicia has a string of pearls.
Properties: Ring; trays; bowl and plates.
Setting: Basically the same set for both dining rooms. A long table and chairs are at center, and a tapestry may be added for Scene 2.
Lighting: No special effects.

THE COBBLER WHO BECAME AN ASTROLOGER

Characters: 3 female; 8 male.
Playing Time: 20 minutes.

Costumes: King, Royal Astrologer, Jeweler, Jeweler's Wife, and Woman wear fine clothes. Titus, Wife, Man and Servant wear clean, plain clothes; Thieves wear rags.
Properties: Shoes; cobbler's hammer; scraps of leather; red ruby in Jeweler's pocket; two bags of gold.
Setting: Scene 1: City street, with cobbler's house at front. Door is in center of house. Bench, with bowl and nut underneath it, is beside door. Scene 2: The Palace Throne Room. Throne or elegant chair is on a small platform at center.
Lighting and Sound: No special effects.

DAME FORTUNE AND DON MONEY

Characters: 3 male; 5 female; 10 or more male and female for Thieves, Sheriff, Judge, Banker, Lawyer, and Villagers.
Playing Time: 20 minutes.
Costumes: Dame Fortune wears long skirt and mantilla. Don José and Don Money wear suits, ruffled shirts, and boots. Manuel wears ragged clothes in first scene, everyday Spanish dress in second scene. Others wear everyday Spanish dress, with shawls for women and sombreros for men, kerchiefs for Two Thieves.
Properties: Newspaper; knitting; document; money (one peseta note, a gold coin, sack of coins, ten hundred-peseta notes); cloth sacks; fan; bolts

of cloth; long loaves of bread; cakes and pies; big ledger.

Setting: Town square of a Spanish village. Cutaway stores of baker and cloth merchant at rear. A bench is down right; a seat, judge's desk and chair are down left. Exits are right and left.

Lighting and Sound: No special effects.

TARO THE FISHERMAN

Characters: 6 male; 3 female; 7 or more male and female for Children and Sea Citizens.

Playing Time: 15 minutes.

Costumes: Goro, Taro, and male children wear shirts, tights, T-shirts, brightly colored sashes, and bandanas. They are barefoot or wear sandals. In Scene 3, Taro and Goro have white beards and wigs. The female children wear kimonos, brightly colored sashes, and have flowers in their hair. Sea King wears mantle and crown, and holds a trident. Big Turtle, who is on all fours, has a cushion strapped to his back, marked in diagonal squares to represent a turtle's shell. Princess wears mermaid's costume, and crown of pearls. Sea Citizens wear cloaks; on the front of each cloak is a picture representing a sea creature.

Properties: Fishing pole; small turtle, of cardboard or felt; roll of parchment; bowl of fruit; cane.

Setting: Scenes 1 and 3: Seashore, near a fishing village in Japan, with rocks down right, and baskets for fish and fishnets scattered on stage.

Backdrop shows sea and sky. Scene 2: Kingdom under the Sea, with a backdrop showing seaweed, shells, rocks, etc. A small table, holding box, is at right. A throne is at center, and two chairs are on either side of it.

Lighting: No special effects.

Sound: Musical scales; lively music, as indicated in text.

BIG PAUL BUNYAN

Characters: 6 male; 2 female; 2 male or female for Bees; as many male and female extras for Townspeople, Farmers, and Lumberjacks as desired. 3 actors for Babe (non-speaking parts).

Playing Time: 20 minutes.

Costumes: Paul has black beard, wears red plaid shirt with shoulder pads, jeans, and platform boots. In Scene 1, he wears baby bonnet. Babe, as a baby ox, is played by one actor wearing blue sleepers, with an attached hood and pointed ears; as a full-grown ox, by two actors wearing blue ox costume with mask and horns. Traveling Lady and Mrs. Bunyan wear long old-fashioned dresses. Bum and Buzz wear striped shirts, leotards, hoods, and wings on their backs. John Shears, Meery, and Farmers wear overalls; Lumberjacks wear plaid shirts, jeans, boots, and knit caps. Some may have beards.

Properties: Toy ax; wooden whistle; carpetbag; wheelbarrow with rope attached; blanket; kettle; cut-out of tree; snowshoes; ladle; 3 or 4 fruit crates; two pails; parsnips.

Setting: Tree stump stands at left. Scene 1: Maine. Backdrop of rocky sea coast. Scene 2: Cave at left, with a cut-out opening standing at center. Inside is campfire with large kettle hanging over it. At right are blue snowbank cutouts. Scene 3: Barnyard of Paul's farm. A corral type fence runs across back of stage and halfway down each side. Up right is a large cut-out of a beehive. Babe's stable is at left.

Lighting: Blue floodlight in Scene 2.

Sound: Offstage voices.

THE THREE EVILS

Characters: 5 male, 2 female; 6 male or female for Elders, Clerk, Guards; at least 4 male and female extras for Villagers.

Playing Time: 20 minutes.

Costumes: Villagers wear appropriate peasant clothing. Jo Chou, silk Chinese clothing and hat with two feathers in it. Elders, somber robes. Mandarin Wu wears bright, embroidered robe, in Scene 1; adds ragged cloak in Scene 2.

Properties: Scepter; sword; pole; basket of eggs; basket of fruit.

Setting: Scene 1, Chinese courtroom, with large carved chair on low platform up center. Mats on floor next to chair. At right are small chair and table with pen, ink and scroll on it. Scene 2: In front of Jo Chou's house. Gateway, with two boulders on either side.

Lighting: No special effects.

Sound: Roaring of water.

THE CLEVER DOG OF HAWAII

Characters: 1 male, 2 female; 7 male or female for Storyteller, Dog, Workers, and evil spirits.

Playing Time: 20 minutes.

Costumes: Hawaiian dress. Women wear a long piece of cloth wrapped in sarong-style, and flowers in hair; men, loincloths or swimsuits. Queen Lukia wears tapa cloth (coarse fabric with geometric pattern) on her head and sponges in ears, in Scene 2. Homoku has long white beard and wig, bushy white eyebrows. All wear flower leis and are barefoot. Dog wears brown leotard, brown hood with felt ears and yarn tail. Evil spirits wear colorful papier-mâché masks that have wild eyes, horns, and red protruding tongues.

Properties: Large toy fish; hoes; coconut (large rubber ball wrapped in burlap); large conch shell (real, papier-mâché, or cardboard).

Setting: Queen's royal taro field, in the Waipio Valley in Hawaii. Mountains, fiery volcano, palm and banana trees are shown on backdrop. Thatched hut is at right, may be painted on backdrop. Taro plants (cut-outs) are up left. Similar plants are painted on backdrop as continuation of royal patch. Note: Plants may be in pots, and pots can be camouflaged by arranging brown wrapping paper around them to look like dirt mounds.

Lighting: No special effects. If desired, red light may be used for volcano in backdrop by cutting out area above volcano, inserting red cellophane, and shining light through cellophane.

Sound: Trumpet to stimulate sound of conch shell horn, amplified and seeming to come from above audience, as indicated in text. Slow, steady, drumbeat, as indicated in text.

THE GREEN GLASS BALL

Characters: 7 male; 5 female; male or female for donkey; as many extras as desired for other villagers.

Playing Time: 20 minutes.

Costumes: Peasant dress. The Old Woman wears ragged clothes. Donkey wears a donkey mask. Terry carries a hoe.

Properties: Tinker's pack, containing grindstone and iron kettle; pot; sack of potatoes; basket containing cardboard knives; cabbages; kettle; sack of apples; wooden doll; pebble; black kettle for Old Woman; green glass ball.

Setting: A small village in Ireland. No furnishings are necessary. Scene 2 is played before the curtain, so that Donkey may disappear through curtain opening at center.

Lighting: No special effects.

THE PIE AND THE TART

Characters: 3 male; 1 female.
Playing Time: 10 minutes.

Costumes: Period dress. Pierre, Louis, ragged, torn jackets, breeches, and caps or berets. Marianne, long dress, apron, white cap. Gautier, white coat, chef's high white hat.

Properties: Pie; apple tart; stick.

Setting: A street scene. At left, there is a working door. Sign over door reads, GAUTIER, PASTRY COOK. There is a wall, right. At center, bench. Outlines of buildings are drawn on backdrop.

Lighting: No special effects.

NIGHT OF THE TROLLS

Characters: 3 male; 1 female; 4 male or female for Bear and Trolls; extras for additional Trolls. If desired, Eric may be played by a girl (Erica) with appropriate text changes.

Playing Time: 15 minutes.

Costumes: Simple peasant clothes for Eric and Larssens. Bear wears appropriate animal costume and mask. Trolls wear hideous masks. King wears crown.

Properties: Whistle or recorder; large bundles; rubber "ax."

Setting: Scene 1: Mountain country of Norway. Backdrop shows snowy mountains and pine trees. Scene 2: The Larssens' cottage, with table with cloth reaching to floor, shelf with pitcher and bowl, and benches, cupboards, fireplace, etc. Heavy wooden door is at one side.

Lighting: No special effects.

Sound: Loud knocking, as indicated in text.

Big Cat, Little Cat, Old Man Monkey

Characters: 2 male; 3 male or female.
Playing Time: 15 minutes.
Costumes: Cats may wear tights with tails and T-shirts and animal masks. Narrator wears Japanese dress. Monkey and Owl may wear kimonos and animal masks.
Properties: Ball of yarn; pack containing two cakes, one larger than the other; small pair of balance scales.
Setting: A bare stage with stool for Narrator.
Lighting: No special effects.

Barnaby the Brave

Characters: 7 male; 3 female; 3 male or female for Trumpeter, Banner Bearer, Thief.
Playing Time: 20 minutes.
Costumes: Barnaby wears baker's hat and apron; Granny wears skirt and apron with pockets; Margaret wears dress with apron; all others wear appropriate dress. Red wigs for Redheaded Man and Redheaded Woman.
Properties: Play paper money; two stacks of pies; one pie "filled with blackbirds," (these may be cardboard cutouts of birds); trumpet; change purse containing play money; long, hollow loaf of french bread containing play paper money; coil of rope; covered dish containing sausage.
Setting: Scenes 1 and 5: A village. Sign on backdrop reads, VILLAGE OF NORTHCHESTER. Also painted on backdrop, at right, is a bake shop (sign above it reads, BAKE SHOP) and at left, a cottage. Bake shop and cottage have working doors. Scenes 2 and 3: The same, except that signs read WELCOME TO SOUTHCHESTER and GRANNY'S PIE SHOP. Scene 4: The same, except that sign to right reads JAIL and other sign reads CRIMECHESTER followed by several lines of print that is too small to be read by audience.
Lighting: No special effects.
Sound: Cock crowing, trumpet fanfare, as indicated in text.

Why the Sea Is Salt

Number of puppets: 9 hand puppets.
Playing Time: 15 minutes.
Description of puppets: Granny and Gillie are "moving mouth" or sock hand puppets. Sharkie, Flipper and Charlie are stick puppets, made of paper on heavy wire. Oliver, Martha, and Mervin are hand puppets in Norwegian costume. Dwarf has a long white beard, a stocking cap, and tattered clothes. In Scene 5, Dwarf wears a sailor's cap.
Properties: Box of "crackers"; model of turkey on heavy wire or dowel; "magic mill," a small coffee grinder, or a box with a revolving handle on top. There is a window in front of the mill, and a black circular disk with eggs painted on it inside the mill. Turn disk from behind mill to give effect of mill grinding out hard-boiled eggs.
Setting: Scenes 1 and 6, the ocean floor. A sea scrim or

curtain of blue netting with seaweed shapes sewed to it is dropped over the stage. Scenes 2 and 4, Martha and Oliver's poor cottage in Norway. There is a table at center stage. Tabletop is made to flip over; in Scene 2, the bare side of table top is shown, and in Scene 4, the table top turns over and reveals dishes and tablecloth which have been glued on. The turkey is also attached to table but can be removed and held by dowel or wire, so Oliver can pick it up and take it outside. The backdrop has a window cut into it, and painted on the backdrop is a shelf holding an empty breadbox. Scene 3: Outside Mervin's mansion. At one side of stage there is a corner of the mansion, with a working door in it. At the opposite side of stage there is a cut-out of a tree. This scene may be played before the curtain. Scene 5: On the sea. This scene may be played on top of the puppet stage, with the sea scrim in place, with the curtains closed. Then when the ship sinks, open the curtains, and lower ship into the viewing area of the stage for the last scene. The ship is a cardboard cut-out with a cloth sail on a dowel. Put a handle on the back of the ship so that you can hold it easily. Attach a cut-out of the magic mill to the ship. Attach a triangle of shiny white fabric to the back of the ship cut-out, with a thread at the top of the triangle, so that the fabric can be pulled up from behind the ship slowly, to give the effect that salt is rising in the ship.

MONKEY BUSINESS

Characters: 6 puppets; 4 storytellers, male or female.
Playing Time: 15 minutes.
Costumes: Storytellers, robes and turbans. Puppets: Rajah, brocade robe, jewelled turban; Gardener, white Nehru cap, robe; Scholar, robe, beard, turban, spectacles; Monkeys, fur suits, ears and tails.
Properties: Watering can, scroll, gate, sign reading. NO MON-KEYS ALLOWED.
Setting: Garden backdrop for puppet stage. There are three trees set against the backdrop, in earthen pots.
Lighting: No special effects.
Sound: Cymbal clashes. Recorded sitar music may precede the play.

THE STRONGEST BEING

Number of puppets: 4 hand or rod puppets; 4 rod puppets.
Playing Time: 15 minutes.
Description of puppets: Sun, Cloud, and Wind are cut from heavy paper, painted in bright colors, with faces, and mounted on sticks. Wall is made of thick cardboard, and has face. Small hole is at center. Musume, Otosan, Okasan, and Dedmu may be hand or stick puppets, and should wear traditional Japanese clothing.
Setting: Japanese garden, with tree large enough to hide behind at right. Backdrop shows blue sky and at right, corner of house.
Sound: Wind whistles.

The Perfect Gift for a Princess

Number of puppets: 9 hand or rod puppets.

Playing Time: 15 minutes.

Description of puppets: Royal attire for King, Queen, Princess. Cook wears apron, chef's hat; Gardener, overalls; Annie, long dress; Jack, Messenger, tights and tunics. Troll, green pointed hat, long white beard.

Properties: Two knapsacks, one with small bottle of milk inside; birthday cake; ring; necklace; bouquet of flowers; box with snugabed (stuffed animal) inside.

Setting: Scene 1, Princess Clare's bedroom, with cot. Scenes 2 and 4, throne room. There are two thrones center. Scene 3, the Enchanted Forest. There are bushes scattered about, a circle of stones center, in the middle of which is a fire. Large cookpot sits over fire. Basket, bowl, and spoon are nearby.

NOTE: Backdrops for all scenes may be paper cutouts pinned to sheeting and dropped from a rod behind puppets.

How the Little Dipper Came to Be

Number of puppets: 6 hand or rod puppets or marionettes.

Playing Time: 15 minutes.

Description of puppets: Clara wears ragged dress. Mother wears nightdress. Old man, in tattered clothes, has white hair. Dog puppet has tongue hanging out. Owl is large, and must fly. Night is a beautiful and mysterious woman with a long cape, and a hood over her hair.

Properties: Tray of food; three dippers, each painted differently—dull gray, shiny silver, and bright gold (may be attached to Clara's hand with clip or string, which can be pulled to make dipper "fly" out of window); chest of diamonds.

Setting: Cottage bedroom, with center window and bed, should be able to be removed quickly, in view of audience. Either have it fold aside or painted on cloth so it can be pulled to one side. It could also be taken down or pulled up. When it is removed, backdrop showing garden with night sky is visible. "The Little Dipper" can be painted on a drop, or small Christmas tree lights can poke through drop—turn them on when needed. The forest is a series of cut-out trees that are rearranged to make different parts of the forest. In Scene 2, there is a well.

Lighting: Lighting should be dim for the woods scenes.

Sound: Simple, soft music for background and between scenes.

Spinning a Spider's Tale

Number of puppets: 10 hand or rod puppets.

Playing Time: 12 to 15 minutes.

Description of puppets: Anansi has black cloak with foam padding underneath and fishing line tied around waist that can be pulled tight as indicated in text; his wig is black and is easily removed to reveal a shiny, bald head. He wears large flamboyant hat and dashiki in Scene 2. Osebo is covered in leopard skin, with ears and whiskers; Onini puppet looks like a snake; Mmboros have hornet wings and antennae. Aso, Sons, and Villagers are dressed in colorful dashikis.

Properties: Drum and low stool for Storyteller; rope for Scene 1; tripod, pot, ladle, table, bowls for Scene 2.

Setting: Forest in Ghana, Africa. Backdrop is painted with green trees and bushes. A cutout of a tree, large enough for puppets to hide behind, with low, hanging branches, right. A low stool for Storyteller is in front of stage, left.

Lighting: No special effects.

Sound: Drumming, as indicated in text.